UNWELCOME GUESTS:

Canada West's Response

to American Fugitive Slaves,

1800-1865

Jason H. Silverman

National University Publications
ASSOCIATED FACULTY PRESS, INC.
Millwood, N.Y. • New York City • London

For Donna

Associated Faculty Press, Inc.

Series in Comparative Studies in Race and Ethnicity

Jason H. Silverman
Series Editor

Silverman—Unwelcome Guests: Canada West's Response to American Fugitive Slaves, 1800-1865

Library of Congress Cataloging in Publication Data

Silverman, Jason H.
  Unwelcome guests.

  (Series in comparative studies in race and ethnicity)
(National university publications)
  Bibliography: p. 165
  Includes index.
  1. Fugitive slaves—Ontario—History—19th century. 2. Blacks—Ontario—History—19th century. 3. Ontario—Race relations. I. Title. II. Series.
F1059.7.N3S55 1984   971'.00496073   84-9263
ISBN 0-8046-9377-3

CONTENTS

About the Author

JASON H. SILVERMAN is Assistant Professor of History at Winthrop College, Rock Hill, South Carolina. He has formerly taught at Yale University, where he was also an editor of the Frederick Douglass Papers, and received his doctoral degree from the University of Kentucky. A specialist in Southern, Black, and Ethnic history, he is the coauthor of *The War of The Confederacy*, coeditor of *From Louisiana to Canada: The Autobiography of William King*, and author of numerous articles in such journals as *The Yale Review*, *The Canadian Historical Review*, and *The Journal of Negro History*. He serves as series editor for Associated Faculty Press' "Comparative Studies in Race and Ethnicity."

ACKNOWLEDGMENTS

One incurs many debts along the way in the process of researching and writing. When your work takes you into two countries, as mine has done, debts mount even further. Little messages on note cards or scraps of paper remembering archivists, librarians, or colleagues who unselfishly offered assistance, or who went well beyond what was asked of them, tend to multiply rapidly. Yet to thank everyone is, in essence, to thank no one. I now delight, therefore, in acknowledging those people who were of especial help to me during the many stages of this study.

As a graduate student, the kind people of the Inter-Library Loan Office at M.I. King Library, University of Kentucky, cheerfully answered virtually all my requests for rare and obscure titles, while simultaneously trying to figure out the complicated loan policies of Canadian institutions. It is no exaggeration to say that this project could never have begun without their cooperation and perseverance. Many other librarians and archivists throughout the United States and Canada assisted me greatly as well. Thanks must particularly go to the staffs of the Public Archives of Canada, Ottawa; the Ontario Provincial Archives, Toronto; the Regional History Collection, D.B. Weldon Library, University of Western Ontario, London; the Moorland-Spingarn Research Center, Howard University, Washington, D.C.; the Schomburg Center for Black Culture, New York City; and the American Missionary Association Archives, New Orleans. I am appreciative of the assistance provided me at these repositories, and the numerous other libraries and research centers that I visited in the course of my work.

Timely and generous grants from the American Philosophical Society and the

Canadian Embassy enabled me to return to Canada and to purchase research materials that otherwise would not have been available to me. I extend sincere thanks to both for greatly facilitating my efforts; Stuart Hughes, Canadian Vice-Consul General in New York City, proffered help and learned advice on innumerable matters, and became a good and trusted friend.

Portions of this volume have appeared previously in a different form. In this regard I want to thank the editors of the following journals for permitting me to reprint material from my articles: *Canadian Historical Review, The Filson Club History Quarterly, Southern Studies,* and *Ontario History.*

Throughout my academic career, I have been fortunate to have a number of colleagues and friends upon whom to rely. Charles P. Roland directed this study as a dissertation, and he has remained a constant source of encouragement, for which I am truly grateful. John W. Blassingame, David Brion Davis, Robin W. Winks, August Meier, and Eugene H. Berwanger have all read and commented on earlier drafts of the work. I am deeply indebted to each of them for their generosity, incisiveness, and exemplary standards of scholarship, which I have sought to follow. Any shortcomings in this book are the result of my stubbornness—not their recommendations.

Others have contributed in equally important ways. Raymond F. Betts, good friend and former teacher, has always been there when I needed him. Over the years, his and Gene Berwanger's faith and confidence in me have consistently provided sustenance when my energy and enthusiasm faltered. In their inimitable ways, Thomas H. Appleton, Paul Doutrich and Jon Safren helped me to keep things in proper perspective. Their friendship mitigated the pressures and anxieties of academia more times than any of us would care to remember, and I shall always be grateful. My typist, Janet Soresino, undaunted by adverse conditions, performed her task with customary efficiency. Kenneth Brown's and Richard Koffler's support for my work have been especially gratifying. I am thankful for their willingness to commit Associated Faculty Press to this study and appreciative of the opportunity to work with them.

My greatest debt, however, is as always, to my wife and partner, Donna. Without her, neither this book nor the dissertation upon which it was based would ever have been completed. She typed, researched, edited, proof-read, composed, and revised. For these, and countless other reasons, I affectionately dedicate this book to her.

New Haven, Connecticut
March 1984   J.H.S.

PREFACE

Studying blacks in Canada poses a rather interesting question. Why investigate a group that, at most, has never exceeded 2 or 2.5 percent of the total population? Perhaps the pioneer of black Canadian history, Robin W. Winks, said it best when he wrote that "history is not, after all, democratic and to dismiss the many thousands of Negroes who have walked across the Canadian stage since 1628—however silently—is to dismiss a human, interesting, and clearly visible segment of the wider Canadian story." Perhaps it is more than that, however. To study the white Canadian response to American fugitive slaves and the history of black institutions in Canada is to determine the true accuracy of the long-perpetuated believe that black life improved significantly north of the forty-ninth parallel (I use this phrase euphemistically to refer to Canada, realizing full well that for sheer technical accuracy most of the area covered in this study lies below that latitude). This determination is important not only for students of the black experience but for those of American, Canadian, and comparative race relations as well. In view of the continuing scholarship on race relations in nineteenth-century Spanish America and on the institution of slavery in the United States, it is imperative to provide the missing element, so to speak; a study of black/white relations just across our northern border. By so doing, a more complete picture of black life in the Americas during the pivotal period of slavery and emancipation can be discerned.

It was with this purpose in mind that I originally pursued the story of the fugitive slaves in Canada. Conventional historiography tells us that throughout the antebellum period, Canada was a sanctuary for American slaves. Seemingly, a promised land where refugee blacks could escape slavery and build a new life in freedom, Canada represented a vivid alternative to the manifestly racist policies of the United States. Encouraged by propagandist and success stories of the Underground Railroad, American blacks, both slave and free alike, recognized the existence of a potential haven north of the border and began emigrating steadily to Canada after 1830. After the Fugitive Slave Law of 1850 made it considerably more difficult for runaway slaves to find refuge in the northern United States, black migration to Canada increased significantly. So extensive was this black exodus that by some contemporary estimates the number of fugitive slaves residing in Canada West (Ontario) alone by 1860 approached some 110,000.

Canadians welcomed the refugees, so the traditional story goes, and "demonstrated their brotherly feelings in tangible ways," according to contemporary accounts. The fugitive slaves also were happy, content, and, in some instances, prosperous in their newly found Canadian Canaan. Fugitive slaves, living in the freedom of Canada, we were told, existed "as well as any people in the world."

This version portrays an idyllic but not altogether accurate picture of fugitive slaves' lives in Canada during the first two-thirds of the nineteenth century. That Canadians gave refuge to thousands of fugitive blacks is undeniable; that they did so because of philanthropic or humanitarian reasons is not. As the number of blacks entering Canada multiplied, so too did negrophobia on the part of white Canadians. This sentiment manifested itself in educational, social, and religious discrimination and segregation that permeated all levels of black life. In the end, the ostensible Canadian Canaan at times strangely resembled the antebellum North or the Jim Crow South.

The American fugitive slaves, then, did not find in Canada what they had been promised. On the contrary, they often found antagonism and resentment. True, the majority of Canadians opposed the institution of slavery, and in fact, slavery became illegal in Canada in 1834, but abolition frequently existed concurrently with a substantial degree of negrophobia and white supremacy. Many Canadians simply shared the deep prejudices and racial practices of their American neighbors. Although freed from slavery in the legal sense, the fugitive black was by no means freed of prejudice in the racial sense. Canada was not the haven that propagandists had advertised, but neither was it the racially and legally oppressive society to the south. The truth lay somewhere in between. Fugitive American blacks might indeed risk their lives escaping to Canada for a respite from the shackles of slavery, and yet find that they were not welcome there.

One

OVERVIEW: THE INTRODUCTION OF BLACKS INTO CANADIAN SOCIETY

Barely nine years after the first blacks arrived at Jamestown, Virginia, a young boy of seven or eight years of age touched foot upon Canadian soil as a slave. A native of Madagascar, the youngster was brought by the privateer, David Kirke, during his invasion of New France,[1] in 1628, and was promptly sold to a Quebec resident. Four years later, the young slave was baptized and assumed the name of Olivier Le Jeune. Apparently kept as a domestic servant for most of his life, it is likely that Le Jeune's official status had been converted to that of freeman by the time of his death in 1654. Yet Le Jeune's circumstantial arrival did not precipitate the inauguration of a large-scale slave trade into Canada, for no other black slaves are known to have lived in New France until the latter part of the seventeenth century.

Prior to 1663, the economy of New France was based solely on private enterprise. The Company of New France, which controlled the colony, had no interest in economic development except as it pertained to the profits of the fur trade. Because the fur trade was a highly individualistic endeavor, slavery was neither required nor requested. Quite unlike the mass-production, agriculturally based economy in the British colonies to the south, which needed many hands, the economy of New France required trappers who operated as independent businessmen in a specialized trade. Hence, slavery was very limited in extent. Lucky was the colonist in New France who could afford the luxury of keeping a slave for personal use. Neither the government nor the Roman Catholic Church encouraged slavery in New France, though they did allow settlers to retain ownership of the few black slaves that were brought into the colony.

Indeed, slavery barely qualified as an "institution" in New France. By 1760, approximately eleven hundred blacks resided there with their white masters and half that number dwelled in or near Montreal, while another quarter lived in other towns. Most were the domestic servants of their predominantly French owners, with only about two hundred blacks working as field hands. In general, whether field hand or domestic servant, black slaves in New France received humane treatment. Slaves were allowed to participate in the sacraments of baptism and the Eucharist and permitted the rite of Christian burial. Their given or Christian names as well as their surnames frequently came from the family names of their owners. Punishment was meted out with equal severity to slaves and freemen alike, with no extant records of unwarranted harsh discipline directed toward slaves. In addition, most blacks remained with the same family until death. Due to their high prices, their limited numbers, their domestic position, and their closeness to the family, black slaves in New France experienced one of the most benign forms of slavery. Neither defended nor condemned, slavery continued in New France as it had begun—uncertainly. Both the colony and the institution evolved irresolutely, and by the mid-eighteenth century both had fallen into decline.[2]

The British takeover of Canada in 1763, however, revived the institution of slavery. The Treaty of Paris, ending the French and Indian War, gave Great Britain possession of all the former French mainland holdings in North America east of the Mississippi River. One unintentional result of this cession was the immediate revival of slavery in Canada, for British law and custom in the colonies supported and espoused the institution. Under the Treaty of Paris, English criminal and civil codes became the law of the land and thereby superseded all French ordinances pertaining to slavery. The Quebec Act of 1774 reinstated French civil law in Quebec, and even when the province was divided, Lower Canada retained French civil law. In regard to slavery, however, British criminal law remained in effect throughout Canada.[3]

The newly appointed British military governor stationed in Quebec, General James Murray, quickly revealed his support of the institution of slavery. In 1763, he wrote to an acquaintance in New York for the express purpose of importing black slaves into the colony to act as domestic servants. Realizing that the French settlers, over whom he was now governor, would never deign to work in such a capacity and that soldiers made unreliable laborers, Murray concluded that "Black Slaves are Certainly the only people to be depended upon" to provide domestic service, agricultural work, and other forms of labor. The cost of such labor appears to have been unimportant to Murray, for he was willing to import a steady supply of black slaves regardless of price.[4] In an attempt to reconcile French customs with British rule, he permitted the French settlers to retain the benign form of slavery that characterized New France. The benevolent condition of slavery was perpetuated, while the extent of slavery expanded under British rule.

By the eve of the American Revolution, British military advisers perceived that an attack on slavery in their southern American colonies might greatly weaken that region's economic stability. To accomplish this end, they dangled a policy of emancipation in front of those slaves who would join the British military during the war. Employed both to furnish British troops with more manpower and to erode the supply of labor in the South, this attempt backfired when few slaves volunteered their services. Worse still, those slaves who did respond, accepting the British military obligation, were often sold back into bondage by their commanding officers. Unscrupulous British officers took advantage of the opportunity to sell black labor for profit, and as a result, blacks across Canada became subject to unlawful abduction and enslavement.

Wartime conditions further muddled the state of slavery in the Canadas. Blacks who had been freed before the war now feared illegal seizure; those who had been captured as a result of the war now experienced further subjugation; and those who had joined the British army, seeking freedom, now found vassalage. A black slave owned by a French merchant in Quebec was abducted and sold by members of the British army. Slaves captured in Kentucky in 1780 by the British were transported to Quebec to be put on the auction block. From New York, Loyalists transported slaves to Montreal to be sold as merchandise.[5] British attitudes and practices during the American Revolution, then, ultimately encouraged the growth of black slavery in Canada.

During this period, owners and slaves alike registered a number of petitions and complaints with the governor of Canada, Sir Frederick Haldimand. The governor, in turn, responded by pressuring Sir John Johnson, superintendent of Indian Affairs, to locate and record the number of illegally seized slaves. Haldimand wrote, "Complaints having been made upon the subject of selling Negroes brought into this Province...I must desire that you upon the most minute inquiry give to the Brigadier-General...a return of all Negroes who have been brought into the Province by parties in any respect under your Directions."

Johnson's reply is perhaps indicative of the lack of concern felt by most British officials. According to his accounting, the disposition of merely fifty slaves was at issue. This conservative number would primarily seem to reflect Johnson's own prejudices as a slave owner, but it emphasizes as well the difficulty of drawing up an accurate estimate. There simply was no reliable method with which to determine the status of a black refugee in Canada during the Revolutionary War. The only recourse for Haldimand was to try to block the continued entry—forcible or not—of black slaves from the American colonies to the south.[6]

Despite Haldimand's efforts, by the end of the Revolutionary War the number of blacks in Canada had grown substantially. Many were brought into Quebec as slaves by displaced Loyalists, while others came with their owners into the area east of Montreal, a region commonly referred to as the Eastern Townships. Paradoxically, hundreds of blacks arrived from the colonies to the south seeking freedom from slavery at just the same time that numerous blacks were being sold into Canada from nearby Vermont—where slavery was outlawed in 1777. By 1784, approximately 4,050 blacks were present in the colonies north of the forty-ninth parallel. Of that number, some 1,800 were slaves, reflecting a 65 percent increase in the slave population during the twenty-one years of British authority. The vast majority of free blacks settled in the maritime provinces, particularly in Nova Scotia. The number of slaves, however, was distributed almost equally between Nova Scotia and the regions soon to be known as Upper and Lower Canada. In view of the continuing influx of Loyalists with their slaves, and the increasing number of free blacks, the black population in Canada may well have been even higher than the official estimate.[7]

The Imperial Act of 1790 bolstered slavery even more. This act let prospective settlers bring into Bermuda, the Bahamas, and Upper and Lower Canada all "Negroes, household furniture, utensils or husbandry or clothing," tax-free. The act further stipulated that such goods must remain the private property of the immigrating individual for at least one year after arrival. In addition, each white male colonist had to take a loyalty oath that was forbidden to all blacks.[8] The Imperial Act of 1790, then, offered effective legal protection to the institution of slavery. It encouraged the importation of black slaves, designated slaves as property, and denied certain rights to blacks, whether slave or free. In so doing, the act discouragd settlement in the Canadas by free blacks, while it promoted the tax-free importation of slaves. As a direct corollary of this act, the slave population again decreased.

Yet although the number of enslaved blacks increased after the arrival of British rule, the population in general grew even more dramatically. At its largest, New France had boasted a population of 55,000. By 1790, some 200,000 colonists resided in Canada. This increase can be attributed to such factors as the immigration of Loyalists from the United States, and the continuing influx of people from the British Isles. Whatever the reasons, the number of settlers multiplied fourfold. The expansion of slavery was hardly noticed, for the number of white colonists exceeded the number of blacks by approximately 100 to 1.[9] In spite of their growth in population, blacks still comprised only a tiny percentage of the residents of Canada.

Accompanying the relative expansion of slavery in British North America, there was a change in the type of work that blacks performed. Those blacks who arrived after 1783 provided more in the way of skilled labor than their predecessors. Instead of being subject to the limitations of domestic or field work, many of them practiced respected trades. Blacks, both slave and free, found occupations as blacksmiths, millwrights, caulkers, carpenters, sawyers, and coopers. A number of slaves became printers under the training of William Brown, founder of the *Quebec Gazette,* and others served as assistants to various printers after Brown's example. Others worked in Canadian taverns as waiters and churners.[10] By 1799, blacks even held positions as surveyors in Upper Canada. Slaves constructed roads through what was formerly the frontier, and in at least one instance, under the direction of a black foreman. Several blacks acted as the contractors for construction crews.[11] It became increasingly apparent that the nature of black servitude in the Canadas had modified.

The frequency and method of manumission changed as well. In regions where slavery had lost its appeal as a viable source of labor, a slave often received freedom in exchange for a "covenant of paid services" with the former master. Many blacks became apprenticed to their former owners in a mutually agreeable pact wherein they learned a valuable trade while remaining in an ensured environment. This kind of negotiation occurred in Upper Canada as late as 1824, when a mulatto youth was placed under the authority of a proprietor who promised to "well instruct and use him" as a journeyman for ten years.[12]

The character of slavery in the Canadas remained fairly benign throughout, with slaves rarely subjected to ill treatment. Absent were the brutal overseer, the cruel concept of slave breeding, and the threat of armed slave revolt. British law in conjunction for the most part with common sense prevented unjust punishment. In 1792, for example, the judge of the Court of Common Pleas of upper Canada, William Dummer Powell, handed down the death penalty to a black convicted of burglary—a crime ordinarily resulting in capital punishment. Just three years later, Judge Powell intervened in the case of a young black who, convicted of the same crime, had been given the same sentence. Addressing Lieutenant Governor John Simcoe on behalf of the youthful offender, Powell successfully argued for leniency, claiming that the youth could not be held fully accountable for his actions because of the detrimental effects of slavery on his impressionable character. In yet another case, two slaves owned by William Jarvis, secretary of the Province of Upper Canada, received the benefit of trial by jury. The two slaves had been seized while committing an act of burglary, but instead of being judged and sentenced by their owner, they were accorded the full privileges of a court trial.[13] Entitled to legal recourse, slaves seldom experienced gross mistreatment.

The few purported cases of extreme abuse in the Canadas prompted scandal and legendary tales. One alleged incident related that Peter Russell, the administrator of Upper Canada, left his slave Jupiter bound in a warehouse for a day. An associate of Russell's, Mathew Elliot, placed a lashing ring on his property with the intent of instilling a fear of whipping in his slaves.[14] While no mistreatment actually occurred at the Elliot home in Sandwich, a public flogging did take place in Quebec; ironically, it happened to a slave owned by editor William Brown. Local legend in Bath, Upper Canada, maintained that a slave was once tied to a tree and whipped. Thereafter, the tree became a landmark.[15] Such reports of mistreatment, however, often had more the character of rumor than of fact.

Indeed, both legend and documentation vividly illustrate the humane treatment that slaves received in the Canadas. The blacks of a Fort Cumberland merchant, James Law, experienced a quality of care renowned enough to engender the adage, "As proud as Law's niggers." The ledger of the estate of Peter Russel proved that he had paid a teacher to tutor the son of a slave, and also indicated that he provided generously for his slaves. In a most philanthropic gesture, the solicitor general of Upper Canada, Robert Isaac Dey Gray, purchased the mother of one of his slaves, brought the family together, and ultimately freed them at his death. He bequeathed a trust fund of 1200 pounds to the woman servant, and left to her sons fifty pounds and two hundred acres of land.

Numerous other estates, including that of Isaac Bennett, set up provisions for the education and emancipation of slaves. In an especially charitable household, the slaves of Henry Denny Denson received medical attention from the family doctor and were given presents by their master at Christmas. The brutalizing effects of separation on slave families were avoided in the Canadas as almost all families stayed together. Records reveal the separation for sale of only two couples, and disclose the sale of only one young child away from his parents.[16]

The benevolent form of slavery that developed in the Canadas may have discouraged mistreatment, but the fundamental inhumanity of slavery remained. Though slaves might have been the recipients of kindness from their owners, they nevertheless performed arduous and strenuous tasks. Slaves died young according to church records, and longed for freedom according to the number of runaways listed in the advertisements of newspapers. The idea that one man owned another continued, for the majority of wills provided for the disposition of slaves along with that of cattle, furniture, land, or other property. William Jarvis only agreed to manumit his slave, Henry Lewis, under duress. The circumstances—runaway Lewis got in touch with Jarvis from New York in order to legally effect the purchase of freedom—dictated his approval. Jarvis may not have intended to free Lewis at that or any other time, but like other slaveholders, he was pleased to receive some financial remuneration from his investment. Even after manumission, some owners attempted to exploit their former slaves for financial advantage. The administrator of the government of Upper Canada, Peter Russell, tried to persuade one recently freed black to act as a surrogate buyer in order to expand Russell's land ownership. Despite the benevolences usually bestowed upon them, then, black slaves in the Canadas yearned to be something more than chattel.[17]

Their condition of enslavement obviously determined that blacks existed in a socially, educationally, and economically restricted environment. Even the humane treatment and the greater technical skills afforded to slaves in the Canadas could never eradicate the stigma of slavery. While many blacks obtained a basic education or learned a marketable trade, most remined in bondage, or if free, in a state of near peonage. They possessed neither status nor property because of the involuntary conditions under which they existed. Put simply, the inferior status of blacks laid the foundations for race relations in future generations. Realizing their plight and foreseeing no immediate cure in the Canadas, a number of openly malcontent blacks decided that their destinies lay across the ocean on African shores.

Toward this end, two "back-to-Africa" movements emerged. Both originated in Nova Scotia and had as their object the return of hundreds of blacks to Africa, specifically to Sierra Leone. The first took place in 1791-1792, when some 1200 to 1500 adult blacks journeyed to Sierra Leone. Of that number, approximately one-third to one-half had been born in Africa. A second and smaller group of blacks, numbering about 550, determined to leave Nova Scotia in 1800, after residing there for just a few years. Most people in this assemblage were Jamaican Maroons who had arrived in Nova Scotia seeking freedom. Both of these "back-to-Africa" movements received funding from white philanthropists who helped to plan the ventures after learning of the blacks' resolution to leave. Although the crossings occurred without event, the settlements in Sierra Leone proved less than successful because of disease, skullduggery, and bad management. These two isolated examples of colonization movements served to dramatize the extent of dissatisfaction on the part of free and enslaved blacks in the Canadas, but alone could not begin to resolve the existing difficulties in race relations there. A more localized panacea soon addressed the problem.[18]

The incipient yet burgeoning antislavery movement in Canada furnished an answer. The lieutenant governor of Upper Canada, John Graves Simcoe, led the official attack against slavery in that province through its legislature. Even before arriving in Upper Canada, during his short stint in 1790 in the British House of Commons, Simcoe had castigated the institution of black slavery. His private correspondence revealed his opinion that both the unwritten British constitution in specific, and Christianity in general condemned slavery. The future Lieutenant Governor of Upper Canada vowed to withhold his signature from any legislation that "discriminates by dishonest policy between the natives of Africa, America or Europe." Though he desired to uphold the Imperial Act of 1790 and its countenance of immigration to his new residence, Simcoe knew that to do so might strengthen slavery in Upper Canada. Because of his constant and candid opposition to slavery, Simcoe considered the issuance of a manifesto liberating all slaves. The impracticality of such a proclamation at the beginning of his term as lieutenant governor, however, temporarily deferred it. In the meantime, Simcoe encouraged free blacks to enter and settle in Upper Canada, not in segregated communities but in the mainstream of Canadian life.[19]

Soon after, in March 1793, Simcoe sought to challenge the legality of slavery and to turn public opinion against the institution in Upper Canada. The opportunity arose during the first convening of the Executive Council where it was revealed by Peter Martin, a free black in the employ of the province's superintendent of Indian Affairs, that an enslaved black girl had been fettered, despite her vehement opposition, and carried over the Niagara River into American enslavement. Another witness attested that many Canadian slave-holders planned to follow suit by selling their slaves across the border. The members of the Executive Council—including Simcoe, Chief Justice William Osgoode, and slaveholder Peter Russell—decided that the owner of the unfortunate slave girl should be indicted for disturbing the peace.[20]

The prosecution of William Vrooman, the owner, by the attorney general of Upper Canada, however, could produce no positive result except to focus public attention on the matter. Chief Justice Osgoode and Peter Russel knew before the meeting of the Executive Council that such was the case, having been informed by Attorney General John White that Vrooman had no more disturbed the peace than if he had sold a recalcitrant cow. Indeed, the attorney general stated that any other similar selling of slaves could legally continue under the current statutes.[21]

So advised, Lieutenant Governor Simcoe urged the revision of those laws. Under Simcoe's direction, Attorney General White introduced a bill in the House of Assembly to abolish slavery gradually. White pushed the legislation through the lower house, experiencing "much opposition but little argument." The source of opposition to the act basically came from two quarters: farmers who utilized slaves in the fields but thought slavery should be limited; and mercenary dealers who purchased black slaves from Indians in order to realize high resale value. Six of the sixteen members in the House of Assembly owned slaves, as did three members in the Legislaive Council. Nonetheless the political aplomb and persuasive persistence of Simcoe and White combined to win unanimous passage for the act.[22]

The bill to abolish slavery in Upper Canada ironically did not free a single black slave. As an act formulated "to prevent the further introduction of slaves" into the province, it merely mirrored the political circumstances under which it was born. Certain officials had initially hoped that the legislation would abolish slavery in Upper Canada altogether; but that idea could not be passed in a bill that required the voting approval of slaveholders. Thus, it seemed a compromise with no clout. And although the act gained royal approval in July 1793, it might not have stood if contested in court. The bill overtly contradicted the clause regarding slaves in the Imperial Act of 1790, by asserting that "no Negro or other person who shall come or be brought into this Province...shall be subject to the condition of a slave or to bounden involuntary service for life." Fortunately, the act drew no challenge, and slavery had been abolished in all British territories by the time Parliament examined contradictory colonial enactments.[23]

The details of Simcoe and White's bill, however, did concern the perpetuation of black slavery in Upper Canada. While it maintained the bondage of those already enslaved, the act ruled that no person could be put into that condition in the future. All offspring of slaves born after this enactment would be freed on their twenty-fifth birthday, and were to be provided "proper nourishment and clothing" until that time. The children born to the next generation would be totally free. Yet the bill contradictorily dissuaded manumission by stipulating that the former owner of a freed slave must offer the security to prevent the latter from becoming a public charge, though indentured servitude was limited to a maximum of nine years. Perhaps most important to the future of slavery in Upper Canada, there could be no further importation of slaves.[24] Simcoe seemed to have achieved at least part of his intended goal.

The act proved to be so unpopular with slaveholders, on the other hand, that it resulted in the removal of White as attorney general in the next election. Misinterpretation occurred as well, as the wife of Provincial Secretary William Jarvis wrote to a relative in England that Simcoe had "by a piece of chicanery freed all the Negroes" and by so doing had "rendered himself unpopular." Even with the protection of their present property then, disgruntled slaveowners resented the provision. When Simcoe left Upper Canada, a number of the unhappy slaveholders tied to reverse the bill. In 1798 Christopher Robinson, representative from the districts of Addington and Ontario, introduced legislation directly negating Simcoe's act. This new bill reaffirmed the Imperial Act of 1790 by allowing black slaves to be brought by immigrants into Upper Canada. The measure passed the House of Assembly by a vote of eight to four, but was tabled in the upper chamber throughout the remainder of that legislative session. Thanks in part to the work of two liberal-minded delegates, Robert

Hamilton and Richard Cartwright, and to the resolve of Simcoe's staunch defender, Solicitor General Robert Isaac Dey Gray, no other measures in support of slavery materialized. Simcoe and White's work stood in Upper Canada as a portent of slavery's future in the Canadas.[25]

The institution of slavery died slowly in Upper Canada after the passage of Simcoe's act in 1793. The lack of newly imported slaves insured slavery's decline, while numerous Canadian slave owners continued to dispose of their slave property by selling them across the border into New York, until that too became illegal in the state in 1799. In contrast to the number of slaves being sold across the border, very few slaves were still spirited into Canada. Consequently, Canadian slavery saw many of its numbers disappear via natural causes, auction blocks, or runaways. Enough slaves escaped into the freedom of the Northwest Territory, Michigan Territory, Vermont, and New York by 1807 to prompt the slaveholders of the western district of Upper Canada to solicit governmental assistance. Ten Canadian slave owners formally petitioned Lieutenant Governor Francis Gore to block "the Facility of Escape to the American States" that had effectively depleted their supply of black slave laborers. British remonstrances to the United States produced no amelioration of the situation for the slaveholders, and, Lieutenant Governor Gore apparently allowed the issue to stall at that pooint. Upper Canada's prevention of future enslavement had successfully limited slavery within its own borders.[26]

Other provinces in British North America experienced slightly more difficulty in attempting to abolish slavery. With White's aid, Simcoe had been able to jockey his bill quickly through the small legislature of Upper Canada. The much larger legislative assembly of Lower Canada, with fifty members in its lower house and fifteen in its upper, confounded any similar effort. The Lower Canadian House of Assembly characteristically split into political factions on most issues, and the dissolution of slavery proved no different. Pierre-Louis Panet, representative from Cornwallis, had introduced a bill to abolish slavery in Lower Canada in February 1793, prior to Simcoe's attempt in Upper Canada. The Panet bill languished in committee, however, and without a powerful sponsor to force the issue, died there. In the end, the legislature of Lower Canada would never pass a measure to dismantle legally the institution of black slavery.[27]

It remained for the press and the courts of Lower Canada to reflect the conscience of its citizens on the slavery issue. The printer of the *Quebec Gazette,* William Brown, and his successor, John Nielson, both owned slaves in Lower Canada. By 1789, Brown had emancipated his slaves and his nephew Nielson followed suit a few years later. Besides their individual examples as proponents of slave manumission, the two editors stirred antislavery public opinion. Beginning in 1790, the *Quebec Gazette* included antislavery poetry in its columns as well as accounts of middle passage barbarism, printed in both English and French. These and associated stories consistently appeared in the *Gasette*, calculated by Brown and Nielson to precipitate opposition to slavery.[28]

The courts of Lower Canada found an antislavery champion, similar to editors Brown and Nielson, in James Monk, chief justice of the King's Bench. While Brown and Nielson raised antislavery consciousness, Monk provided the initiative to repress the growth of slavery in Lower Canada the first time slaves were brought before his bench. In a 1798 case, Monk judged that an act of 1562, governing the punishment of slaves, journeymen, and servants had stipulated that disciplinary action must be taken in houses of correction. The act, he argued, did not empower the court to place those individuals in prisons or jails—only in houses of correction. Upon this technicality, and in view of the fact that no "houses of correction" existed in Lower Canada, the slaves in question were awarded release. To entrench his antislavery stand, Chief Justice Monk issued an obiter dioctum stating that slavery did not officially exist in the province. And he admonished slaveholders that this interpretation would hold for any future cases brought before his court involving slaves.[29]

It did not take slave owners long to respond. In April 1799, the representatives of Montreal and Quebec, Joseph Papineau and John Black respectively, tendered a lengthy suit to the House of Assembly. The petition represented the response of Lower Canada's slaveholders to Monk's position on slavery and proposed that houses of correction be constructed in the province to prevent slave release on that legal technicality. Further, it maintained that, contrary to Monk's opinion, existing legislation upheld the institution of slavery in Lower Canada.[30] The suit concluded with a plea to the House of Assembly either to act to protect slavery and slave owners' rightful property, or to react by ending slavery altogether. Even the petitioners recognized that their slave population might revolt under an ambiguous status.

As a result, a bill was fashioned after Simcoe's act in Upper Canada. The act defined limitations on black slavery, and included a clause restricting the importation of slaves. James Cuthbert, member for Warwick, proposed the legislaiton early in 1800, but it received no consideration. Measures proposing the same ideas were introduced repeatedly in subsequent years, each, however, failing to pass. The faction supporting the institution of slavery never could reach a compromise with those favoring abolition, while social differences between representatives of rural districts and those from Montreal and Quebec precluded agreement as well. While everyone seemed to support the establishment of houses of correction, and a bill for their organization passed into law in 1799, a provision requiring slave committal failed. The ineffectual legislature thus enabled Monk and the judiciary of Lower Canada to control the fate of slavery.[31]

Not until 1829 would the Executive Council of Lower Canada officially endorse Monk's obiter dictum. The action arose after a Canadian, Paul Vallard, assisted a mulatto slave in escaping from Illinois into Lower Canada. Proceeding through formal channels, United States Secretary of State Henry Clay appealed for Vallard's extradition so that he could be prosecuted for theft. The administrator of Lower Canada, Sir James Kempt, requested a ruling from his Executive Council which, in turn, advised him that a person could be extradited only if the act of which he was accused by the United States was also illegal in Canada. The Executive Council finally acknowledged that "the state of slavery is not recognized by the Law of Canada...Every Slave therefore who comes into the Province is immediately free whether he has been brought in by violence or has entered it of his own accord." Neither Vallard nor the former slave were returned to the United States. The Executive Council, by substantiating Monk's opinion, effectively rendered the institution of slavery untenable in Lower Canada.[32]

The antislavery movement proceeded in similar fashion in the province of Nova Scotia. A proclamation had been issued in the House of Assembly there in 1787 that effectively denied the existence of slavery in the province. In addition to this support for abolition, the judiciary reinforced antislavery sentiment. The successive chief justices, Thomas Andrew Strange and Sampson Salter Blowers, dominated court decisions regarding slavery in Nova Scotia from 1791 to 1833. The two chief justices devoted their adjudication to the gradual "wearing out" of slavery. Carefully avoiding the question of the legality of the institution, Strange and Blowers nevertheless engaged in a courtroom war of attrition upon slaveholders. With the aid of religious Leader Reverend Dr. James MacGregor, they exploited public antipathy toward slavery. By the turn of the century, slavery had virtually disappeared from Nova Scotian life.[33]

The champions of the antislavery movement in the Canadas, then, were the magistrates. Forceful judicial decisions undertook to dismantle, albeit, slowly, the institution of slavery. Where conflicting legislation or public pressure forestalled abolition, judicial activity directed the course of events.[34] By the decade of the 1820s, slavery in the Canadas had essentially disappeared due to the restrictions placed on its growth prior to the turn of the century. The last isolated extant notices of slaves for sale appeared in Nova Scotia in 1820 and in Quebec in 1821; and, referral to slave property occurred rarely in wills after that time. Although a small number of blacks remained enslaved, the growth of slavery had been stymied by effective judicial intervention.[35]

The final death knell to black slavery in British North America came on 28 August 1833. The Parliament of Great Britain on that date enacted the Imperial Act decreeing the permanent and complete abolition of slavery in all British colonies, effective one year later on 1 August 1834. The Imperial Act stated that every slave more than six years old would provide apprenticed labor to his owner, but limited the length of apprenticeship to six years. After this period of apprenticeship, former slaves had no further obligation to the slaveholder. The act allowed for slave children less than six years old to be apprenticed until reaching the age of twenty-one, at which time they, too, became totally free. It created a pool of twenty thousand pounds to compensate slave owners for their loss of property. This money would be divided into nineteen shares to be distributed among the sixteen British colonies in the Caribbean, Bermuda, the Cape of Good Hope, and Mauritius. No provision was made for the provinces of British North America to receive financial remuneration. By that omission, as well as by the fact that the Canadas were excluded from any mentioin in the act, the British Parliament obliquely voiced its position on slavery there. Obviously, the British government believed that slavery had already perished in Canada, causing no need for compensation to former slaveholders.

Parliament had made a correct assumption, for although a few slaves in the Canadas might have been eligible for apprenticeship, none actually entered into it. Of the approximately eight hundred thousand slaves freed by the Imperial Act of 1833, no more than about fifty resided in British North America at the time of its passage.[36] And when John Baker, a former slave of Robert Isaac Dey Gray who had been liberated in 1804, died in 1871, no other freed slaves survived him in the Canadas.[37]

The interrelation of several factors contributed to the decline of the institution of slavery in Canada. Its economic impracticability provided the basis for slavery's demise. Slavery had been a means of furnishing labor, but not a cheap one, as the cost of clothing and feeding slaves continued to rise. Moreover, manual labor in the Canadas never demanded a large enough work force to make slavery very profitable. Instead of appreciating, slave values depreciated, so slave breeding was economically unfeasible. Too, numerous slaves tried to escape through the frontier; to free states in America; or to the sea from the maritime provinces.[38] Investment in slave property seemed risky and frequently expensive, while indentured servitude could provide an effective alternative source of labor without the economic and moral ramifications of slavery. In the end, the Canadas simply consisted of too individualized a labor force where slavery began as a temporary convenience and ultimately became extraneous baggage.

Although slavery ceased to exist, blacks were nevertheless irrevocably present in the Canadas. Their numbers swelled after the War of 1812, when at least two thousand refugee blacks from the United States sought freedom in Canada. Unskilled and uneducated, the majority of the refugees settled in Nova Scotia, and lived in perpetual poverty because they either could not or would not be gainfully employed. Shunned by former Loyalist slaves, they worked at occasional odd jobs rather than becoming farmers or fishermen, they never became involved in politics, nor sought to better themselves through education. As a group, the refugees became associated with charity; a stigma that manumitted Loyalist slaves had managed to avoid, and one that led to friction between the two groups of blacks. More significantly, white Canadians perceived the refugees as representative of the bad characteristics of blacks in general. To Canadian whites, the indolence of the newly arrived blacks reflected on the entire race, and they looked upon the refugees with increasing impatience. Yet, as long as the blacks were limited in number, the problem could be ignored.

The introduction of blacks into Canadian society, then, was intimately associated until 1820 with the development of slavery. Virtually no free blacks had chosen to settle in Canada before the Revolutionary War, so the only contact that white Canadians had with blacks was with their slaves. When free blacks entered Canada at the time of the American Revolution, the relationship between whites and blacks had not yet been strained basically for several reasons: blacks provided needed labor and, in some cases, skilled labor; both free blacks and slaves continued to benefit from the impartial application of the law in Canada; and finally, slaves were still accorded good care, with no blacks experiencing unusually harsh punishment. Perhaps most important to this relationship, however, was the fact that the black population in Canada remained insignificantly small when compared to the number of whites. Blacks were barely visible in Canadian society as a whole. Not until the refugees from the War of 1812 arrived were there overt signs of tension between the races.

From this environment emerged the myth of a Canadian Canaan for fugitive slaves from the United States. Nonetheless, a humane form of slavery did not necessarily imply pro-black attitudes among white Canadians; nor did a strong antislavery movement mean Canadians were predisposed toward blacks. Canadians supported human rights but blacks in 1820 remained on the lower rungs of society's ladder. With few skills and little training, blacks in Canada were never rich. Still, most blacks in Canada had received emancipation by the 1820s and looked forward to a life of freedom. This was the magnet that during the next four decades would induce thousands of fugitive slaves to cross the border into Canada.

NOTES

1. Throughout this study, the term Canada is used to designate the area encompassed by the Dominion of Canada. When technical accuracy was required, more precise terms have been used. New France refers to the French colony prior to 1763. Upper

Canada was created in 1791 and constituted what is now the province of Ontario. Lower Canada, created the same year, is the present-day province of Quebec. From 1841 to 1867 these were Canada West and Canada East respectively. During both periods they were referred to collectively as the Canadas. On 29 March 1867, under the British North America Act, the Dominion of Canada was created uniting Ontario, Quebec, New Brunswick, and Nova Scotia.

2. For more on slavery in New France, see Hubert Neilson, "Slavery in Old Canada: Before and After the Conquest," *Transactions of the Literary and Historical Society of Quebec,* Series 2, 26 (1906), pp. 19-45.

Several general histories of blacks in Canada include accounts of this topic as well. See Ida Greaves, "The Negro in Canada," *McGill University Economic Studies,* no. 16 (Montreal, 1930), pp. 9-21;

Headley Tulloch, *Black Canadians: A Long Line of Fighters* (Toronto, 1975), pp. 71-91;

Leo W. Bertley, *Canada and Its People of African Descent* (Pierrefonds, P.Q., 1977), pp. 25-37; and

Ontario Educational Communications Authority, *Identity: The Black Experience in Canada* (Toronto, 1979), pp. 1-10.

By far the most scholarly treatment of blacks in Canada is, however, Robin W. Winks, *The Blacks in Canada: A History* (New Haven, 1971). For information on slavery in New France see especially pp. 1-23, though Winks's entire study is a veritable storehouse of information concerning all aspects of the role of blacks in Canadian history.

3. Winks, *Blacks in Canada,* p. 25;

William Renwick Riddell, "The Slave in Upper Canada," *Journal of Negro History* 4 (October 1919), pp. 372-77'

Idem, "The Slave in Canada," *Journal of Negro History* 5 (July 1920), pp. 275-76; John K.A. Farrell, "Some Opinions of Christian Europeans Regarding Negro Slavery in the Seventeenth and Early Eighteenth Centuries," *The Canadian Historical Association Report* (1958), pp. 13-22.

4. James Murray to John Watts, 2 November 1763, in the James Murray Papers, Letter Book #2, pp. 15-16, located in the Public Archives of Canada, Ottawa.

5. Winks, *Blacks in Canada,* pp. 29-31.

See also William Renwick Riddell, "Notes on the Slave in Nouvelle France," *Journal of Negro History* 7 (July 1923), pp. 316-30;

Idem, "Le Code Noir: Application of in Canada," *Journal of Negro History* 10 (July 1925), pp. 321-29.

Loyalists were those who remained faithful to Great Britain during the American Revolution and consequently were often forced to flee from the colonies to Canada for their safety.

6. Sir Frederick Haldimand Journal found in *Canadian Archives, B*, no. 217, p. 21, Public Archives of Canada, Ottawa.

7. *Report on Canadian Archives, 1889* (Ottawa, 1890), p. 39.
   See also T. Watson Smith, "The Slave in Canada," *Collections of the Nova Scotia Historical Society for the Years 1896-1898* 10 (1899), pp. 1-161; and
   William Renwick Riddell, "Some References to Negroes in Upper Canada," *Ontario Historical Society Papers and Records* 19 (1929), pp. 144-46.

8. This act of 1 August 1790 is cited as 30 George III, c. 27, and is found in its entirety in Miscellaneous Documents, no. 16, part 2, located in the Public Archives of Canada, Ottawa.

9. Department of Agriculture, *Censuses of Canada: 1665-1871* (Ottawa, 1876), pp. xlii, 61, 74-80.

10. Neilson, "Slavery in Old Canada," pp. 31-34; and
    Winks, *Blacks in Canada*, pp. 46-46.

11. Agreement between Jack Mosee, William Willis, and Thomas Ridout, 2 February 1799, Report No. 3; and
    Agreement between Parker Mills and David William Smith, Report No. 5:
    both found in the Crown Land Papers, General Correspondence, located in the Ontario Provincial Archives, Toronto.

12. Riddell, "The Slave in Canada," pp. 293-99.
    See also "Copies of Original Documents from the Collection of the Society," *Lennox and Addington Historical Society, Papers and Records* 2 (1910), pp. 41-42.

13. William Dummer Powell to John Simcoe, n.d., 1795, in the William Dummer Powell Papers, vol. 1, p. 6; and
    the record of the Court of Common Pleas, 18 March 1788, 19 July 1793, and 18 December 1799 in Miscellaneous Documents, no. 16, part 2:
    both located in the Public Archives of Canada, Ottawa.

14. Both Russell and Elliot held slaves in substantial numbers. Russell is said to have owned 99 slaves while Elliot possessed somewhere between 50 and 60 slaves. riddell, "The Slave in Canada," credits Elliot with "more than 50 slaves" on p. 326, n. 17, and on p. 333 with "some sixty."
    See also the Russell Family Papers, Ontario Provincial Archives, Toronto, for more information on Peter Russell's treatment of his slaves.

15. Riddell, "The Slave in Canada," pp. 334-35;
    Smith, "The Slave in Canada," pp. 34, 49, 76-77;
    Neilson, "Slavery in Old Canada," p. 33;
    Jesse E. Middleton and Fred Landon, *The Province of Ontario: A History* (Toronto, 1927), p. 101; and
    James E. Jones, *Pioneer Crimes and Punishments in Toronto and the Home*

District (Toronto, 1924), pp. 11-12.

16.   The account book of Peter Russell, entries for 4 and 11 September, 16-17 October, 2 and 19 November, 17 December 1803, and 20 January, 26 February, 10 July, 6, 14, and 21 November 1804;
Peter Russell to William Cooper, 28 April 1799:
both in the Peter Russell Papers, Ontario Provincial Archives, Toronto;
Elizabeth Russell Diary, 6 January 1808 in the Toronto Public Library;
Henry Lewis to William Jarvis, 3 May 1798, in the William Jarvis Papers, box 55, Toronto Public Library;
Miscellaneous Documents, vol. 21, no. 1, in the Public Archives of Canada, Ottawa.

17.   Richard Norton Wilkinson, last will and testament, 28 April 1804, "Individuals," vol. 6, Public Archives of Canada, Ottawa:
Burger Huycke, last will and testament, 1787, Miscellaneous Documents, vol. 30, no. 2, Public Archives of Canada, Ottawa.

18.   For a detailed account of the Canadian "back to Africa" movements, see James W. St. G. Walker, *The Black Loyalists: The Search for a Promised Land in Nova Scotia and Sierra Leone, 1783-1870* (New York, 1976).
The Maroons were descendants of black slaves who had escaped from the Spanish before the British conquest of Jamaica.

19.   Riddell, "The Slave in Upper Canada," pp. 372-86;
Smith, "The Slave in Canada," pp. 43-48, 90-122.

20.   Earnest A. Cruikshank, ed., *The Correspondence of Lieut. Governor John Graves Simcoe, with Allied Documents relating to His Administration of the Government of Upper Canada* (Toronto, 1923), vol. 1, p. 304 (hereafter cited as *Simcoe Correspondence*).

21.   Ibid. See also the John Graves Simcoe Papers, Ontario Provincial Archives, Toronto, for more information on White.

22.   William Renwick Riddell, *The Life of John Graves Simcoe, First Lieutenant-Governor of the province of Upper Canada, 1792-6* (Toronto, 1926), p. 201, quoting White's diary for 14 March 1793;
Cruikshank, *Simcoe Correspondence,* vol. 2 (1924), pp. 53-54; and
C.C.James, "The First Legislators of Upper Canada," *Transactions of the Royal Society of Canada,* 8 sec. 2 (1902), p. 104.

23.   This Act of 9 July 1793 is cited 33 George III, c. 7, and is found in its entirety in Miscellaneous Documents, no. 16, part 2, in the Public Archives of Canada, Toronto.
See also Riddell, "The Slave in Canada," pp. 318-19; and
Jason H. Silverman, "Kentucky, Canada, and Extradition: The Jesse Happy Case," *The Filson Club History Quarterly* 54 (January 1980), p. 51.

24.   Ibid; Greaves, "The Negro in Canada," pp. 13-14.

25. Hannah Jarvis to Samuel Peters, 25 September 1793 in the William Jarvis Papers, Toronto Public Library;

Robert Isac Dey Gray to Katharine Valentine, 16 February 1804, Miscellaneous Documents, 21, Public Archives of Canada, Ottawa:

William Renwick Riddell, *Upper Canada Sketches: Incidents in the Early Times of the Province* (Toronto, 1922), pp. 57-59;

Idem, *The Legal Profession in Upper Canada in its Early Periods* (Toronto, 1916), pp. 155-56;

Idem, *Life of Simcoe,* p. 427; and

Idem, "The Slave in Canada," pp. 322-24, n. 13, and p. 385, n. 20.

26. John Pearson to William Jarvis, 16 April 1798, and J. Walton to Jarvis, 7 May 1798, William Jarvis Family Papers, Toronto Public Library;

Elisha Anderson affidavit, 14 April 1796, Upper Canada Land Petitions, Book A, p. 1;

David M. Erskine to Francis Gore, 26 May 1807, Upper Canada Sundries, vol. 6:

both documents in the Public Archives of Canada, Ottawa:

Cruikshank, *Simcoe Correspondence,* vol. 4 (1930), pp. 61, 154.

27. Riddell, "Notes on the Slave in Nouvelle France," pp. 316-30;

Neilson, "Slavery in Old Canada," pp. 19-45;

Greaves, "The Negro in Canada," pp. 16-20; and

Winks, *Blacks in Canada,* pp. 99-101.

28. Riddell, "The Slave in Canada," pp. 305-16;

Tulloch, *Black Canadians,* pp. 91-96; and

Bertley, *Canada and Its People of African Descent,* pp. 25-42.

29. The statute of 1562 is cited as 5 Elizabeth, c. 4, and was not repealed until 1814 with 54 George III, c. 96:

both laws in their entirety are located in the Public Archives of Canada, Ottawa.

30. The laws referred to in the petition were an ordinance of 1709, and the Imperial Acts of 1732 and 1790, none of which really applied to their case. For a detailed account of this episode see Riddell, "The Slave in Canada," pp. 305-12.

31. Riddell, "The Slave in Canada," pp. 308-12; and

Winks, *Blacks in Canada,* pp. 99-102.

32. The original record is located in the Public Archives of Canada, Ottawa, but it is more conveniently found in William Renwick Riddell, "An International Complication Between Illinois and Canada Arising Out of Slavery," *Journal of the Illinois State Historical Society* 25 (October 1932), pp. 125-26.

33. For a detailed account of the crusade against slavery in Nova Scotia, see Riddell, "The Slave in Canada," pp. 359-76;

Smith, "The Slave in Canada," pp. 100-61;

Greaves, "The Negro in Canada," pp. 17-20;

I. Allan Jack, "The Loyalists and Slavery in New Brunswick," *Transactions of the*

Royal Society of Canada 2d series, 4 (1898), pp. 137-85.

34. This is particularly true for Nova Scotia, New Brunswick, and Lower Canada. Besides the sources listed above for blacks in these areas, see Robin W. Winks, "Negroes in the Maritimes: An Introductory Survey," *Dalhousie Review* 48 (Winter 1968), pp. 453-71; and

William Spray, *Blacks in New Brunswick* (Fredericton, 1972).

35. Riddell, "The Slave in Canada," p. 373.

Smith, "The Slave in Canada," pp. 95, 116;

Neilson, "Slavery in Old Canada," p. 41n; and

J.C. Hamilton, "Slavery in Canada," *Magazine of American History* 25 (March 1891), pp. 233-38.

36. The Statute of 1833 is cited as 3, 4 William IV, c. 73 and is found in its entirety in the Public Archives of Canada, Ottawa. British Honduras, although not yet a colony, was treated as such for the purpose of share dividing in this act.

37. Baker's story is told in J.C. Hamilton, "The African in Canada," *Proceedings of the American Association for the Advancement of Science* 33 (1890), pp. 366-68.

38. See particularly Winks, "Negroes in the Maritimes," pp. 453-71;

Spray, *Blacks in New Brunswick,* pp. 1-25;

Jack, "The Loyalists and Slavery in New Brunswick," pp. 137-85; and

Donald Clairmont and Dennis Magill, *Nova Scotian Blacks: An Historical and Structural Overview* (Halifax, 1970), pp. 5-36, for more on this.

Two

A QUESTIONABLE HAVEN

If blacks had been introduced into Canadian society through slavery, their numbers ironically increased concurrent with the death of that institution. Even as slavery ceased to flourish, the free black population grew. Manumitted Loyalist slaves, refugees from the War of 1812, and black fugitives from the United States comprised the larger black populace in Canada after the turn of the century. Manumission in Canada prior to 1833 frequently occurred as a result of judicial and economic pressures, helping to hasten the end of the practice of slavery. In the meantime, more than two thousand blacks sought refuge in Canada during and immediately following the War of 1812. The British promise of transportation and full legal rights as free settlers to all relocating United States citizens fostered this influx of blacks.[1] Unorganized, uneducated, and unskilled, these refugees swelled the ranks of unemployed free blacks in Canada and thereby spurred the development of white Canadian concern about further black arrivals. The people who exacted the most vociferous response from white Canadians, though, were the fugitive slaves from the United States.

Prompted by the uncertainties of life in the United States, blacks began to settle in Canada in the early 1820s. The vast majority chose to live in Upper Canada, the most convenient and accessible Canadian province. Substantial black settlements arose at several locations in Upper Canada during the next two decades, most notably at Amherstburg, Oro, and Wilberforce. The Wilberforce community, in particular, served to establish white Canadian resentment and suspicion of the black fugitives. Given every opportunity to prosper, this black community achieved little success and became burdensome to white Canadians.

As a result, the response of white Canadians to black colonists became increasingly negative. In the failure of blacks to assimilate successfully into the existing agricultural economy lay the foundation of social racism in Upper Canada. Legally, however, black fugitives retained governmental support in Upper Canada to the extent that numerous extradition requests were successively denied. Despite social disaffection, then, black fugitive slaves continued to cross the border into the refuge of Upper Canada.

This desire to reach Canada is best observed in the testimonies of the fugitives themselves. John Warren, a recently arrived fugitive living in Canada, explained that he had "heard of a free State where black people were free, and had no master or mistress, and just wanted to go there." In conjunction with aversion to slavery, most blacks feared that they would be eventually wrenched from their families by being sold South. James Sumler, an ex-slave who fled from Virginia to Toronto, had witnessed the sale of his brother into slavery in the Deep South and believing that his "chance would come next," he and his family headed for safety in Upper Canada. Yet the American South was not the only propelling region for blacks; discrimination in the North encouraged free blacks to seek sanctuary in Canada as well. Aby Jones noted that he only had nominal freedom in the Northern states and this constituted "as much liberty" in the United States "as was allowed to a free man of color. I saw at once that I was not really free; that there was a distinction made. I wished then to emigrate to some place where I could be really a FREE MAN." Blacks in the North were denied the right to inherit property, and were denied a litany of other legal rights. For example, in Indiana blacks were prohibited from testifying in court. There the property of Aaron Siddles "was not safe, for any loafing white might destroy or steal, and unless a white man were by to see it, I could get no redress."[2] Such prevailing attitudes prompted Siddles to move to Chatham. In the end, Northern blacks feared abduction and enslavement. Even before 1830, some two hundred black refugees in Upper Canada requested land where they might band together to avoid kidnap and a return to the American South and slavery.[3] Hoping for freedom from fear, freedom from unjust laws, and freedom from slavery itself, black Americans crossed the border into Canada looking for a new life.

The first fugitive blacks to relocate in Upper Canada stopped just inside the Canadian border for several reasons. First, the itinerant blacks had limited funds with which to travel, and thus were encouraged to terminate their journey as soon as safety was ensured. As farmers, it also seemed more prudent to remain in an area where soils were comparable to those in the United States. Finally, the proximity to the border provided the refugee blacks with an escape hatch by which they could return to the United States if necessary or desired. As a result, small black settlements materialized just across the Detroit River at Amherstburg, Windsor, and Colchester; beyond the Niagara River at Welland and St. Catharines; and in the nearby fertile peninsula, paralleling Lake Erie, at Chatham, Dresden, and London. Other bands of fugitives dispersed gradually into Oro, Toronto, and the Queen's Bush. Drawn by similarities of experience, later arrivals tended to settle near the original settlements but apart from Loyalist ex-slaves.

Before 1830, black fugitives entered Upper Canada in small and unorganized groups. Only the fortunate, shrewd, and courageous gained access to the province for the journey required great perseverance and determination. Most of the refugees came from the upper South, and had spent some time in a free Northern state. They thereby received some valuable experience by working in a free-soil economy and adapting to a colder climate. Those who elected to continue northward into Upper Canada did so voluntarily prior to 1830, for they could have remained as free blacks in the northern United States, albeit tenuously. A later wave of black immigrants would enter the province prompted primarily by fear for their freedom, rather than by conscious decision. Thus, the willingness of the first black fugitives contrasted with the negative propulsion of later black refugees. There seemed to be every positive motivation for success on the part of the first ex-slaves to arrive from the United States.

The introduction of tobacco in 1819 into Upper Canada by former slaves from Virginia and Kentucky helped to make Amherstburg a thriving area during the decade of the 1820s. Located near Fort Malden on the Detroit River, Amherstburg became a focal point for immigrating blacks as its tobacco crop developed into a major economic resource. Soon, enough tobacco had been harvested for export to Montreal, where it brought a high market value. A cash crop, demanding a larger labor pool than previously available, tobacco drew fugitive blacks toward Amherstburg where ready employment awaited. One British observer in 1824 commented that fresh black recruits joined the labor force at Amherstburg weekly. By mid-decade, thanks in part to an eager and competent black labor force, 600 hogsheads of tobacco were exported annually, while each acre of the fields yielded 800 to 1,500 pounds of tobacco.[4]

But the tobacco raised at Amherstburg was meant for sale only in Canada, and by 1827, the Canadian tobacco market was glutted. The price dropped from 6d. to 3d. per pound when the Montreal market became overstocked and the quality of the leaf dropped as well. William Berczy, a white tobacco farmer of Amherstburg, attributed this decline to "the negligence of the growers and the over anxiety of the merchants to make large returns." The stemming and curing of the tobacco had been done carelessly, and when a few merchants shipped some of this tobacco to England, the British brokers encountered much difficulty in selling it due to its inferior quality.[5] Discouraged by the low price and the restricted market, farmers in and around Amherstburg largely abandoned cultivation of the crop. In the process, black labor became superfluous when whites themselves undertook whatever aspects of the limited tobacco harvest remained.

This situation had left the fugitive slaves unemployed. By 1827, the number of refugee blacks in Amherstburg and in the adjacent community of Colchester had grown to approximately six hundred, or 20 percent of the population. They had been drawn to that particular area because of the demand for labor in the tobacco fields, and now, with no other skills, no education, and no organization, they were left to fend for themselves. The Reverend R. Rolph provided the only leadership within the black community, and his call for self-exertion and self-help went largely ignored. Recently arrived fugitives were in no condition to start new lives, for according to one observer, they were "without money, food or clothing suited to the rigors of a Canadian winter." Struggling Colchester thus became a "wretched settlement" of unemployed blacks while the whites in Amherstburg considered their black neighbors as "being thievish and otherwise immoral." Still, no widespread segregation developed, probably because as the assessment rolls and census indicate, blacks lived in small groups of fewer than forty. Nevertheless, white Canadians began viewing their black neighbors with contempt. The impoverished blacks simply formed such a large percentage of the population that they could be neither ignored nor approved.[6]

Those blacks who traveled farther into the province of Upper Canada took up residence in the peninsula farming communities of Chatham, Fairport (later Dresden), Hamilton, and Brantford. The seventy-five refugee blacks in the township of Chatham by 1827 justified support from Dr. Bray's Associates, a philanthropic society for aiding black immigrants, but the fugitives remained poor and indigent.[7] Almost a decade later, the homes of these Chatham residents were described as "sad dirty hole(s)," where cholera struck first in the town. In Brantford, located on the Grand River, fifteen black families experienced covert resentment as white Canadians suggested that they move elsewhere in the province.[8]

A unique black colony in Upper Canada was located at Oro, in a rather remote area on the western side of Lake Simcoe, far removed from the larger Upper Canadian towns. This location, however, was of strategic importance to Canadians for Oro lay between York (now Toronto), then capital of Simcoe County, and the military outpost at Penetanguishene on Lake St. Claire. Because the water route in between was quite vulnerable to American attack or blockade, Canadian authorities wanted to construct a safe and convenient overland route. Toward this end, the Executive Council of Upper Canada[9] decreed in an order of 26 April 1819 that tracts of land at Oro would be made available "to such persons qualified to receive Grants from the Crown as are willing and able to perform

Settlement Duty."[10] This land could be bought at the fixed price of five pounds for each one hundred acres with two hundred acres being the maximum amount permissible per person. Hardly a humanitarian gesture, the offer was made to entice laborers and expedite work on the Penetanguishene Road. Once the construction was completed, workers could remain to farm in the area. Even so, no whites responded, but four blacks immediately petitioned for the grants.

All blacks who so applied for land received one hundred acres on Wilberforce Street in Oro. That this occurred was no strange coincidence. Though the original order had provided for tracts of two hundred acres on the first range, blacks were nonetheless restricted to smaller tracts of land, specifically located in the second range. Despite this overt prejudice, by 1826 twenty-three black families had requested land. In all, only three households at Oro were white Canadians; the rest were all black immigrants.[11] Sir Peregrine Maitland, the lieutenant governor of Upper Canada, by then had perceived the "considerable advantages from the measure, both in view of policy and (particularly) in that of humanity."[12] Appearing to be a great humanitarian, Maitland had, in reality, simultaneously found a way to supply labor while keeping blacks employed but segregated.

The only black settlement to be sponsored by the government, Oro Township nearly failed by 1827. Poor administration compounded by the fact that only eight of the applicants had actually moved to Oro prevented the concept of a true black community from developing there. In that year, however, new life was breathed into the township by the appointment of Peter Robinson as commissioner of Crown Lands.[13] Robinson quickly inaugurated a new system to encourage the colonization of Oro by allowing blacks to purchase land at a nominal fee of one shilling per acre, as compared to the newly instituted four shillings required of whites. Too, the payment was not due until the settlers actually applied for the land patent. With this as an incentive, more black families began moving to Oro.

By 1830, the black population at Oro had reached one hundred and fifty. Most had come from the United States, as common laborers or field hands though the assessment rolls indicate that the community also had a barber, washerwoman, cooper, brewer, and logger.[14] Little is known about the previous education of Oro's black residents, but the community itself had neither a school nor a teacher. The black settlers designated fugitive slave John Little as their leader. With the aid of a white missionary couple, the Reverend and Mrs. Ari Raymond, blacks tried to adapt to farming along the western shore of Lake Simcoe. Helped by government land grants and assisted by German immigrants, who offered seed on credit to the incipient farmers, the black community seemed on the verge of flourishing. A few even optimistically mentioned the possibility of dispatching a black representative to the Upper Canadian Parliament. But Little knew nothing of organization or leadership, and the Raymonds left after several years. Robinson's new system had indeed drawn more blacks to Oro; still, the fugitives had never paid for the land and remained as illegal squatters. They had cleared enough land to eke out a living, but not enough to make Oro a prosperous or thriving community. Fugitive slave R.S.W. Sorrick, replacement for the Raymonds, stayed only a short while before he, too, left Oro. With him in 1847 went the majority of the black inhabitants of the area in quest of a milder climate, leaving fewer than sixty black settlers at Oro Township beyond 1850. Indigent whites were then encouraged to go there, and as the white population grew, the black population decreased. Those few black settlers who stayed at Oro wrestled an existence through the 1860s, after which time Oro essentially lapsed as a black settlement.[15]

Oro's failure as a black community derived from a combination of several factors. The blacks who migrated there were, by and large, unskilled laborers with little experience in farming. They had no organization, and precious little advice from the missionaries. No government agent was sent to Oro to help the blacks locate their lots or plan their farms. While the people complained of the bitter cold at Oro, the Executive Council did "not deem it expedient to advise the selection of Lands in any other part of the Province with a view to the formation of a settlement of Colored People." To avoid encouraging an influx of blacks from the United States, the council felt that blacks had already received the same terms and opportunities as any other settler and thus denied all petitions to move the black settlement to better locations. Lacking assistance, organization, education, and skills, the blacks at Oro had little chance of success. And with the white Canadian "repugnance to their forming communities near them," Robinson observed that Oro's success "might lead to the assembling of so great a number of persons of colour from the United States as to alarm the present (white) Inhabitants."[16] In the final analysis Oro fostered but one product: social disaffection on the part of both blacks and whites.

The arrival of fugitive slaves in Upper Canada partially corresponded to the extent of segregation or controversy surrounding blacks in the northern United States. The segregated educational facilities, denial of property transfer, and absence of certain rights in the courts of law that occurred in the North by 1830 encouraged blacks to relocate in Upper Canada. Still, racial tensions in the northern United States at that time lacked the intensity and breadth to force collective movements of fugitive slaves and free blacks out of the country. The large migration would come after new waves of immigrants created competition for free black labor in the northern cities, and when discrimination replaced toleration.

The first major effort made by blacks to establish their own community in Upper Canada occurred as a direct response to legislated discrimination in Ohio. Although separated from the slave states by the Ohio River, Cincinnati and other riverfront towns maintained many of the social beliefs of their neighbors to the south. Slavery had been abolished in Ohio in 1802, but new legislation was passed in 1804 and 1807 to retain control over black laborers. These codes stated that any black seeking employment in the state of Ohio must present a court-issued certificate of freedom. To provide security against fugitives, in addition, the law stipulated that each black man must post a five hundred dollar bond within three weeks of arrival. These legal restrictions had gone unenforced for years. But by 1829, the black population in Cincinnati had grown to almost three thousand, and Southern neighbors began to protest against the lure of easy freedom. Cincinnati leaders determined to enforce the requirements of Ohio's black laws. Further, the city fathers passed legislation prohibiting black participation in the militia and in jury duty, and prohibiting blacks from carrying arms.

The strict implementation of Ohio's black laws was designated to begin in 1830. Black residents of Cincinnati were allowed sixty days to obtain certificates of freedom and to post the necessary security bond. Worse, burgeoning white resentment exploded violently when angry whites mobbed blacks, and rioting ensued. The free blacks in Cincinnati realized that the rigorous administration of these laws meant disaster for them. As a group, they decided that "we, the poor sons of Aethiopia, must take shelter where we can find it.... If we cannot find it in America, where we were born and spent all our days, we must beg it elsewhere." The impetus for mass migration had thus been provided. A committee was appointed to organize the group movement and two black representatives, Israel Lewis and Thomas Cresap, journeyed to Upper Canada to "beg it elsewhere" and to locate a suitable area for black settlement.[17]

To Cincinnati blacks, Upper Canada seemed the most logical place to relocate. At that time, the Canada Company, which held vast amounts of land in the province, wished to sell a large tract of land on Lake Huron. Cresap and Lewis first sought the sanction of Upper Canada's lieutenant governor, Sir John Colborne. On behalf of the Canadian government, Colborne cordially received the two black agents and offered an encouraging message: "Tell the Republicans on your side of the line that we do not know men by their color. If you wish to come to us, you will be entitled to all the privileges of the rest of his Majesty's subjects." Cresap and Lewis then approached the Canada Company, and struck a bargain very quickly. Although negotiations had not yet been finalized, the first black refugees began to relocate on a tract near present-day Lucan in October of 1829. Named in honor of William Wilberforce, renowned British abolitionist, the

Wilberforce Settlement was born.[18]

Colborne's enthusiastic response, however, may have been misleading. By the spring of 1830, the representatives in the House of Assembly of Upper Canada concluded that, despite their good intentions toward black refugees, "... the sudden introduction of a mass of Black Population, likely to continue without limitation, is a matter so dangerous to the peace and comfort of the inhabitants, that it becomes necessary to prevent or check, by some prudent restrictions, this threatened evil." This attitude was also evident in the *African Repository*, a contemporary journal published by the American Colonization Society, which regarded the arrival of blacks en masse as the intrusion of unwelcome guests toward whom "neither the Government, the people, nor the climate of Canada, are favourable."[19] The implicated fears of white Canadians might have served to slow the incoming tide of Cincinnati blacks were there time, but the negotiations between Cresap and Lewis and the Canada Company had been successfully concluded.

Like Oro Township before it, the Wilberforce Settlement nearly failed before beginning. The arrangements with the Canada Company called for the purchase of four thousand acres of land for six thousand dollars with payment due by November of 1830. The original black settlers then intended to sell portions of this property to new arrivals and purchase additional land with the capital gained. Yet the free blacks of Cincinnati who planned to inhabit the Wilberforce Settlement had no financial resources with which to begin. Without recounting black assets, Cresap and Lewis had grandly assured the Canada Company of payment. With nowhere else to turn, the Cincinnati blacks approached the Ohio legislature hoping that that body would obligingly donate funds toward black dispersion in Upper Canada. Ohio lawmakers had no such intention, however, especially since Cincinnati's mayor was attempting to slow black removal. It remained for the Quakers of Ohio and Indiana to assist the would-be settlers and with the aid of their agent, Frederick Stover, the Quakers bought eight hundred acres on behalf of the Cincinnati blacks. Receiving payment for less than one-quarter of that which had been expected, the vexed Canada Company refused any future dealing with black settlers.[20]

Despite the setback, land had been acquired in Upper Canada specifically for immigrating blacks. The Wilberforce Settlement took shape as the blacks organized a permanent governing body, the Board of Managers. Austin Steward, previously a grocer of Rochester, New York, was lured to Wilberforce to become chairman of the board, a position he retained until returning to Rochester in 1837. The governing body also included a secretary-treasurer and several representatives whose awesome responsibility it was to ensure continued funding and endorsement for the Wilberforce Settlement.[21]

The future of the settlement looked even more promising after Wilberforce received the support of noted antislavery advocate Benjamin Lundy. Lundy publicly endorsed the Wilberforce Settlement, observing that "full confidence may be placed in those at present selected to manage the public concerns of the settlement; and the true friends of the oppressed could scarcely render a more acceptable service to the cause of philanthropy, than by assisting, with pecuniary and other means, the persecuted colored man in obtaining residence there." His analysis resulted from a personal inspection in 1832 and helped to promote considerable public discussion of the general concept of black relocation and specifically of black resettlement in Upper Canada.[22]

No accurate records concerning the size of the black population at the Wilberforce Settlement are extant. Sources indicate that approximately a thousand black refugees fled from Cincinnati during the winter of 1829-1830. Of this number, it has been estimated that one-third to one-half directed their travel northward into the various regions of Upper Canada. As closely as can be determined, Wilberforce received about two hundred of those black settlers. The Settlement maintained a constant black populace of that size until 1836, when the number of residents began to decrease. Roughly half the original population, or around one hundred blacks, remained in 1840, and that number dropped to fifty-two by the early 1850s.[23]

Momentarily ignoring the population figures, the popularity of the Wilberforce Settlement seemed undeniable. Positive statements by contemporaries lauding its success abounded after the initial period of acclimation. The virtually destitute black refugees who in 1830 faced an "unbroken wilderness" with the protection of merely "a few rude log huts" quickly constructed new housing and tilled the soil. By the end of 1831, Austin Steward, the chairman of the Board of Managers, revealed that Wilberforce was almost self-sufficient. The community had a temperance society, a Baptist and a Methodist church, and both a Sunday School and a day school. Its bucolic nature at once encouraged cooperation and competition among residents. As Benjamin Lundy recorded, the blacks at Wilberforce boasted one hundred head of cattle along with a few horses and pigs. The settlement had a general store and a grist mill, and was surrounded by native timberlands waiting to be cut. The merchandising of produce or timber products could be accomplished easily through trade in previously established markets. According to Lundy's observations, the schools proved to be popular enough to attract white children from outlying areas. Both Steward and Lundy, then, published highly laudatory comments about the early progress of the refugees at Wilberforce. They stressed that the community was comprised of "industrious and thrifty farmers . . . in no way inferior to the white population, when given an equal chance with them."[24]

Yet quite different accounts emanated from other sources as well as from the participants themselves. Observing the Wilberforce Settlement in 1833, the Reverend William Proudfoot of neighboring London noted that "the soil is very good, but the dwellings of the negroes, (are) wretched, badly built and very small." The settlers with whom the Reverend Mr. Proudfoot spoke complained of lack of funds, supplies, and new recruits, even accusing the Canada Company of rushing away any recent arrivals. Proudfoot left with a distinct impression of rampant disaffection on the part of the black colonists. Patrick Shirreff, a Briton touring through North America, recounted many of the same problems. From his point of view, the expectations of the black settlers had been too high, and he compared their situation with that of Irish immigrants who had abandoned their country only to become impoverished and improvident in Canada.[25]

Hiram Wilson also issued a negative report about the Wilberforce Settlement. Normally a strong ally of blacks in Canada, the abolitionist took exception to the Wilberforce community. In a communication with antislavery editor William Goodell, Wilson pointedly remarked:

> That the true friends of colored Americans may not be forever gulled and deceived by colonization humbugs...permit me to state that the Wilberforce colony is a miserable concern.... There are not more than 18 or 20 families there. Some of them are wretchedly poor—others in a more thriving condition, but all much the worse for the begging campaigns of (agent) Israel Lewis and others. Had they been taught as in other parts of the province, to sustain themselves by their own industry, instead of looking for foreign aid, their condition would be much better than it is.

Wilson's inspection also provided critical information regarding the educational system at Wilberforce. Contrary to the allegations of Lundy and Steward, Wilson denied the existence of any school in the settlement as late as 1837. The one school that was organized disbanded within three years. By the end of the decade, therefore, Wilson concluded that Wilberforce as a black community "is now inferior to several other settlements."[26]

The causes of the eventual failure of the Wilberforce Settlement lay essentially in the dealings of the key members of the community, the Board of Managers. Unfamiliarity with farming methods surely contributed to their struggle, but the basis for the collapse of all their grandiose schemes was mismanagement. It was, above all, a lack of good leadership and organization that drove the Wilberforce Settlement toward collapse.

Indeed, the Cincinnati blacks had gone from unemployment in Ohio to destitution in Upper Canada. Only a few of their leaders were educated, and according to one observer, while most of the Wilberforce blacks enjoyed reading the Bible, "none of them could do little more than spell out more simple portions, a word at a time." The leaders of Wilberforce simply did not teach their constituents the requisite skills for their new way of life. Consequently, whites perceived the refugees who went to Upper Canada as irresponsible. "The greater number (of blacks) were people of bad character, idle and dissolute," wrote an agent of the Canada Company, "they depended on their agents to raise money from outside sources, rather than learning to use the resources at hand."[27]

Lack of experience, skills, and education were not the only problems at Wilberforce. Antagonism soon arose between two significant members of the community. Israel Lewis, who had been appointed one of the settlement's agents, had wielded great influence at Wilberforce since its inception. In addition to arranging the contract with the Canada Company, Lewis had convinced Austin Steward to quit his grocery in Rochester and serve as Wilberforce's chairman of the board. But Lewis had not anticipated Steward's ambition. Steward, realizing the political potential of his position as chairman and aiming for a seat in the legislature of Upper Canada, usurped the remainder of Lewis's power. A frustrated Lewis began to behave erratically. He purportedly threatened another officer with a gun, kept inaccurate financial records, imported a mistress, and destroyed the subscription registers. His irresponsible behavior brought him censure from the governing board in 1831, to which he reacted with a suit claiming defamation of character. His designation as agent was eventually restored, however, and he quickly departed to represent the settlement in the United States.

There Lewis begged for donations and unabashedly kept the seven hundred dollars amassed for the Wilberforce Settlement. Charged with repudiation of a debt by Steward, Lewis countered with an accusation of theft against the former grocer. Court records indeed revealed that Steward had faced a grand jury indictment on the charge of felony, but the case closed with his acquittal.[28] Amidst the charges and countercharges of their leaders, the Wilberforce Settlement struggled to survive. Warned to keep this growing schism between its leaders out of the press so as to avoid disrepute, the affair instead became a major scandal among antislavery advocates.

In view of the resultant scandal, the Wilberforce settlers decided in 1832 to remove Lewis from his official capacity, choosing the Reverend James Sharpe of London, Upper Canada, as his replacement. But before the year ended, the management of Wilberforce again condemned Lewis, stating that he "has refused to account for the money, generously contributed by the public for our relief," and was thereby "practicing a deception upon our friends in the United States, by taking up donations, pretending that such gifts will be faithfully applied to our relief." The warning appeared in abolitionist newspapers across the land. Meanwhile, Arthur Tappan, founder of the newly formed New York Anti-Slavery Society, disclosed that Lewis had already received some fifteen hundred dollars illegally. Numerous members of Wilberforce then issued another statement concerning the actions of their former representative, terming his behavior "scandalous" and "ridiculous in the highest degree." Their reprobation decreed that "no man who has the good of our colored brethern at heart, can, after residing at Wilberforce, and reviewing with an impartial eye the conduct of Lewis, give him his support."[29]

Still Wilberforce lacked adequate leadership. Angered, Israel Lewis exploited his former power within the settlement to foster further strife. Along with another former agent of Wilberforce, Baptist preacher Benjamin Paul, Lewis attempted to found an organization entitled the Wilberforce Colonization and High School Company of Upper Canada with the ultimate goal being the establishment of a manual labor school at Wilberforce. In truth, Lewis's penultimate goal was to solicit funds for this endeavor. Declaring himself both president and agent of the colonization company, Lewis was duly authorized to sell stock certificates on the company's behalf. Toward this end he traveled to New York where in 1834 he again began soliciting funds for the people of Wilberforce. Whatever monies he collected on this trip never made it back to Wilberforce, however. Lewis disappeared from public view, to die years later a pauper in Montreal, but in the meantime bequesting to Wilberforce the debts he had incurred by default.[30]

The Wilberforce settlers, determined to erase the tarnish on their community's name, decided to repay those who had been deceived by Lewis. With this in mind, another agent, Nathaniel Paul, sailed to England where he successfully solicited funds for Wilberforce. Paul additionally lectured throughout England on behalf of British abolitionists. Word of a forthcoming address by Paul was publicized by the notable British abolitionists, George Thompson and John Scoble, whose advertisements preceded or coincided with the visit. Rewarded with good attendance, Paul received substantial monies for Wilberforce while spreading valuable information on antislavery activities and generally promoting a positive image for blacks.[31]

Because of his warm reception, Nathaniel Paul remained in England for four years, twice as long as his Wilberforce constituents had anticipated. Anxious to learn of Paul's efforts on their behalf, the board of managers dispatched Canadian Henry Nell to England to retrieve Paul. Nell fulfilled his office by inducing Paul to return to Upper Canada, then almost seriocomically Nell himself disappeared in England with the sum of money entrusted to him for his return to North America.[32]

When Paul returned to Wilberforce, he accounted fully for his whereabouts and expenses while in Britain. His ledger showed the receipt of more than eight thousand dollars for the Wilberforce Settlement, but actual expenses amounted to seven thousand. Considering the back salary due him of fifty dollars per month, Paul's activities left Wilberforce with a loss of almost sixteen hundred dollars. Without collecting that sum, Paul abandoned the settlement and lived the remainder of his life in Albany, New York. Chairman of the Board Steward, ambivalent toward Paul's efforts but perhaps smarting from the disappearance of Nell, gave the former agent credit for his honest accounting by noting, "He *did* return when sent for, and he did account for the money he collected, though he retained it all." By his colleagues, Paul was neither applauded nor condemned, but the New York *Evangelist* offered severe criticism. Reviewing the fund raising enterprises of former agents Lewis and Paul, the *Evangelist* concluded "that the disastrous results of past efforts, together with the unsettled state of (Wilberforce), will prevent any further contributions in aid of an enterprise, which adds to the many proofs, that colonization, in any shape, is not the way to benefit the people of color."[33]

Indeed, black settlers at Wilberforce did not benefit in any long-term sense from the experiment. Most of the members of the governing board had either died or deserted from Wilberforce within its first decade of operation. Steward had left for Rochester in 1837, and vocal advocate Benjamin Lundy died two years later. A plan so grandly begun quietly and quickly declined. The population dropped from its peak of about two hundred at inception to half that number in 1840, and halved again by the 1850s. Those who stayed were primarily the unskilled, uneducated, and unorganized. To protect its interests, the Canada Company even offered to repurchase the improved tracts, hoping to sell the adjacent land to white settlers.[34]

Wilberforce not only failed to improve the situation of fugitive blacks; it actually worked to their detriment. The experiment had proved to be a big financial hazard to the Canada Land Company, which not only lost the sale of large tracts of land but alienated prospective white patronage. Thereafter, white Canadians had an example by which to discourage other sales of land to black immigrants. The judges of the Western District of Upper Canada, concerned about the possibility of a sudden influx of blacks to Wilberforce and similar communities, sought "some legislative check... (to) be placed upon the rapid importation of this unfortunate race, such as have of late inundated this devoted section of the province, to the great detriment to the claims of the poor Emigrant from the mother country." The most far-reaching effect of Wilberforce's failure, then, could be seen in the concomitant increase in white Canadian prejudice. Wilberforce's grandiose but impractical plan seemed to prove to white

Canadians the incapability of black self-sufficiency and the unfeasibility of future planned black settlements. The fatal lack of black leadership and organization— not inherent racial debilities—nevertheless portended badly for the progress of fugitive blacks. The Wilberforce Settlement, distinguished by its good farmland, timber, and marketing location, had every chance of success but met with disaster internally, rather than externally. Indeed, through the downfall of Wilberforce, the refugees had acquired the reputation among white Canadians as being "in no way above the mass of indigent Irish settlers who were arriving at the same time, and contrasts between poor whites and the philanthropically aided black farms were not to the Negroes' credit."[35]

Throughout Upper Canada, negrophobia began to surface as the reports of Wilberforce's failure spread. If former Loyalist slaves and free blacks had experienced toleration and even some degree of human respect from white Canadians, fugitive blacks arriving from the United States in the 1840s, after Wilberforce's decline, received an increasingly hostile reaction. Armed with the knowledge of Wilberforce's debacle, white Canadians commenced treating all blacks as social inferiors. The "unwelcome intruders" met in Upper Canada with "no small disfavour" from whites. The same magistrates that had requested a legislative check on the importation of blacks remonstrated in 1835 against the withdrawal of troops from Amherstburg. The local residents feared "the very numerous & troublesome black population coming into the District from the Slave States & who are the most depraved & reckless description generally speaking; and who are almost daily violating the laws & even threatened to put civil authority at defiance." Within five years, lieutenant governor Sir George Arthur, originally sympathetic toward the black refugees, protested that any additional immigration of ex-slaves would foster extremely serious racial tension in Upper Canada.[36]

White Canadian prejudice toward the fugitives after Wilberforce's demise manifested itself on many fronts. Perhaps the most obvious evidence of prejudice could be seen in stereotypical segregation. One observer in Upper Canada noticed that blacks resided in the "least valuable corners of the towns." Their increasing numbers prompted William Davies of Toronto to pejoratively claim that he saw "Free Niggers...at every step." Canadians responded to these blacks with such descriptions as "scarcely useful," "little better than a nuisance," "despised and deserted," and "as a class,...not at all a desirable population" which must be "shunned and kept at a distance." According to a Chatham foundress sympathetic with the refugees, Canadians had simply grown weary of the steady stream of emigrating blacks. Even Henry Highland Garnet, staunch antislavery advocate of New York, recognized that "color phobia" had become as enervating to blacks in Canada as it was in the United States. As white Canadians in Chatham and surrounding areas requested an end to continued black immigration, negrophobia resounded in Upper Canada.[37]

The negative white response to fugitive blacks was mitigated to an extent by anti-American sentiment. White Canadians were willing to tolerate black refugees in order to prove their moral eminence over American civil liberties, and they self-righteously chided the United States for perpetuating the institution of slavery. Such criticism took various forms. Some newspapers, for instance, supported Canadian abolitionism while simultaneously criticizing American race relations. The Toronto *Globe* accorded Canadians the responsibility of "preserving the honour of the continent" in countering the American "Peculiar Institution." Both the Niagara *Reporter* and the Huron *Gazette* joined the *Globe* in condemning American slavery and in applauding Canadian and British abolition. Furthermore, the Montreal *Witness* assumed the offensive concurrently against both the United States and slavery as if the terms were interchangeable. Other papers recalled that slavery had been abolished years earlier in Canada, and that fugitive slaves received equal protection and rights with whites in the provinces of Canada. In a different form of anti-Americanism, maps of the United States were forbidden in some schools in Upper Canada. The impression given was that compassion characterized the common Canadian response to black immigrants, while Canadian disdain of the United States was couched in attacks on American slavery. When racial problems did emerge, Canadians credited the "American Virus" as the cause. In fact, the Montreal *Witness* reasoned that Canadians "must necessarily trace the prejudice of colour to the neighboring states."[38]

Despite the obvious growth of negrophobia on the part of white Canadians, black fugitives continued to arrive in Upper Canada. Instead of being driven from Canada because of the prejudice, however, the blacks remained and attempted to prove their loyalty to wary Canadians. To so demonstrate, the black vote when cast supported the existing political conditions in Upper Canada. In an effort to uphold the status quo, blacks aligned themselves with conservatives. An infuriated political radical, William Lyon MacKenzie, denounced the black population as so "extravagantly loyal" that they would "uphold all the abuses of government and support those who profit by them." When MacKenzie launched his Reform movement, he again criticized fugitive blacks for being "opposed to every species of reform in the civil administrations of the colony."[39] Another observer, American abolitionist James G. Birney, commented in his correspondence on the extensive black conservatism in Upper Canada. An appreciative parliamentary legislator, politically conservative, remarked that "there are not in his Majesty's dominions a more loyal, honest, industrious, temperate, and independent class of citizens than the colored people of Upper Canada." Blacks consistently endorsed Conservatives, particularly in the southwest corner of Upper Canada which lies closest to the United States. A grateful Mayor of Toronto, recognizing black political support for his candidacy, threatened to stop the performances of a circus in the city unless the usual black songs were omitted "to save the feelings of the gentlemen of colour."[40]

Proving their political loyalty, blacks steadfastly remained in Canada. The failure of Wilberforce could not dishearten those who had experienced freedom in Upper Canada, regardless of an increasing display of white Canadian prejudice. In an insidious form of negrophobia, some Canadians attempted to recruit blacks in colonization schemes to the West Indies or Africa, though such efforts never succeeded as the ex-slaves appreciated their legal protection in Upper Canada. Believing themselves safe from the slave catcher, possessing the franchise, and receiving civil rights heretofore denied, fugitive slaves in Upper Canada wished to savor their freedom. Yet beginning in the 1830s and 1840s, the notion of a legal Canadian sanctuary for black refugees was tested by a series of American extradition requests. In the process, the security of blacks in Upper Canada would be threatened, and negrophobia would find cause to expand.

Constant rumors of the abduction of Canadian blacks to the United States and slavery recurred, with some basis in fact. Positive proof of kidnapping occurred in 1836, when a slave catcher abducted two fugitive blacks from St. Catharines. Another documented case cited that a refugee black and his benefactor, Charles Bâby, together fought off a kidnapping attack on the former slave. These persistent, clandestine activities served to erode the feeling of security among blacks in Upper Canada. The process of extradition, too, contributed to black uneasiness. As such, the twelve thousand fugitives residing in the province after the Imperial Act of 1833 had abolished slavery, feared for their own safety. The applicable legislation seemed in need of review as the increasing likelihood of abduction or legal extradition made black life in Canada tenuous at best.[41]

From the Canadian viewpoint, the question concerning American extradition requests for fugitive slaves seems to have been answered first by John Beverly Robinson, attorney general of Upper Canada, who stated in 1819 that despite "whatever the condition of these Negroes in the Country to which they formerly belonged, here they are free—For the enjoyment of all civil rights consequent to a mere residence in the country and among them the right to personal freedom as acknowledged and protected by the laws of England...must ...be extended to (them) as well as to all others under His Majesty's Government in this Province." He concluded by noting that any interference with the civil rights of Canadian residents would be prosecuted to the full extent of the law. Canada had become a haven for the hunted.[42]

The Parliament of Upper Canada, however, passed an act in February 1833 that provided for extradition of fugitive criminals from foreign countries. Under this statute, anyone in the province charged by the executive of a foreign nation with "Murder, Forgery, Larceny or other crime which if committed within the province would have been punishable with death, corporal punishment, the pillory, whipping, or confinement at hard labour" could be arrested, detained, and ultimately returned at the discretion of the provincial governor and his executive council.[43] This law obviously threatened the freedom of all runaway slaves from the United States: first, because many slaves indeed committed such crimes in the process of escaping; second, because slave owners might bring false charges in order to regain their property. Three test cases soon came from Kentucky, which requested in rapid succession the extradition of runaways Thornton Blackburn, Solomon Mosely, and Jesse Happy.

In the case of Thornton Blackburn and his wife, extradition was refused. They had been taken into custody in Detroit in accordance with the United States Fugitive Slave Law and a certificate issued for their return to Kentucky. On the day he was to be transported south, however, Thornton Blackburn was rescued by the aid of a violent mob and crossed into Canada where his wife had escaped in disguise a day earlier. Canadian authorities denied that Blackburn had taken part in the rioting or forcible rescue since he was merely trying to escape from slavery. By Canadian definition then, Blackburn could not be charged with any of the offenses stipulated in the act of 1833 which would have required his extradition. The attorney general of Upper Canada argued further that if Blackburn and his wife

> . . . should be delivered up they would, by the laws of the United States be exposed to be forced into a state of slavery from which they had escaped two years ago when they fled from Kentucky to Detroit; that if they should be sent to Michigan and upon trial be convicted of the riot and punished, they would after undergoing their punishment be subject to be taken by their masters and continued in a state of slavery for life, and that, on the other hand, if they should never be prosecuted, or if they should be tried and acquitted, this consequence would equally follow.

As a result, no extradition occurred in the Blackburn case.[44]

The next request from Governor James Clark of Kentucky concerned Solomon Mosely, who stole his master's horse, rode the horse to Buffalo, N.Y., where he sold it, and escaped across the Niagara River to Upper Canada. Mosely's lawyer made no attempt to deny the theft but chose to emphasize the ulterior motive of the Americans to return Mosely to slavery, noting that "four men have travelled 1500 miles at the expense of at least $400 to bring to justice a Slave charged with stealing a horse of only the value of $150." Nevertheless, the attorney general, the executive council, and the lieutenant governor of Upper Canada all agreed that the crime had been proved and was one of the offenses provided by the act of 1833 for extradition of fugitive criminals. Despite their abhorrence of slavery, Canadian officials could find no legal technicality upon which to deny extradition, so Mosely was ordered to be returned to Kentucky. His return, though, was prevented by mob force which allowed him to escape, and thereafter Mosely lived free in England and Canada with no further legal action taken against him.[45]

The case of Jesse Happy brought a more definitive ruling on extradition as this matter received the careful consideration and attention of the attorney general, Executive Council, and lieutenant governor of Upper Canada, the secretary of state of the Colonies, the foreign secretary, and ultimately the law officers of the Crown. Jesse Happy escaped from Kentucky in 1833 on his master's horse. He left the animal and arranged for its recovery before crossing the border into Upper Canada, and Thomas Hickey, the owner, subsequently reclaimed the horse. Two years later, the grand jury of Fayette County, Kentucky, indicted Happy on the charge of horse stealing. Two more years passed before Thomas Hickey swore out an affidavit against Happy, in which Hickey did no more than describe the ex-slave. Yet it was upon this indictment and affidavit that Governor Clark of Kentucky based his demand in August of 1837, for extradition of Jesse Happy as a fugitive criminal. A Canadian justice of the peace forthwith issued a warrant for Happy's arrest and detention on 7 September 1837. Consequently, Happy was taken into custody and confined in the Hamilton jail.[46]

The attorney general of Upper Canada, the Honorable Mr. Hagerman, rendered a routine decision the next day when he reported that the evidence pointed toward the accused's guilt and judged that legally the prisoner could be extradited. That Mr. Hagerman had misgivings concerning the case appeared in an obiter dictum to the ruling in which he commented: "It has been intimated to me that the accused is a fugitive slave and if delivered up will not only be subject to punishment for the felony charged against him but after such punishment shall have been inflicted he will be returned to Slavery—"[47] A cursory examination of the evidence apparently proved unsatisfactory to the attorney general, who forwarded this report with postscript to the executive branch of the provincial government.

The Executive Council met on September 9 to deliberate the proper course of action in Happy's case. They reviewed the evidence, the attorney general's report, and a report from Chief Justice John Beverly Robinson, the former attorney general of Upper Canada and author of the statute of 1833. Robinson's report noted that the purpose of the act was to ensure reciprocity in the surrender of fugitive criminals, particularly between Upper Canada and the adjoining states of Michigan and New York. He disagreed that the one phrase allowing discretion by the Executive Council of the province was intended to be applied toward fugitive slaves. Taking a purely legalistic position, he argued against the exemption of ex-slaves from the provisions of the statute by claiming:

> We have not a right to say, and certainly not the power to insist, that slavery shall not be tolerated in (other) countries; and since we cannot abolish slavery there, I do not think that we can properly proceed towards accomplishing such a result...by deciding that slaves who murder their masters, or burn their houses, or steal their goods, shall find a secure refuge in this Province,—while the white inhabitants of the same Countries shall, under similar circumstances be surrendered, on the requisition of their Government.

Thus Robinson disposed of the moral argument that returning the party to the United States would again subject him to the institution of slavery and negated the problem of double penalty since Canadian officials could take no legal responsibility toward any consequences to the party after trial. The chief justice then denied that if fraudulent charges came against one fugitive slave, such charges would be repeated in similar cases. He implied that presupposing insincere and unauthentic warrants on the part of the United States would result in similar reaction to Canadian requests for extradition of fugitive criminals. The danger, as he saw it, was in encouraging a breakdown in the exchange of criminals who might flee from one country and ``could be secure of protection in the other against the consequences of their most atrocious crimes.'' Robinson concluded that, contrary to popular opinion, Canadian protection of a fugitive slave ``is to stand between him and public justice...and if he ought to abide the test of a public trial, we cannot properly avert the possible consequences to him of a state of slavery which we had no hand in creating.'' Yet perhaps the chief justice's true sympathies appeared when he made the extra-legal remark that such protection of fugitive slaves would increase the migration of blacks to Canada which ``to say the least, it is not desirable to encourage.''[48]

Compared then to the Mosely case which was characterized by prompt and correct documentation, the case against Jesse Happy lacked credence since ``the Alleged Offence purports to have been committed more than four years ago'' with no legal recourse sought until August 1837. In addition, the Executive

Council felt uneasy about subjecting Happy to the possibility of double penalty. Concerned that the ulterior motive on the part of the former owner was to return the man to slavery, the council professed that "were there any Law by which after taking his trial and if convicted undergoing his sentence he would be restored to a State of Freedom—the Council would not hesitate to advise his being given up, but there is no such provision in the Statute (of 1833)." The council hesitated to decide the matter as peremptorily as the attorney general and therefore closed their report with a request for further information from Happy and a request for guidance on these questions from the government "as a matter of general policy."[49]

Sir Francis Bond Head, lieutenant governor of Upper Canada, received his Executive Council's report and determined to resolve the question of extradition of fugitive slaves by appealing to a higher court. Early in October 1837, he wrote to Lord Glenelg, the secretary of state for the colonies, requesting specific instructions for such cases. In a lengthy harangue which belied the author's attitude, Lieutenant Governor Head argued:

> It is quite true that if a white man who has stolen a horse from the Commonwealth of Kentucky comes with it or without it to this Province, he is. . .liable to be given up on demand to the neighboring authorities, and it certainly does seem to follow that a black man ought not to expect, because our laws grant him personal freedom, that he should moreover claim from them emancipation from trial for crimes for which even British-born subjects would be held responsible; yet on the other hand, it may be argued that a slave escaping from bondage on his master's horse is a vicious struggle between two parties of which the slave owner is not only the aggressor, but the blackest criminal of the two—it is the case of the dealer in human flesh versus the stealer of horse flesh.... The clothes and even the manacles of a slave are undeniably the property of his master, and it may be argued that it is as much a theft in the slave walking from slavery to liberty in his master's shoes as riding on his master's horse; and yet surely a slave breaking out of his master's house is not guilty of the same burglary which a thief would commit who should force the same locks and bolts in order to break in.

He continued by declaring that the Canadian government would be justified in refusing extradition until American law would guarantee the return of the subject to Upper Canada, thus precluding the possibility of double indemnity. Sir Francis Bond Head included documentation for both the Mosely and Happy cases in his communication to the secretary of state to show impartiality in his rulings, even though his true sentiment toward the morality of extraditing fugitive slaves was clearly evident in his letter.[50]

While awaiting a reply from the secretary of state, the Executive Council of Upper Canada met again to consider the disposition of Happy's case. They also considered new evidence wherein a witness corroborated Happy's claim that he carefully planned the animal's return to the rightful owner. They then ruled "that the horse may not have been stolen but merely wrongfully used for the purpose of Escape." Even were he not a runaway slave, they concluded, there was "so much doubt over the case that the Council cannot report...that the evidence is sufficiently satisfactory...to recommend the delivery up of the Prisoner." It was implied that the members of the council could not accept the indictment by Kentucky's grand jury at face value in view of the contradiction of sworn statements by Canadian residents. This report reiterated the earlier request for a legal ruling from a higher governmental authority on the subject of extradition of fugitive slaves. It, nevertheless, rendered the council's final decision to release Happy from custody based on insufficient evidence. This correspondence, forwarded to Lieutenant Governor Head, prompted the release of Jesse Happy from the Hamilton jail in mid-November 1837.[51]

Meanwhile, Secretary of State Glenelg received the request for advice and directed the problem to British Foreign Secretary Lord Palmerston. Noting that he was aware of no positive rule governing the extradition of fugitive slaves, Lord Glenelg submitted that in his view each case should be decided at the discretion of the officials involved. If his interpretation held true, Glenelg continued, the suit on restitution of Jesse Happy should be refused on three grounds: first, that Happy did not take the horse with felonious intention and did not appropriate the property permanently; second, that no legal action had been pursued for four years after perpetration of the alleged crime; and third, that "the punishments to which Slaves are liable by law in the United States for offences of this nature are such as our own principles of jurisprudence compel us to regard as indefensible, and disproportioned to the crime." Lord Glenelg thus supported the action taken in this instance by the Executive Council and the executive of Upper Canada.[52]

Lord Palmerston agreed to lay both the general matter and the specific case before the law officers of the Crown. The opinion was handed down by law officers Sir John Campbell and Sir Robert Mousey Rolfe early in 1838. As a general policy, they advised that "no Distinction should...be made between the Demand for Slaves or for Freemen." If the alleged offense "had been committed in Canada," warranting apprehension and prosecution in accordance with Canadian statutes, "then on the requisition of the Governor of the Foreign State, the accused party ought to be delivered up, without reference to the question as to whether he is, or is not, a Slave." They also stipulated, however, that the evidence to be used in cases concerning extradition of fugitive slaves "must be evidence taken in Canada, upon which (if False) the Parties making it may be indicted for Perjury." This would ensure against further examples of faulty, inaccurate, or incomplete documentation. In addition, the power of discretion could still be used by Canadian officials to refuse extradition whenever special circumstances so demanded. Noting the lack of evidence of criminality in the case of Jesse Happy—especially since the accused obviously had no intention of appropriating the animal—the law officers ordered his release. The officers did not discuss the moral ramifications of slavery as exemplified by the double indemnity argument. They merely interpreted the legal technicalities fixed by the statute of 1833 and ignored the politics of abolition.[53]

Lord Palmerston accepted this response without comment and forwarded the substance of the opinion to Lord Glenelg. Consequently, Lord Glenelg enclosed a copy of Palmerston's text in his 9 March 1838 reply to Sir George Arthur, lieutenant governor of Upper Canada. The new lieutenant governor used the opinions of the law officers as precedent-setting standards and as a general instruction "for the guidance of the local Government on future similar occasions."[54]

Thereafter, the law officers' ruling was strictly upheld in the cases pursued after this decision. No further extradition charges against fugitive slaves appear in official records for almost five years until the Nelson Hackett case arose. Hackett, a slave in Arkansas, stole a horse, a coat, a saddle, and a gold watch, and escaped to Canada West.[55] His master pursued proper legal channels, and Canadian officials adhered to the standard set in the Happy case. They granted extradition based on the reasoning that at least one of the aforementioned thefts had been committed with felonious intention. The other most noteworthy extradition case concerned a slave, John Anderson, who killed a white master when escaping. Indeed, the Anderson case became somewhat of a cause célèbre in Canada in the early 1860s. Anderson was first convicted and prepared for extradition, but mass meetings protested the decision as did the voice of the Reform press, the *Toronto Globe.* The official organ of the British and Foreign Anti-Slavery Society, the *Anti-Slavery Reporter,* lobbied for Anderson's release. Gerrit Smith, notable New York abolitionist, twice visited Canada West to speak on Anderson's behalf. The Anti-Slavery Society of Canada sponsored rallies and resolutions in favor of overturning the verdict. Finally, on 16 February 1861, Anderson was acquitted on the basis of faulty warrant. The courts again followed the letter of the law officers' judgment in the Happy case by accepting only formally correct documentation.[56]

The clarification of rulings on the extradition of fugitive slaves helped to increase black security in Upper Canada. Knowing that each case would be judged on its own merits, the black refugees benefited from proper legal proceedings wherein their rights as free men, equal with whites under Canadian law, were protected. The chances of extradition proved slim overall, making the risk of return to the United States seem slight. For this reason, and because of the propelling influence of widespread racial tension in the northern United States beginning about 1830, the black population in the Canadas exploded between 1815 and 1840. At the time when Wilberforce had just been founded, the number of fugitive slaves estimated to reside in the Canadas was less than ten thousand. As Wilberforce declined and the extradition laws came to be defined by usage, approximately sixty thousand refugee blacks claimed Canadian citizenship. The Canadian extradition decisions, concurrent with the heightened enforcement of black codes in the United States, had served to draw fugitive slaves toward a Canadian Canaan.

The conscientiousness of the Upper Canadian judiciary may have fostered this population accretion, but it could not have occurred without the tacit consent of white Canadians. After all, fugitive blacks demonstrated their political loyalty to British North America by supporting the conservative majority. Additionally, the multiple extradition appeals on the part of Americans had publicized for Upper Canadians the issue of black emancipation raging south of the province. Philanthropic white Canadians, anxious to encourage abolition throughout the whole of North America, founded the Anti-Slavery Society of Canada.[57] The conspicuous series of extradition requests, then, had important political and moral ramifications in Upper Canada as anti-American sentiment and antislavery became synonymous. The moral indignance of white Canadians was raised as the insidious institution of slavery prospered in the United States. The combination of these factors compelled Canadians to accommodate thousands of fugitive slaves.

From their limited experience with Loyalist ex-slaves, white Canadians had scanty knowledge of what to expect from the refugee blacks. The first black immigrants furnished necessary cheap labor in Amherstburg and Oro, the qualification being that blacks were not specifically required to fulfill the need, just their labor. The Wilberforce Settlement proposed to provide a sanctuary in Upper Canada for Cincinnati blacks, but it was planned externally—not by Canadians. While white Canadians originally received fugitive slaves with ambivalence or toleration, blacks were never recruited or expected in great numbers. The subsequent economic failure of those three predominantly black communities lowered the white Canadian opinion of black refugees. By 1840, the generalized response of white Canadians was to associate all blacks with improvidence, ignorance, and indigence.

The admission of blacks into Upper Canada had implied their social acceptance as well. That assumption, however, had proved to be overstated at best. Canadian recipience of the fugitive slaves did not guarantee their assimilation into the mainstream of society, nor did opposition to slavery necessarily represent pro-black sentiment. Antislavery advocates exploited the legal sanctions offered to fugitive slaves, but the influx of blacks prompted the original forbearance on the part of white Canadians to turn increasingly into intolerance. The introduction of more black settlements in Upper Canada would only intensify white Canadian negrophobia. While Upper Canada was undeniably a legal haven, in every other respect it had become a questionable one.

NOTES

1.   For a detailed account of the refugee blacks from the War of 1812, see Winks, "Negroes in the Maritimes," pp. 453-71;

Idem, *Blacks in Canada*, pp. 114-41;

Walker, *Black Loyalists*, passim;

Clairmont and Magill, *Nova Scotian Blacks*, passim;

Jack, "Loyalists and Slavery in New Brunswick," pp. 137-85; and

Spray, *Blacks in New Brunswick*, passim.

2.   Benjamin Drew, *A North-Side View of Slavery. The Refugee: or, The Narratives of Fugitive Slaves in Canada. Related by Themselves* (Boston, 1856), pp. 98, 150, 186, 272-73.

3.   "Petition of Coloured People Prepared at Ancaster, Upper Canada, July 25, 1828," *Journal of Negro History* 15 (January 1930), pp. 115-16.

4.   John Howison, *Sketches of Upper Canada* (Edinburgh, 1821), p. 201;

Joseph Pickering, *Inquiries of An Emigrant: being the Narrative of an English Farmer from the Year 1824 to 1830* (4th ed., London, 1832), pp. 96-97;

Audrey Saunders Miller, ed., *The Journals of Mary O'Brien, 1828-1838* (Toronto, 1968), p. 75; and

Fred Coyne Hamil, *The Valley of the Lower Thames, 1640 to 1850* (Toronto, 1951), pp. 123-26, 145.

5.   William Berczy to (?) Mudge, 3 April 1829 in Upper Canada Sundries, vol. Q, part 1, pp. 244-49, Public Archives of Canada, Ottawa.

6.   James Logan, *Notes of a Journey through Canada, the United States of America, and the West Indies* (Edinburgh, 1838), p. 70;

Amelia M. Murray, *Letters from the United States, Cuba and Canada* (London, 1856), p. 117;

Fugitive Slave Files and Assessment Rolls located in Fort Malden National Historic Park, Amherstburg, Ontario; and

Fred Landon, "Amherstburg, Terminus of the Underground Railroad," *Journal of Negro History* 10 (January 1925), p. 4.

7. Dr. Thomas Bray, founder of the Society for the Propagation of Christian Knowledge and of the Society for the Propagation of the Gospel in Foreign Parts, dedicated his life "to the church, to care of the poor, and to the reformation of prostitutes." Just prior to his death, Bray, along with several friends, created an association whose primary goal was the "Instructing [of] Negroes in the British Plantations in the Christian Religion." Toward this end, he left £960 for his colleagues to provide books for several communities and to supplement black schools in Nova Scotia, the Bahamas, and Pennsylvania. H.P. Thompson, *Thomas Bray* (London, 1954), p. 97.

    The figure for the number of blacks in Chatham comes from the Census of Canada in the Public Archives of Canada, Ottawa.

8. Sydney Jackman, ed., *A Diary in America, with Remarks on Its Institutions, by Frederick Marryat* (New York, 1962), pp. 165, 170;

    Hamil, *Valley of the Lower Thames*, p. 173;

    Jonathan W. Walton, "Blacks in Buxton and Chatham, Ontario, 1830-1890: Did the 49th Parallel Make a Difference?" (Ph.D. dissertation, Princeton University, 1979), pp. 1-19;

    John K.A. Farrell, "The History of the Negro Community in Chatham, Ontario, 1787-1865" (Ph.D. dissertation, University of Ottawa, 1955), pp. 34, 120, 166;

    Michael B. Katz, *The People of Hamilton, Canada West: Family and Class in a Mid-Nineteenth Century City* (Cambridge, Mass., 1975), pp. 61-68; and

    the Black History files in the Hiram Walker Historical Museum, Windsor, Ontario.

9. The members of the Executive Council who issued the land grants to blacks were Chief Justice William Dummer Powell and James Bâby, both of whom were slave owners, John Strachan (later Bishop of Toronto), William Claus, and Lieutenant Governor Sir Peregrine Maitland. Most evidence indicates that Maitland was the mastermind of the black settlement plan and that he labored assiduously to ensure its success. For more on Oro Township, see

    Gary E. French, *Men of Colour: An Historical Account of the Black Settlement on Wilberforce Street and in Oro Township, Simcoe County, Ontario, 1819-1949* (Stroud, Ontario, 1978).

10. Land Book K, p. 92 of the Crown Land Papers, Ontario Provincial Archives, Toronto.

11. French, *Men of Colour*, pp. 15-17.

12. George Hillier (Civil Secretary to Maitland) to Henry Goulburn, 24 September 1819, in Colonial Office Records #42, Q 326, vol. 363, p. 117, Public Archives of Canada, Ottawa.

13. French, *Men of Colour*, p. 30. Peter Robinson was the brother of John Beverly Robinson, attorney general and later chief justice of Upper Canada.

14. French, *Men of Colour*, pp. 30-33; and
    Lillian F. Gates, *Land Policies of Upper Canada* (Toronto, 1968), pp. 173-81.

15. W.E. O'Brien, "Early Days in Oro," Simcoe County Pioneer and Historical Society,
    Pioneer Papers, no. 1 (1908), pp. 22-27;
    Miller, *Journals of Mary O'Brien*, p. 95;
    Andrew F. Hunter, *A History of Simcoe County* (Barrie, Ontario, 1909), vol. 2, pp.
    143-45;
    William Loe Smith, *The Pioneers of Old Ontario* (Toronto, 1923), pp. 306-7;
    Thomas Rolph, *A Descriptive and Statistical Account of Canada: Showing Its
    Great Adaptation For British Emigration* (London, 1841), pp. 184-85;
    Land Petitions of 13 and 14 June 1836 in Upper Canada Land Petitions, #395,
    Public Archives of Canada, Ottawa; and
    Land Declaration, Oro, 1836, in Crown Land Papers; and
    Mrs. Edward George O'Brien Journal, 7 March 1830:
    both in Ontario Provincial Archives, Toronto.

16. Upper Canada Land Petition #B-15-115, in Ontario Provincial Archives, Toronto;
    and
    letter of Peter Robinson, 4 December 1830, in Correspondence, Record Group, 5,
    vol. A-1, p. 58791, Public Archives of Canada, Ottawa.

17. Wilbur H. Siebert, "Fugitive Slaves in Canada," in the Siebert Papers, Ohio State
    Historical Society, Columbus;
    Richard C. Wade, "The Negro in Cincinnati, 1800-1830," *Journal of Negro History*
    39 (January 1954), pp. 43-57;
    Fred Landon, "Negro Colonization Schemes in Upper Canada before 1860,"
    Transactions of the Royal Society of Canada, 3d series, section 2, 23 (1929), pp.
    73-80; and
    Leon F. Litwack, *North of Slavery: The Negro in the Free States, 1790-1860*
    (Chicago, 1961), pp. 73-74.

18. Resolution of a court of Directors of the Canada Company, 26 April 1827, in Upper
    Canada State Papers, series Q, p. 13, Public Archives of Canada, Ottawa;
    Wade, "The Negro in Cincinnati," pp. 43-57.
    For more on the origins of the Wilberforce Settlement, see
    Fred Landon, "The History of the Wilberforce Refugee Colony in Middlesex County,"
    Transactions of the London and Middlesex Historical Society 9 (1918), pp. 30-44;
    Idem, "Wilberforce, an Experiment in Colonization of Freed Negroes in Upper
    Canada," *Transactions of the Royal Society of Canada*, 3d series, 2d section, 31
    (1937), pp. 69-78;
    Idem, "Fugitive Slaves in Ontario: A Digest of Two Papers," *Northwest Ohio
    Historical Society, Quarterly Bulletin* 8 (April 1936), pp. 1-12; and
    William H. and Jane Pease, *Black Utopia: Negro Communal Experiments in*

America (Madison, 1963), pp. 46-62.

For corollary information see

Fred Landon, "Agriculture Among the Negro Refugees in Upper Canada," *Journal of Negro History* 21 (July 1936), pp. 304-12; and

Marilyn Bailey, "From Cincinnati, Ohio to Wilberforce, Canada: A Note on Antebellum Colonization," *Journal of Negro History* 58 (October 1973), pp. 427-40.

19.   *African Repository and Colonial Journal* 6 (March 1830), pp. 27-29.

20.   *The Friend,* 9 January 1830;

Austin Steward, *Twenty-two Years a Slave, and Forty a Freeman; Embracing a Correspondence of Several Years, While President of Wilberforce Colony, London, Canada West* (Rochester, 1857), pp. 190-91; and

The Emancipator, 15 September 1836.

21.   *Liberator,* 17 September 1831 and 12 May 1832.

22.   *Liberator,* 12 May 1832.

Lundy was one of the earliest and most vocal antislavery advocates and the man responsible for recruiting William Lloyd Garrison to the abolitionist cause. Particularly interested in colonization, Lundy visited Upper Canada in 1832 to investigate the life of the fugitive slaves. He printed the diary of his trip in his newspaper, *The Genius of Universal Emancipation,* and his conclusion that "no place perhaps in the northern or north-western part of America presents a stronger and richer soil" helped to remove fears about little-known Canada.

See Fred Landon, ed., "The Diary of Benjamin Lundy Written During His Journey Through Upper Canada, January 1832," *Ontario Historical Society Papers and Records* 19 (1921), pp. 110-33;

Idem, "Benjamin Lundy Abolitionist," *Dalhousie Review* 7 (July 1927), pp. 189-97;

Idem, "A Pioneer Abolitionist in Upper Canada," *Ontario History* 52 (June 1960), pp. 77-83; see also

Benjamin Lundy, *The Life, Travels and Opinions of Benjamin Lundy* (Philadelphia, 1847).

The Fred Landon Papers, Regional History Collection, D.B. Weldon Library, University of Western Ontario, London, contain more on Lundy and should also be consulted.

23.   For varying estimates of the population of the Wilberforce Settlement throughout the 1830s and 1840s, see periodic issues of *The Friend,* the *African Respository and Colonial Journal, Niles Register, The Genius of Universal Emancipation,* the *Colored American,* and *The Liberator,* all of which reported frequently on the settlement; and

Thomas Rolph, *Emigration and Colonization: Embodying the Results of a Mission to Great Britain and Ireland, During the Years 1839, 1840, 1841 and 1842*

(London, 1844).

24. *The Liberator*, 17 September 1831;
Landon, ed., "Diary of Benjamin Lundy," pp. 110-33; and
Steward, *Twenty-two Years a Slave*, pp. 185, 202.

25. William Proudfoot, "The Proudfoot Papers," *Ontario Historical Society Papers and Records* 27 (1931), pp. 435-97; 28 (1932), pp. 71-114; 29 (1933), pp. 141-60; 30 (1934), pp. 124-43; 31 (1935), pp. 91-114; 32 (1936), pp. 92-104; and
Patrick Shirreff, *A Tour Through North America* (Edinburgh, 1835), p. 178.

26. *The Friend of Man*, 14 March 1838, 1 May 1839, and 31 July 1839;
Colored American, 16 February 1839;
Rolph, *Emigration and Colonization*, p. 311; and
Canada Mission, *Sixth Annual Report* published in *The Liberator*, 17 March 1843.

27. Report of Mr. Prior, agent of the Canada Company, 28 April 1835, in Colonial Office Records, series Q, vol. 386, part 1, no. 37, Public Archives of Canada, Ottawa;
Landon, "The History of Wilberforce Refugee Colony," p. 33, and, "Fugitive Slaves in Ontario," pp. 5-6.

28. This account, albeit hostile to Lewis, is generally drawn from Steward, *Twenty-two Years a Slave*, and from statements of Lewis and Steward reprinted from *The Liberator*, 13 April 1833, more conveniently found in
Carter G. Woodson, ed., *The Mind of the Negro as Reflected in Letters Written during the Crisis, 1800-1860* (Washington, D.C., 1926), pp. 179-81. See particularly pp. 180-81 and 184-84 of Woodson for examples of inconsistencies in Steward's stories. See also
Howard W. Coles, *The Cradle of Freedom: A History of the Negro in Rochester, Western New York and Canada* (Rochester, 1941), pp. 41-77;
Pease and Pease, *Black Utopia*, pp. 46-62; and
Robin W. Winks, ed., *Four Fugitive Slave Narratives* (Reading, Mass., 1969), pp. 9-15 of the Peases' introduction to Steward's autobiography.

29. *The Liberator*, 9 March and 13 April 1833;
Woodson, *Mind of the Negro*, pp. 525, 189-90; and
"Letters of Negroes Largely Personal and Private," *Journal of Negro History* 11 (July 1926), pp. 176-77.

30. *The Liberator*, 23 February, 2 March, and 9 March 1833, 8 March 1834, 2 and 16 July 1836;
The Friend of Man, 1 May, 31 July, and 14 August 1839;
The Emancipator, 9 June 1836;
Steward, *Twenty-two Years a Slave*, pp. 233-34; and
Woodson, *Mind of the Negro*, pp. 181-83, 626-27.

31. *Oberlin Evangelist*, 28 August 1839;
The Friend of Man, 14 August 1839;

The Liberator, 14 January 1832, 7 February and 14 March 1835;

Charles Stuart, *Remarks on the Colony of Liberia, and the American Colonization Society: With Some Account of the Settlement of Coloured People, at Wilberforce, Upper Canada* (London, 1832), pp. 11-16;

Steward, *Twenty-two Years a Slave*, p. 187;

"Letters of Negroes," pp. 179-80;

Woodson, *Mind of the Negro*, pp. 628-29, 662-63; and

Walter M. Merrill, *Against the Wind and Tide: A Biography of William Lloyd Garrison* (Cambridge, Mass., 1963), pp. 72, 343.

Before leaving England, however, Paul and Garrison fell into dispute. Paul had lent Garrison money for the latter's return voyage to the United States and when he tried to collect in America, Garrison refused to pay, claiming the money was not a loan but rather a donation to their common antislavery cause.

32.   *The Emancipator*, 15 September 1836;

Steward, *Twenty-two Years a Slave*, pp. 261-62, 311-42.

33.   *New York Evangelist*, n.d., copied in *The Emancipator*, 15 September 1836;

Steward, *Twenty-two Years a Slave*, pp. 263-67, 251;

Woodson, *Mind of the Negro*, pp. 637-38;

The Liberator, 22 June and 23 November 1833.

34.   "Reminiscences of Two Negroes at Lucan," Record Group 19, Box 31, Public Archives of Canada, Ottawa;

Shirreff, *A Tour Through North America*, p. 178; and

Letters Concerning Wilberforce, in Fred Landon Papers, Regional History Collection, D.B. Weldon Library, University of Western Ontario, London.

35.   Rolph, *Emigration and Colonization*, pp. 313-14.

36.   Upper Canada State Papers, vol. 387, part 2, pp. 314-14, Public Archives of Canada, Ottawa;

The African Repository and Colonial Journal 6 (March 1830), pp. 27-29;

Hamil, *Valley of the Lower Thames*, pp. 313-14;

James R. Brown, *Views of Canada and the Colonists* (Edinburgh, 1851), pp. 62-63, 289; and

Jason H. Silverman, "The American Fugitive Slave in Canada: Myths and Realities," *Southern Studies* 19 (Fall 1980), pp. 215-27.

37.   Henry Highland Garnet, *The Past and the Present Condition, and the Destiny of the Colored Race* (Troy, N.Y., 1848), pp. 25-29;

John Shaw, *A Ramble Through the United States, Canada, and the West Indies* (London, 1856), p. 49;

William S. Fox, ed., *Letters of William Davies, Toronto, 1854-1861* (Toronto, 1945), p. 45.

38.   See the following issues of Canadian newspapers for examples of anti-American

editorials and comments:

Montreal *Witness*, 5 January, 18 May, 8 and 22 June, 6, 20, and 27 July, 3 and 10 August, 21 September, 12 October, 16 November, 12 and 21 December 1846;

Toronto *Daily Globe*, 6 July and 8 September 1857; and 27 April and 9 September 1858;

John Charlton Papers, ms, Autobiography, p. 167, Ontario Provincial Archives, Toronto;

Winks, *Blacks in Canada*, pp. 262-63;

Montreal *Witness*, 1 May 1848; and

Ged Martin, "British Officials and Their Attitudes to the Negro Community in Canada, 1833-1861," *Ontario History* 66 (June 1974), pp. 79-88.

39. William Lyon Mackenzie, editor of the *Colonial Advocate*, one of the largest newspapers in Upper Canada, was the first mayor of Toronto. He also was the leader of a reform movement that sought to prevent the union of Upper and Lower Canada, supported the abolition of slavery, and opposed the return of fugitive slaves by extradition to the United States. In 1837 he led an unsuccessful rebellion against British rule. In their encounters against Mackenzie's forces, the British skillfully and successfully employed five companies of black soldiers. For more on this, see

Greg Keilty, ed., *1837: Revolution in the Canadas* (Toronto, 1974);

Ernest Green, "Upper Canada's Black Defenders," *Ontario Historical Society Papers and Records* 27 (1931); pp. 365-91;and

Fred Landon, "Canadian Negroes and the Rebellion of 1837," *Journal of Negro History* 7 (October 1922), pp. 377-79.

40. Petitions of 20 July and 14 October 1841, 9 March 1842, and 21 April 1848 in the Toronto City Council Papers, Ontario Provincial Archives, Toronto;

American Anti-Slavery Society, *Fourth Annual Report* (1837), pp. 350-51;

Dwight L. Dumond, ed., *Letters of James Gillespie Birney, 1831-1857* (New York, 1938), vol. 1, pp. 395-96.

41. Upper Canada State Papers, vol. C, pp. 247-65, Public Archives of Canada, Ottawa;

Chatham Journal, 23 December 1843;

Amherstburg Echo, 7 September 1888;

William Lewis Bâby, *Souvenirs of the Past* (Windsor, 1896), pp. 132-40; and

British and Foreign Anti-Slavery Society, *Third Annual Report*, p. 164.

42. Upper Canadian Archives Sundries, 1819, Public Archives of Canada, Ottawa.

43. The Statute of 1833 is cited 3 Will IV c. 7, and is found in its entirety in Public Archives of Canada, Ottawa. The Executive Council was appointed by the Provincial Governor. For more on the extradition of fugitive slaves from Canada see

Roman J. Zorn, "Criminal Extradition Menaces the Canadian Haven for Fugitive Slaves, 1841-1861," *The Canadian Historical Review* 38 (December 1957), pp.

284-94; and

Alexander L. Murray, "The Extradition of Fugitive Slaves from Canada: A Reevaluation," *The Canadian Historical Review* 43 (December 1962), pp. 298-314.

44. Upper Canada State Papers, vol. 61, pp. 31-48, 137-63; and

Minutes, 6 September 1834, in Record Group 1, vol. E, p. 54:

both in Public Archives of Canada, Ottawa.

The quote is from the Report of Attorney General Robert S. Jameson in "Canadian Archives, State J," p. 137, also in Public Archives of Canada, Ottawa.

45. Upper Canada State Papers, vol. 40, pp. 217-232, in Public Archives of Canada, Ottawa;

Janet Carnochan, "A Slave Rescue in Niagara, Sixty Years Ago," *Niagara Historical Society*, publication no. 2 (1897), pp. 8-18;

The Friend of Man, 11 October and 22 November 1837; and

Alexander L. Murray, "Canada and the Anglo-American Anti-Slavery Movement: A Study in International Philanthropy" (Ph.D. dissertation, University of Pennsylvania, 1960), pp. 125-28.

46. See *Commonwealth v. Happy* (1835), VI-C-124, Box 94, Drawer 835-37;

Hickey Affidavit (1837), VI-C-124, Box 96, Drawer 851-58:

both in the Fayette County and Circuit Court Records, State Archives and Record Center, Frankfort, Kentucky.

See also J. Mackenzie Leask, "Jesse Happy, A Fugitive Slave from Kentucky," *Ontario History* 54 (June 1962), pp. 87-98; and

Fred Landon, "The Fugitive Slave in Canada," *The University Magazine* 18 (April 1919), pp. 270-79.

47. Colonial Office Records, 42 series, vol. 439, p. 182 (hereafter cited as CO 42/439/182).

48. CO 42/439/199-204.

49. CO 42/439/190-92.

50. CO 42/439/170-73.

51. CO 42/445/35-38.

52. CO 42/439/176-79.

53. CO 42/453/84-87. Sir John Campbell was the attorney general in the Law Offices of the Crown.

54. Dispatches from the Colonial Office, 1841-1865, in Record Group 7, vol. G, p. 1, Public Archives of Canada, Ottawa.

55. Upper Canada became Canada West in 1841. For more on the Hackett case, see Roman J. Zorn, "An Arkansas Fugitive Slave Incident and Its International Repercussions," *Arkansas Historical Quarterly* 16 (Summer 1957), pp. 133-40.

56. Riddell, "The Slave in Canada," pp. 355-57;

Fred Landon, "The Anderson Fugitive Slave Case," *Journal of Negro History* 7 (July

1922), pp. 233-42.

57. For more on the antislavery movement in Canada, see

Robin W. Winks, " 'A Sacred Animosity': Abolitionism in Canada," in *The Anti-Slavery Vanguard: New Essays on the Abolitionists*, ed., Martin Duberman (Princeton, 1965), pp. 301-42;

Fred Landon, "The Anti-Slavery Society of Canada," *Journal of Negro History* 4 (January 1919), pp. 33-40;

Idem, "Abolitionist Interest in Upper Canada," *Ontario History* 44 (October 1952), pp. 165-72; and

Idem, "The Anti-Slavery Society of Canada," *Ontario History* 48 (Summer 1956), pp. 125-31.

Three

FREE BUT UNWELCOME

By the 1840s, the situation for free blacks in the northern United States had deteriorated as the enforcement of black laws heightened. Indeed, at the beginning of the decade approximately 93 percent of the northern free black population resided in states that either partially or completely disenfranchised them. In New Jersey, Pennsylvania, Connecticut, Indiana, and Rhode Island, blacks were completely denied the right to vote, and in order to vote in New York, blacks had to meet a three-year residence requirement and own $250 worth of property. Only in the states of Maine, Vermont, Massachusetts, and New Hampshire did blacks vote with the same privileges as whites. Although no state entirely denied blacks due process of law, many significantly restricted black legal rights. For example, Illinois, Ohio, Indiana, and Iowa prohibited black testimony in cases involving whites, and before 1860, only Massachusetts allowed blacks to serve as jurors. In some states, blacks were not allowed to be clerks or typesetters, to buy or sell alcoholic beverages, or to trade tobacco or other farm products without a license. Despite restrictions on the type of employment they could pursue, blacks were required to work or were subject to bound apprenticeship. By 1835 many northern states also limited or prohibited free black immigration, so that blacks could not move freely from one county to another without fear of being arrested as fugitives. Racial animosity increased, often exploding into violence. Between 1834 and 1841, at least six major race riots took place in various areas of New York, Ohio, and Pennsylvania. Black churches and homes were burned, and many blacks were beaten.[1] Because of this racial enmity, hundreds of destitute blacks fled to Canada West during the 1840s.

In order to help the fugitives adjust to their new country and lifestyle, several black communities were founded in Canada West after 1840. The first black settlement organized after Wilberforce was the community at Dawn. The circumstances surrounding the establishment of this settlement remain obscure since sources are few and unreliable. It appears, though, that Hiram Wilson, one of the rebels who relocated to Oberlin College after Lane Seminary declared its unwillingness to support abolition, initiated the plans to create a permanent manual labor school at Dawn. Predicated upon the principle that education would best train the fugitives for living as free men, the school would act as a halfway house for fugitive slaves, providing them the practical skills necessary for employment.

Wilson's concern for fugitive slaves had earlier taken him on an inspection tour of Upper Canada to examine their progress. Dismayed at what he discovered, Wilson then sought to improve the black situation in Canada. Supported by the American Anti-Slavery Society, as well as by forty-three Oberlin College students, he proceeded to found a number of schools in various black communities in Upper Canada. Although the schools were open to all who wished to attend, they were primarily intended to provide educational facilities for fugitive slaves. This work on behalf of fugitive slaves earned Wilson quite a reputation among abolitionists; it also put him heavily in debt by the end of 1839. The American Anti-Slavery Society promptly called for the "liberal patronage of every true-hearted abolitionist" to help alleviate Wilson's financial worries and by 1841, prominent abolitionist Gerrit Smith was spearheading a committee that devoted itself to the distribution of funds, Bibles, and garments to the schools originally sponsored or motivated by Wilson.[2]

Wilson's renown as an educator of fugitives in Canada West received the attention of James Canning Fuller, a magnanimous Quaker from Skaneateles, New York. Wanting to help the fugitive slaves in Canada, Fuller nevertheless disapproved of any plan administered by United States citizens. He would, on the other hand, collaborate with Wilson in supporting an educational institution for fugitives that would be governed by Canadians. Fuller agreed to the establishment of the British-American Institute, a school created expressly to promote the "Education Mental Moral and Physical of the Coloured inhabitants of Canada not excluding white persons and Indians." For this purpose Fuller solicited funds in England in the summer of 1840 and returned to British North America to a post on the new school's board of trustees.[3]

The concept of a manual labor school received the enthusiastic support of Josiah Henson, an influential former slave residing in Canada West. Uneducated and virtually illiterate, Henson had escaped in 1830 from the United States and fled to Canada where he became known as the prototype for Harriet Beecher

Stowe's protagonist, Uncle Tom.[4] His charismatic personality enabled him to be universally accepted as a black leader in Canada West, and by the mid-1830s, he commanded enough respect among his fellow fugitives to be entrusted with the purchase of land on their behalf. Accepting this responsibility, Henson located and rented land near Colchester, where a small community of blacks then settled. Discovering that most of the inhabitants of this settlement raised tobacco and had no other visible means of income, Henson emphasized to his constituents the inherent limitation and folly of cultivating only one cash crop, and encouraged them to diversify. This common-sense approach was quickly vindicated when the tobacco market became glutted; shortly thereafter, Henson joined Wilson in commending the idea of the British-American Institute at a "convention of coloured people" in Canada West. With Henson's influence, the black delegates supported the plan, and concluded that "we look to the school, and the possession of landed property by individuals, as two great means of elevation of our oppressed and degraded race."[5]

Receiving the support of Hiram Wilson, James Canning Fuller, and Josiah Henson, the British-American Institute became a reality. Two hundred acres near Chatham were purchased in November of 1841 for eight hundred dollars, and just over a year later, the manual labor school accepted its first students. The next year Henson became manager of the Institute and took up residence in the community. From all appearances, the plans for the school and settlement were succeeding.

Optimistically named Dawn, the entire community would revolve around the British-American Institute. In this manner Dawn filled the needs of the school as opposed to the reverse. A single branch of the school administration performed the organizational responsibilities for the settlement; community activities complemented school activities, with very little distinction or separation between the two. The black residents of Dawn, then, reinforced the formal and informal synonymity of their community with the school. Even the churches and businesses of Dawn operated as adjuncts of the British-American Institute.[6] Only through the satisfactory management of the school would a sound basis be established for the success of this settlement of fugitive slaves; and, it was assumed that as manager of the British-American Institute, Josiah Henson would supply that leadership necessary to ensure Dawn's survival.

Dawn did indeed prosper during its first few years: its population grew to almost five hundred people; over one hundred acres were cleared for use in farming; and Henson oversaw the construction of a saw mill "at considerable expense." The citizens of Dawn generously supplied impoverished new arrivals with clothing and housing. Classes at the British-American Institute were attended by anywhere from 56 to 116 adult pupils, and there were other classes for children, encouraging Henson to describe the settlement in his autobiography as virtually self-supporting.[7]

Despite Henson's optimism, he knew little about directing an organization such as the British-American Institute, and consequently, by 1847, the institute was heavily in debt. That summer, Henson was called before a convention of dissatisfied blacks at Drummondville. Resolving that "the British-American Institute...is not conducted to the satisfaction of the People of Colour in this Province," the convention appointed a five-man committee to audit the school's books and papers. Though the report of the next convention is not extant, it is clear that Dawn faced ominous financial problems. Within fourteen months of the committee's report, not a single member of Dawn possessed financial credibility. Hiram Wilson left the settlement to return to the United States, depriving Dawn of his leadership, while the remaining trustees stated publicly and pointedly that they would not be responsible for debts incurred by any of their colleagues. Convinced that it was the saw mill and not the school that created the financial woes of Dawn, the governing board of the community planned to send emissaries outside the province to raise funds to pay the mill's outstanding debt of $7,500.[8] By so doing, they hoped that the community's reputation and solvency could be simultaneously retained.

Henson shouldered his responsibility in having created the debt, and in 1849 traveled to England to solicit funds to ease the financial difficulty. He collected more than $1,500, but the effort faltered when rumors began to circulate that he was not an authorized agent for either Dawn or the British-American Institute. The British and Foreign Anti-Slavery Society created a committee to investigate the charges, and sent its secretary, John Scoble, to Canada West where he discovered that Henson was indeed a duly accredited agent; in the interim, however, the circumstances of the black residents in Dawn had worsened. "In a languishing state," was how the black *Voice of the Fugitive* described the school at Dawn, "everything is going down hill, so that it is, in fact, unworthy of the name of an Institution. The party that now have it in charge, are doubtless unable to carry it on with propriety."[9] With the death of James Canning Fuller, the remaining trustees refused to assume any responsibility, and Henson was nearly impeached for mismanagement.

Because of the fiscal malfeasance, the British and Foreign Anti-Slavery Society assumed control over the failing British-American Institute and appointed John Scoble, a white Englishman, as the new manager. Scoble immediately alienated the black community by taking the best house, equipment, and livestock for himself, and selling timber from the settlement for personal gain. Meeting at Dresden to discuss the situation, a group of blacks charged that "the conduct of said Mr. Scoble...was distasteful to the people of this community... his pomp and pride of deportment, and his petulant and over-bearing spirit—was such as totally unfitted him for the office he assumed, and the work he was sent to accomplish." Far from assisting the school or the community, Scoble's behavior contributed to the bad publicity and reputation of both. Four times before 1861, Scoble was reprimanded for poor administration and one trustee, James C. Brown of Toronto, even instituted court action to remove Scoble from his post. Scoble survived until 1868 when the trustees finally succeeded in dismissing him. For Dawn, however, that was too little and too late, for the settlement had already essentially ceased to function as a sanctuary for fugitive slaves.[10]

Like Wilberforce before it, Dawn succumbed to poor leadership and management. Never possessing enough money to keep the institution out of debt, what meager funds existed came from external sources, rather than being generated from within the community. While the idea of the manual labor school had certainly seemed practical, the founders failed to consider the necessity of long-range financial solvency. Ironically, the very institute, meant to train blacks for economic survival, failed itself to succeed financially. "It seems a great mistake in judgement," reported the American Missionary Association, "to build a high school or college, instead of laying out the money collected in establishing and maintaining common schools, especially when the funds are committed to trustees who are incompetent." With those scathing remarks, the Association dismissed Dawn as an utter failure, unworthy of any assistance.[11] The idea of a self-supporting settlement for fugitive slaves had met with another defeat.

Dawn's ignominious demise continued the trend of failure begun with Amherstburg, Oro, and Wilberforce. It prompted even those who most wanted black communities to flourish to criticize such endeavors. Thomas Henning, secretary of the Canadian Anti-Slavery Society, observed that unskilled, unedu-cated fugitive blacks would never be able to prosper by farming in Canada West, for they simply could not understand all the "Burkean nuance property-holding implied." Boston abolitionist Benjamin Drew was particularly predisposed toward the fugitives, yet he, too, was forced to concede that Dawn left upon him "an unfavorable and melancholy impression." After interviewing fugitive slaves in Canada West on behalf of the American Freedmen's Inquiry Commission, Samuel Gridley Howe reached the same conclusion. Viewing Dawn as the quintessential, self-segregated community failing because of dependence on others, Howe wryly commented that "taken as a whole, the colonists have cost to somebody a great deal of effort; and they have not succeeded so well as many who have been thrown entirely upon their own resources."[12]

Besides discouraging proponents of self-sufficient black communities,

Dawn aroused renewed white antagonism toward blacks who solicited funds. This prickly issue had begun with the begging of agents Israel Lewis and Nathaniel Paul on behalf of Wilberforce and continued when Josiah Henson collected donations to defray the costs of the floundering saw mill at Dawn. Black editor of the *Provincial Freeman,* Mary Ann Shadd, noted that "great injury (was) done to the colored people, by Mr. Henson's self-assured character of a public benefactor and authorized beggar for them."[13] Most significant, Shadd's comment reveals that many blacks viewed begging as distasteful and improper. Nevertheless, whites observed that the practice continued, and feared that soliciting would increase with the establishment of other black communities. At best a volatile subject, begging had become associated exclusively with blacks, and in the process lowered white Canadian opinion of fugitives and reinforced the belief that they were improvident. The experience of Josiah Henson and the Dawn Community had merely exacerbated and entrenched white Canadian prejudice toward fugitive slaves in Canada West.

Because of the large concentration of approximately four thousand destitute fugitives living in the Amherstburg area, yet another black community was planned. Despite the dismal record of the fugitive slave settlements, a convention of blacks was held in 1846 in nearby Windsor at which it was suggested by the Reverend T. Willis and by Isaac Rice, a white missionary, that a new black community be created. With the support of abolitionists Lewis Tappan and Charles Stewart, and with the backing of antislavery advocates in nearby Detroit, the plan suggested at the convention began to materialize. The Sandwich Mission, as it was named, proposed not only to establish a black community but to supply to the refugees houses and land, to solicit funds from sources on both sides of the Atlantic, and to provide for the sick and elderly. "We are aiming in this, not only to get homes," commented one observer, "but (to) secure steady education and better gospel privileges, being here as in the states excluded from white schools and white Temperance Societies." The consumption of alcoholic beverages was forbidden, and the improvement of the lots was to commence within a stipulated length of time. A board of trustees, appointed by backers from Detroit, was to manage the Sandwich Mission and arbitrate any conflicts between settlers in order to avoid public recrimination. Choosing a site about ten miles north of Amherstburg, some twelve hundred acres were soon purchased for resale to the new community.[14]

By 1850, however, no substantive resettlement had occurred. An antislavery convention in Detroit the next year reconsidered the original goals of the Sandwich Mission and found a broader base of support in a large group from Michigan calling themselves the Refugee Home Society. Merging with the original organizers of the Sandwich Mission, now called the Fugitives Union

Society, a single organization was formed, the Refugee Home Society, whose members ambitiously planned to purchase fifty thousand acres of land for use by a fugitive-slave community. The other goals were essentially the same as those of the original Sandwich Mission. Within the first two years the management changed three times. But by 1853, under more stable leadership, the society bought almost two thousand acres in Canada West. Of this land, some thousand acres were redistributed among 150 fugitives.[15]

After an uncertain beginning, the settlers experienced debilitating difficulties. Many blacks became incensed when an increase in surveying charges led to an increase in the price of their land and a decrease in the time allotted for improvement. Because only the destitute participated in the Refugee Home Society, many settlers swiftly fell into arrears. Contrary to its charter, the society publicly disgraced the community by suing the debt-ridden fugitives. Deciding in favor of the defendants, the court found that "as the purchase money for the land was begged in the name of the fugitives, they are entitled to the land without payment."[16] As a consequence of this legal action, the society's finances were depleted, incapable of providing either facilities or funding for the education of the fugitives. Nor were the purchased holdings contiguous, making the settlement seem even less like a true community.

Besides financial woes, the Refugee Home Society faced the opposition of blacks in Canada West, led by Mary Ann Shadd and Samuel Ringgold Ward. Accusing the society of selling the land to the fugitives at a higher price than other readily available government land, Ward also contended that the plots assigned by the society were less than adequate in size. Further, he criticized the clause enabling the society to repossess the land as denying the fugitives their rights as landowners. "No other set of land-jobbers than the Refugee's Home Society," wrote Ward, "beg for their capital in the name of the poor whom they thus victimize." To Ward, the Refugee Home Society constituted merely a front for making a quick profit.[17]

Mary Ann Shadd, in more specific fashion, charged the black leader of the society, Henry Bibb, and his Detroit supporters with malfeasance. She castigated the society's agents for taking a commission of between 20 and 63 percent on funds donated to aid the refugees and for abusing the begging system by using the money for extensive private business operations. Resenting the implications of begging as "materially compromising our manhood, by representing us as objects of charity," Shadd assailed the undignified manner in which funds were solicited, arguing against begging because it implied that blacks could not be financially independent. Having scorned organized religion in the past because of her belief that the churches contributed to segregation, Shadd now simply extended her contempt of segregated communities to the Refugee Home

Society.[18] Begging as a means to raise funds and the self-imposed segregation of fugitives were far more destructive than the scalping of land to Shadd, for *they* were the policies that could most damage the image of blacks in the white Canadian mind.

Yet Ward and Shadd were not the only critics of the Refugee Home Society. At two public meetings in Windsor in late 1852 and early 1853, blacks condemned both the society and the continued begging by its agents. Observing the black discontent, Alexander McArthur, a white Windsor resident, wrote to the American Missionary Association corroborating Ward's and Shadd's accusations. McArthur described the black disdain and distrust of Henry Bibb and stated categorically that the Refugee Home Society

> does not work and never can under the present arrangement...the better portion of the fugitives cannot be enduced (sic) to go on the land at all. The measure is unpopular among them, partly because of some odious features in the constitution of the society which restricts them in disposing of the property if they see fit...and partly because of Mr. Bibb's connection with the measure...the whole scheme is destined to prove a magnificent failure. It is another of those bottomless pits which have opened their mouths here on this fugitive mission and swallowed so much of the people's charitable contributions.[19]

Rapidly, the Refugee Home Society was becoming another debacle in the history of black communities in Canada West.

Henry Bibb did not take his opposition lightly, however. As editor of the *Voice of the Fugitive,* Bibb had a ready forum from which to defend his position. He called for a North American Convention of Colored People to include in its goals black ownership of land and the "social, political, and moral elevation" of black fugitives. Merely the first step in a long process of uplifting the former slaves, the Refugee Home Society represented a beginning and not an end. Soon Bibb gained the support of an increasing number of blacks including J. Theodore Holly, a black preacher, formerly of Connecticut, who responded point by point to the accusations against Bibb and the society. Holly claimed that the society's leadership and agents were honest, and that its regulations fostered independence rather than dependence. He noted that initially segregation would benefit newly arrived fugitives, giving the community a sense of identity, yet he assured his fellow blacks that integration would naturally follow. Assimilation "will be done by the colored man himself," wrote Holly, "when (he) is in a state of freedom, after he becomes *thoroughly* educated, and the *personal* sense of slavery shall be lost in a free-born generation of descendants, in political contact with other classes."[20]

A fatal blow befell the society in 1854 when Henry Bibb died. With its black standard bearer gone, the struggling Refugee Home Society lost its public support and joined Wilberforce and Dawn as ignominious failures. Again, poor financial planning and factionalism amongst the blacks themselves had contributed to the society's end. To white Canadians, the issue of begging was thereafter even more firmly associated with blacks. In the aftermath, the concept of a self-supporting black settlement seemed quite remote as the death of the Refugee Home Society left but one image of blacks in Canada West: that of black indigence and ineffectiveness.

The large numbers of destitute blacks entering the province immediately following the passage in 1850 of the American Fugitive Slave Law strongly reinforced the negative image. While the strict enforcement of black laws and the concomitant racial animosity in the Northern states had encouraged blacks to emigrate during the 1840s, the new Fugitive Slave Law virtually propelled thousands of blacks to Canada West. The very nature of the law, which stipulated that the owner of a fugitive slave could recover him either with the authorization of a warrant or "by seizing and arresting such fugitive, where the same can be done without process" threatened all Northern blacks, fugitive slave and free alike.

United States marshals and law-enforcement officers were required to aid the owner both in the pursuit and return of the fugitive to the state or territory from which he escaped. To ensure cooperation, the law declared that the marshals were liable for the slave's value if he escaped a second time, or were subject to a fine for noncompliance. Perhaps the most frightening aspect of the Fugitive Slave Law to blacks lay in the final provision, which stated that "satisfactory proof" of ownership would suffice to prove that the slave had escaped and could be automatically reclaimed.[21] For good reason, blacks feared that the law would result in the claim and enslavement of even free blacks. With little surprise, thousands were driven to seek the safety of Canada West.

Estimates of the number of fugitive slaves in the province at this time varied widely, from as few as fifteen thousand to as many as seventy-five thousand. From the best available sources, it would seem that the fugitive slave population in Canada West in 1852 approximated thirty thousand. With whites numbering almost nine hundred and fifty thousand, the percentage of blacks remained small, about 3.2 percent. As the decade continued and thousands more fugitives fled from the United States to the province, this percentage of blacks increased to 4 or 5 percent of the total population. The impact of the influx of blacks was felt more strongly than the figures might indicate, however, for the refugees tended to locate in specific areas, chiefly where previous fugitives had established. This meant that in the 1850s, blacks comprised approximately 20 percent of the population of Chatham, 25 percent of Amherstburg, and as much as 33 percent of Colchester. So concentrated was the black population that William Davies, a local white resident, speculated that he saw "Free Niggers...at every step."[22] And it was precisely in those areas of highest concentration that white Canadian prejudice and racial animosity grew most rampantly.

Another factor contributing to the escalation of prejudice centered around the labor market of Canada West. Cheap labor was badly needed for railroad construction during the late 1840s and early 1850s, but this need was filled with the immigration of thousands of Irish. Because of their destitute situation at home, the suffering Irish were encouraged to relocate in Canada, where competition among the unskilled workers resulted. Considered inferior by the French-Canadians and the Irish, as well as by a number of the English, blacks seldom received work in preference to other ethnic groups. Indeed, the competition with the Irish hurt blacks even beyond the immediate effect of rendering them unemployed. Irish prejudice proved "to be more hostile to the Negro in Canada West, whether along railway lines or elsewhere, than any other ethnic group within the province."[23]

In view of the problems presented by the unemployed and impoverished fugitive slaves, white Canadians deeply resented the arrival of more blacks. The failure of several organized black communities had entrenched the white belief that the fugitives were ignorant, improvident, and indigent. With little sympathy and patience, then, the white residents of Canada West braced themselves for still another attempt at establishing a black settlement in their midst.

The final such effort was initiated by a white preacher who had been in Canada for only one year. Born in Ireland and educated at Glasgow University, the Reverend William King served as a missionary for the Free Presbyterian Church of Scotland before traveling to Jackson, Louisiana, where he became master of a private boys' school. There King married Mary M. Phares, daughter of a wealthy plantation owner. Returning to Scotland in order to continue his theological studies, King emigrated to Canada West upon the death of his wife in 1846. Before he could continue in his mission as a minister in Canada West, however, King believed it imperative to dispose of the fifteen slaves he had inherited as part of his wife's estate and reconcile his stated antislavery belief with his slaveholder status. In Louisiana, King learned that it was illegal to manumit slaves without providing for their future, and he feared leaving them in a Northern state, such as Ohio, because of the rigid enforcement of the black laws. Finding no sanctuary for his slaves in the United States, King determined to found a permanent settlement for blacks in Canada West. With his own manumitted slaves as the core of this community, the Elgin Settlement, named for the current governor general, was conceived.[24]

King did not make his decision recklessly or lightly. Before undertaking the project, he visited Canada West where he hoped his acquaintances at the Toronto Synod would sponsor the settlement. Presenting a clear picture of his goals to place the fugitives "on land, give them an interest in the soil, and provide them with a Christian education," King asked for assistance. The synod rejected the request, declaring it inappropriate for a spiritual body to originate the community's support; it pledged, however, that it would open a mission at the settlement. For several months thereafter, King diligently canvassed the province for immediate and continued funding.

Unlike his predecessors, King was recognized as a well-educated, responsible, and respectable leader. He enlisted the aid of a committee of prominent people in Toronto, and soon "succeeded in obtaining the subscription of stock to the amount needed." Wanting to have a broad base of financial support before commencing his project, King formed a stock company that would take all fiscal responsibilities at first, and would be phased out as the community learned to manage its finances independently. Stockholders subsequently met in Toronto on 1 June 1849 to organize the Elgin Association and select the site for the black settlement, six miles southwest of Chatham. That fall the Elgin Association purchased forty-three hundred acres in the township of Raleigh, and the first black settlers arrived before the end of the year.[25] It appeared that King's careful planning was about to reach fruition.

Unfortunately, the Elgin Association had chosen an area where the proposed establishment of a black community created a hotbed of controversy. King should have recognized the warning signals, for he wrote in his autobiography:

> I had visited the township of Raleigh before purchasing the land, and preached two sabbaths in Chatham. I was very popular but when it was known that I intended to settle a colony of coloured persons in the township my popularity fell rapidly. The next time I visited the town—I got the cold shoulder—scarcely anyone would speak to me. One man came to me. . .and told me as a friend that my life was in danger, and that I should not expose myself after dark in the town.

Obviously, there was ill feeling on the part of white Canadian citizens toward King's projected community, and King keenly realized that prejudice against the fugitive "has followed him even in this free Country and operates against his moral improvement." Aware that prejudice in Canada West kept many black children out of school, King observed that the animosity was especially pronounced near Chatham, where already 20 percent of the population was black.[26] Undaunted, King persisted in his plan with the faith that a successful settlement would reverse public opinion.

Soon the opposition escalated. Even before the incorporation of the Elgin Association, the white inhabitants of the area objected to the plan, sending a petition to the legislative assembly, in which they stated that the black settlement would be "highly deleterious to the morals and social condition of the present and future inhabitants of this District, as well as to its prosperity in every other respect." Although the white residents indicated their prejudice in presupposing the negative impact of a black community, their fears were based on the past experience of other communities.

Following this petition, Edwin Larwill, Western District Council member and vocal resident of Chatham, assumed leadership of the vanguard of white opposition to the Elgin settlement. According to historians William and Jane Pease, "Little is known about Larwill beyond the fact that he was born in England and was an old-line Tory. He may have been a lawyer, a merchant, or a real-estate agent, for it is known that he held some land, and may have been an active speculator. He was active in local politics, serving during the 1840s both as a member of the Western District Council and as member of Kent County in the Canadian Legislature. It can be said unequivocally about Edwin Larwill that he was...violently and actively anti-Negro."

Larwill offered at least a dozen reasons why the Elgin Settlement should be stopped. Some of his arguments were from an economic standpoint: property values would drop, and better-stock European immigrants would face unfair competition in the unskilled labor market. Others were social in nature: amalgamation would be inevitable; self-government would be impossible. He even offered religious logic: moral people could always manage alone, and racial distinction was part of God's plan. Larwill stated that Canadian public opinion was against black communities, and that the creation of another such settlement might encourage friction with the United States. He declared blacks to be "indolent, vicious and ungovernable," and concluded that blacks suffered greatly in the cold Canadian climate.[27]

Quickly becoming the titular leader of the white Canadians, Larwill engineered yet another petition by residents of Raleigh, Chatham, and vicinity, which ultimately was endorsed by 377 people—a substantial percentage of the white population.[28] This petition opened by agreeing that blacks should indeed seek self-fulfillment and satisfaction like any other human beings, but then qualified it by stating that any "colony of Vicious Blacks would be prejudicial to every interest of Society." In short, some of Chatham's denizens believed blacks should be free, as long as they did not choose to be so in Canada West. The Chatham petition proceeded like a virtual indictment, charging that the existence of this black community would encourage miscegenation, provoke war with the slaveholding United States, devalue property, invite social and political chaos, and discourage "better stock" European immigrants. In a less than subtle manner it concluded: "Would not offices of trust, Honor, and Emolument, ultimately fall to their Share. Imagine our Legislative Halls studded and, our principal Departments managed by, these Ebony Men.... The Genious (sic) of our Institutions would be destroyed."

Opposition to the establishment of a community of former slaves, founded upon fear, was thus fed by racism. The white supremacist petition was finally presented to the Free Presbyterian Synod in Toronto, supporter of the Elgin idea, in an attempt to block the location of blacks so near to Chatham.[29]

With no response from the Toronto Synod, fearful whites called a public meeting at the Royal Exchange Hotel in Chatham to pass all measures necessary "to prevent the partial colonizing of colored people" in the township of Raleigh. Meeting during the heat of August, chairman George Young expressed the immediate need to prevent the fugitive slaves from buying land. In response, William King took the floor to object to the activities, charging that the assemblage "is called to do an illegal act and I protest the whole proceedings as illegal, and if any disturbance should arise, as it is feared there would from the excited state of the public mind you will be held responsible for it." Along with this condemnation, King attempted to defend the Elgin plan by reassuringly stating that there "would be no incursion of coloured riff-raff," since the Elgin community "was only open to the deserving, and these only it was (his) wish to encourage."[30]

King's assurances were made in vain, as he was "frequently interrupted during his remarks, and it was impossible to hear him; the noise and groans being so frequent." The white crowd simply did not wish to listen, nor was the matter open to debate or discussion. They merely wanted to proceed with the prejudicial business at hand and their comments provide quite a revealing picture of the white Canadian mind regarding blacks. Declaring that a black relocation project should not be pursued, or allowed by the government, in an area already settled by whites, Walter McCrae asked if anyone in Canada would welcome "several hundreds of Africans, into the very heart of their neighbor-hood." McCrae reflected on the question of whether other Canadians would want to compete with black settlers for political and social privileges and he raised the dreaded spectre of miscegenation as the "necessary and hideous attendant" of any further concentration of blacks among whites. Believing he represented the vast majority of white Canadians, McCrae closed his remarks with a common plea simultaneously against slavery and blacks. "Let the slaves of the United States be free," McCrae implored, "but let it be in their own country; let us not countenance their further introduction among us; in a word, let the people of the United States bear the burden of their own sins."

After McCrae's impassioned address, his fellow white Canadians appointed a Vigilance Committee, whose purpose it was to monitor and publicize the progress of the Elgin Association. In this manner, they hoped that heightened public awareness of Elgin's proceedings would intensify the already existing anti-black feelings. Meanwhile, a newly created committee drafted further anti-Elgin petitions to be sent to the governor general, the appropriate member of Parliament, the chief executive of the Western District, and the president of the Elgin Association.[31]

Attempting to stave off the rising tide of opposition, William King submitted a statement to the Chatham *Chronicle* in which he tried to clarify his intentions and persuade the people of the advantages of the proposed black community. With deep sincerity he wrote: "The object of the Society is to take the good, give them every encouragement, and make them better.... Many of the colored persons who proposed to settle in Raleigh are British subjects, and many of them are possessed of considerable means. (Our) settlement...will exercise a wholesome moral influence on the colored population...; improve the nature of land in Raleigh; increase the revenue of the Township, and add to the trade of Chatham."

King's appeal was useless, however. A Chatham resident quickly responded to King's remarks in a letter to the editor, signed as "one who was present at the meeting." The anonymous author attacked King's argument about the attraction of prosperous blacks to the community by caustically asking how Elgin could claim the status of a philanthropic organization if it ignored those "destitute of all means of support, uneducated, degraded in mind, and prostrate in infamy."[32] Much to his chagrin, King went unsupported in the *Chronicle* by any local resident. Indeed, the Chatham *Chronicle* had, until this time, seemed unbiased in its reporting. In an attempt to mollify all concerned parties, the *Chronicle* suggested that intelligent blacks recognize the need to move elsewhere, contending that their advancement would be "better consulted and more successfully carried out" in a different location, particularly one well removed from white communities.[33]

The *Chronicle* then published a letter from another mysterious author. Signed by "Cannon," the correspondence, meant ostensibly to be the black aspirations of Elgin, stated that the fugitives planned an active political campaign. Outnumbering whites in the area, the blacks would dominate local politics and essentially take over the entire Western District; once in control, they would assert themselves socially, with miscegenation their ultimate ambition.[34] An unbiased reader might have considered the letter a caricature of the worst fears of white Canadians. But it was written and interpreted from a jaded perspective and taken quite literally by the *Chronicle's* white readership. That there was neither rebuke nor protest against "Cannon's" statements indicated the gravity and extent of racial animosity in the area.

The controversy continued unabated in the press. Perhaps because by now the *Chronicle* assumed a blatantly racist editorial stance, a newspaper from outside the immediate vicinity served as the organ for supporters of the Elgin Association. Publishing a pro-Elgin letter with over a hundred signatures, the Toronto *Globe* reminded its readership that three of the signatories—Archibald McKellar, Thomas Williams, and George Jacobs—were Western District justices of the peace. Addressed to the president and directors of the Elgin Association, the letter declared, "We think it right to inform you, that a large and respectable portion of the inhabitants of the District, offer no opposition, and take no part in such illegal proceedings."[35] Though it gave King great reassurance and though a significant number of people agreed to tolerate the settlement, it nevertheless stopped short of actually promoting the Elgin Association. In the end, the letter condemned the resolutions passed at the Royal Exchange Hotel, doing nothing more to facilitate King's project.

Angered by the letter in the *Globe,* Edwin Larwill responded with one of his own to the editor of the *Chronicle* in which he proclaimed: "It is a deliberate falsehood to say, that a respectable portion of the white inhabitants of this District are in favour of the objects of the Elgin Association. It is belied by the unanimous petition of the Municipal Council,...it is belied by the proceedings at the (Sheriff's) Meeting,...it is belied by the Press,...it is belied by the clandestine manner in which the document sent to the Globe office was signed."[36]

Larwill exhibited particular outrage because the letter in the *Globe* failed to note that many of its signatories were black. Thinking this misled readers into believing that a majority of local whites supported Elgin, Larwill felt it his responsibility to correct the misconception.

While the pro- and anti-Elgin forces aired their opinions openly in the press, Larwill himself took surreptitious action against the fugitives. Taking advantage of his position as councillor of the township of Raleigh, Larwill requested that the governor general delay granting land to the Elgin Association until after the Western District Council met. At that assembly, held in early October 1849, Larwill presented a petition that accused the government of advancing the Elgin project and labeled any suit supporting the community previously received by the government as false. Larwill assured the governor general that there was "but one feeling, and that is of disgust and hatred, that they, 'the Negroes,' should be allowed to settle in any Township where there is a white settlement."[37] By endorsing Larwill's petition, the Western District Council officially went on record as opposing the Elgin Settlement.

Larwill's petition was forwarded on to Parliament for review. The version read in Parliament, however, had an addendum attached, apparently without the council's approval, that featured requests for such anti-black legislation as a poll tax on American blacks in Canada West, "some enactments against amalgamation; and . . . a Bill by which all foreign Negroes shall be compelled to furnish good security that they shall not become a burden." The addendum continued by seeking a ban on the sale of land to blacks, and by asserting that blacks should not be enfranchised. Its author, presumably Larwill, concluded that "the Canadians will never tolerate" the mingling of the races, either literally or figuratively.[38] Although the majority of white residents in the Western District did not necessarily support the provisions for a security bond, disenfranchisement, or an enjoinment on black public officials, the fact that the council had approved and submitted Larwill's petition to Parliament indicated a great deal of negrophobia. That someone or some few wanted to invoke legislative orders reminiscent of the black laws in the northern United States testified to the depth of anti-black sentiment in Canada West.

Notwithstanding the effect of the petition upon white public opinion, the sale of land to the Elgin Association took place within two weeks. Irate, Larwill led an attempt to block approval of the Elgin Association's charter, and the House of Assembly unanimously supported his protest to disallow Elgin's incorporation. Nevertheless, King's plans had been so carefully organized and so fully documented that the Elgin Association received its charter less than a year later—on 10 August 1850.[39]

Within two years the Elgin Settlement boasted a black population of seventy-five families, and soon the number nearly doubled. As the population grew, so, too, did the community's economic prosperity. There were carpenters, cobblers, and blacksmiths, and most landowners cleared their lots for subsistence farming. The settlement included a potash and pearl-ash factory, a two-story brick hotel, and a general store, while all houses met strict standards in size and quality. By 1854, seventy-seven homes existed according to those standards, and eight others by far exceeded the minimum. To encourage community pride, each property and neighborhood was judged in annual competitions. The prizes, coveted by all, encouraged great care of land and homes alike. In fact, one report described a neighborhood of Elgin with gardens "tastefully laid out, . . . filled with vegetables, fruit, and flowers—the houses clean and whitewashed—and many of them trained the vine and honeysuckle on the rustic pillars that supported the piazza in front."

Why, unlike his predecessors, had King been able to inspire such effort and achieve such success? Perhaps the answer can be found in the type of blacks allowed to settle at Elgin. True to his public vow, King admitted only those fugitives who could present evidence of their good moral character, insisting that "such precaution is indispensably necessary to the success of (this) undertaking. If all should be admitted who might come, whether they were temperate or intemperate, industrious or indolent, honest or dishonest, the management of the institution might fall into the hands of bad men, or be so seriously impeded by such men, that it could not succeed, even under the conduct of the best."[40] Because of the soundness of their character, the fugitives at Elgin took easily to the idea of self-help, and wanting to eradicate the pejorative image of previous black settlements, community members abstained from any frivolous behavior. Prompted by peer pressure, Elgin achieved its goal of self-support.

Other important aspects of community life at Elgin contributed significantly toward its success as well. The Buxton Mission, created by the Toronto Free Presbyterian Synod as promised, met the spiritual needs of the fugitives. A Baptist church was established in 1854, and a Methodist church several years later with the fugitives attending all three churches regularly, and participating actively in the Mission's Sunday School. That the Buxton Mission set up a library with over five hundred volumes illustrates the extent of the community's interest in religion.[41]

The books, however, would have been of little help had the community members been incapable of reading. With this in mind, in 1850, King began a school in Elgin for the elementary education of both adults and children offering instruction in English, arithmetic, and geography. Within three years, the curriculum expanded to include Greek, Latin, and algebra to meet the needs of at least 150 students attending the school.[42]

Yet, King did not stop there. He also focused on the fugitives' political education wanting to ensure that they understood self-government. Establishing several governing committees, King encouraged his constituents to become Canadian citizens as quickly as possible in order to vote. He explained to them the purpose of bloc voting and "kept them a compact body, so that the political power they have got will protect them."[43]

The Elgin blacks soon tested their political prowess. Longtime nemesis Edwin Larwill, up for reelection to the councillorship of Raleigh in 1851, ultimately lost his election, in part because of the black votes cast from Elgin. Smarting from this defeat, Larwill then successfully sought a seat as representative to Parliament where he continued to harass Elgin by introducing legislation to review the settlement's records. In a litany of requests aimed at thwarting Elgin's success, Larwill filed for

1st. Copies of the Proceedings of the *Elgin* Association, and Reports thereon for each year since the incorporation of the said Society.... 2ndly. The quantity of the Land purchased by the said Corporation, the conditions of the purchase, the sum given per acre, the time and terms of payment, if they have been complied with, and, if not, why not? And a copy of all such rules and regulations touching the management and disposition of the Lands, properties, estate, and effects of the said Association. 3rdly. The number of public buildings erected, their location, dimensions, uses, and cost of construction.... 4thly. An account of the receipts and expenditures of the said Association.[44]

The attorney general approved of Larwill's request for this audit on the grounds that the Elgin Association was a chartered corporation. In response, King inserted appendices on finances, stockholders, and governing by-laws to the 1854 Annual Report, thus temporarily silencing the vituperative Larwill. The residents of Elgin, however, quickly achieved their political revenge against Larwill the next time he campaigned for reelection. Wielding their bloc vote wisely, the blacks supported Archibald McKellar, who had endorsed Elgin from its inception. With this defeat, Larwill was finally removed from provincial politics.[45]

Elgin's early success continued until the Civil War. Only once did a taint of dishonesty and deception emerge, and even that did not involve King or the settlers directly, but rather some investment agents who absconded with or lost a large sum of the settlement's money. Three hundred black families flourished at Elgin, clearing several thousand acres in the process. The demand for education became so great that two more schools, supported by local taxes, were built in the district, and by the 1860s, black teachers who had been educated at Elgin found employment in these additional district schools. Most significantly, whites began to send their children to the Elgin school because it provided a higher quality of education than its white counterparts. When more than seventy blacks left the settlement for the United States, however, to enlist on the Union side in the Civil War, a disturbing trend had commenced that was ultimately to lead to Elgin's demise by 1873. Elgin's school closed during a smallpox epidemic in the late 1860s; in the aftermath, many blacks decided that it was time to leave. Most returned to the United States to find jobs as teachers, though several became lawyers, doctors, and principals in public schools; the most successful graduates of Elgin were a Congressman and a judge.[46] King's community in Canada West had indeed served these blacks well, but with Elgin's decline went the last effort at establishing a Canadian haven for blacks. The implementation of Lincoln's

Emancipation Proclamation in the United States had simply destroyed that kind of community's raison d'être.

Compared with the other fugitive slave communities, Elgin was by far the most successful. Unlike the former slaves in Amherstburg, these fugitives owned their land and planned a solid economic future. In contrast to Oro, Elgin had superb organization and a better location for farming and trade. Where Wilberforce failed because of poor leadership, Elgin flourished under King's capable direction. While the British-American Institute had a grandiose scheme for the manual labor school at Dawn, Elgin's school program provided the basic education that the fugitives lacked. This, in turn, enabled many to find honorable employment. King's careful screening of applicants avoided the low moral character and begging that characterized the black settlers of the Refugee Home Society. Further, under the guidance of King, the blacks at Elgin learned how to exercise their political power, and learned the responsibilities implicit with civil rights. The primary cause for Elgin's decline, then, cannot be attributed to internal failure; an external event, the abolition of slavery in the United States, allowing the fugitives to return to their homeland, sounded the death knell for Elgin.

Did Elgin achieve its goals? There can be no denying its triumph in comparison with other black communities, yet Elgin, too, failed to achieve its most important ambitions. It never removed the stigma of blacks in Canada West, nor prepared either whites or blacks for an integrated society. Despite the settlement's obvious prosperity and the stature that some of its inhabitants eventually acquired, whites remained suspicious, distrustful, and fearful of fugitive slaves. The Amherstburg *Courier* stated in 1850 that "the white inhabitants are fast leaving the vicinity of the. . .colored settlement," while those white Canadians who remained fought both the establishment and continuance of the black community, as indicated by the popular support given to Edwin Larwill and his various anti-Elgin petitions. Perhaps the town clerk of Malden, one Mr. Brush, summarized the white viewpoint best when he commented in 1863 that "A portion of them (the colored people) are pretty well-behaved, and another portion not. . . . We have to help a great many of them; more than any other class of people we have here. . . . I think the Council have given more to the colored people than to any others."[47]

The image of black indolence and indigence still existed in Canada West, and whites still refused to socially interact with the fugitives. Isolated from its white Canadian neighbors on every level, geographically, spiritually, and socially, the Elgin Settlement functioned as an independent community that relied only upon itself for sustenance and solace. In this regard, Elgin did satisfy one aim; but ironically, that very autonomy fostered future segregation. King had proposed to educate and to prepare the fugitives for living as useful members of a predominantly white society. Because Elgin existed in a vacuum, however, it never confronted the problems associated with integration and for the large percentage of blacks concentrated in the Western District, this was Elgin's tragedy. It contributed to a few individuals' accomplishments while the great majority of fugitive slaves went unaffected. Elgin did not overcome negrophobia on the part of white Canadians, nor did it contribute anything of enduring value to the resolution of racial problems in Canada West. Fugitive slaves continued to be an unaccepted minority, and King unhappily discovered that Elgin alone could not eradicate the prejudice permeating white Canadian society.

In fact, this negrophobia in Canada West was becoming quite evident to contemporary observers. Under the auspices of the American Freedmen's Inquiry Commission, Samuel Gridley Howe visited the province in 1863 to record the conditions of fugitive slaves. While in Canada, Howe noticed the Canadians's pride in their laws that ideally offered equal protection to all races. Yet, he perceptively concluded, the "very frequency of the assertion...proves that it is not considered a matter of course that simple justice should be done. People do not boast that the law protects white men." A sensitive social critic, Howe also noticed the marked difference between white Canadian reaction to a few fugitive slaves in the early years, and to the organized black communities and thousands of black immigrants in Canada after 1850. Initially, blacks were accorded status as a novelty and as such received cordial treatment; after the influx of many more runaway slaves, with the accompanying competition in labor and social standing, Howe detected that blacks had ceased to be "interesting negroes" to white Canadians and were instead regarded as merely "niggers." On the other hand, Howe also discovered a significant degree of black discontent with white Canadians, particularly in Canada West and close to the Elgin Settlement.[48]

Most indicative of this attitude are the responses to Howe's interviews. Thomas Likers, a fugitive slave from Maryland residing in Canada West, concluded that there "was as much prejudice against the black man in Canada as there is in the States, and I have sometimes thought more." J.W. Lindsay, an escaped slave from Tennessee, expressed much the same feeling declaring "the Colored people in Canada have no chance for advancement; not only social advancement but they are barred out from every thing that will give them a living." Lindsay railed particularly against Canadian prejudice in labor and education, observing that "as far as prejudice goes, the slaveholders have not so much absolute prejudice as the people here—not half (as much)." Likewise Lewis Chambers, who worked for the American Missionary Association as a minister to blacks in Canada from 1855 to 1863, described the racism and the prejudice prevalent in Canada: "There is more sympathy for the slave in the States than there is in Canada...the prejudice in Canada is great; it is worse than it is in the States in many respects." Chambers saw blacks driven from their homes, and watched, in horror, his own home burn as the result of arson.[49]

Testimony about Canadian anti-black prejudice in and around the Elgin Settlement emerged in the interview with George Williams, formerly enslaved in Maryland. Cursing the day he moved to Canada, Williams bitterly exclaimed that he would have been "better off" in the United States. Horace Hawkins, a runaway from Kentucky, apparently traveled widely throughout Canada West and discovered "prejudice greater than in the States." He noticed negrophobia almost everywhere he visited in Canada with racial distinctions in the travel industry, to the extent that "a colored man cannot get accommodated at any of the hotels in Canada or any line of railroad or public travel." And, he noticed racial enmity on omnibuses as well as steamboats, where blacks were refused as passengers or given inferior accommodations. By their own testimony, the fugitive slaves attested to a significant degree of negrophobia and white supremacist attitudes on the part of their Canadian neighbors.[50]

It had taken less than fifty years for prejudice to build in Canada West. By the late 1850s, city directories listed black businesses and homes in a separate section while blacks were excluded from religious camp meetings, hotels, and various kinds of employment. Blaming blacks for "all the outrageous crimes, and two-thirds of the minor ones," and claiming their right to "preserve (white) property from deterioration," Canadian whites refused to sell land to blacks or permit them into their neighborhoods. One newspaper perhaps summarized it all when it advised the fugitives that if they stayed in Canada West, they would "ever have to contend with their superiors." The background of the fugitives, their indolence, their communal failures, and their rapid and concentrated influx, had resulted in the province becoming, in the words of one black, "beneath and behind Yankee feeling in its colorphobia."[51] The dream of a Canadian Utopia turned into a nightmare, as blacks, theoretically free, found themselves increasingly unwelcome.

NOTES

1. John Hope Franklin, *From Slavery to Freedom: A History of Negro Americans* (New York, 1980), pp. 160-74; and
    Litwack, *North of Slavery*, pp. 75-93, 263.
2. Papers of the American Anti-Slavery Society: minutes of meetings, 4 December 1833, 23 October 1839, 15 January 1840, in the Library of Congress, Washington, D.C.;

The Emancipator, 22 December 1836;

The Friend of Man, 17 January, 14 February, 9 May, and 28 June 1838;

National Anti-Slavery Standard, 8 July 1841;

The Liberator, 10 April 1846;

American Anti-Slavery Society, *Fourth Annual Report* (1837), p. 19; and

Calendar of Gerrit Smith Papers in the Syracuse University Library, vol. one: General Correspondence (Albany, 1941), pp. 2, 108, 129, 255.

3.   Crown Land Papers, Record Group 1, Ontario Provincial Archives, Toronto;

Voice of the Fugitive, 21 May 1851 and 15 July 1852;

British and Foreign Anti-Slavery Reporter, May 1856; and

Canada Mission, *Sixth Annual Report* published in *The Liberator,* 17 March 1843.

4.   For more on the relationship between Josiah Henson and Uncle Tom, see William H. Pease and Jane H. Pease, "Uncle Tom and Clayton: Fact, Fiction, and Mystery," *Ontario History* 50 (April 1958), pp. 61-73.

5.   Josiah Henson, *The Life of Josiah Henson, Formerly a Slave, Now an Inhabitant of Canada: Narrated by Himself* (London, 1852), and *Truth Is Stranger than Fiction: Father Henson's Story of His Life* (Boston, 1858).

See also the introduction and reprint edition of Henson's autobiography in Winks, ed., *Four Fugitive Slave Narratives;* and

William B. Hartgrove, "Josiah Henson," *Journal of Negro History* 3 (January 1918), pp. 1-21.

6.   Memorial U-6758, entered 10 July 1845, and Memorial 8027, entered 16 June 1846, in the Kent County, Ontario, Registry Office, Chatham, Ontario;

Canada Mission, *Sixth Annual Report* in *The Liberator,* 17 March 1843;

Josiah Henson's deed of property in Fred Landon Collection, Regional History Collection, D.B. Weldon Library, University of Western Ontario, London;

Life of Josiah Henson, p. 70; and

K. Gordon MacLachlan, *A History of Dawn Township and its Origin,* n.d., n.p., passim.

7.   Wilbur H. Siebert's notes on the British-American Institute in his "Fugitive Slaves in Canada, " Siebert Papers, Ohio State Historical Society, Columbus; and

Life of Josiah Henson, pp. 116-17.

8.   Wilbur H. Siebert's notes on Josiah Henson in his "Fugitive Slaves in Canada," Siebert Papers, Ohio State Historical Society, Columbus; and

Report of the Convention of the Coloured Population Held at Drummondville, August, 1847 (Toronto, 1847).

9.   *Voice of the Fugitive,* 15 July 1852; and

Wilbur H. Siebert's notes on Josiah Henson in his "Fugitive Slaves in Canada," Ohio State Historical Society, Columbus.

10.   *Chatham Planet,* 3 February 1859;

Victor Lauriston, *Romantic Kent: More Than Three Centuries of History, 1626-1952* (Chatham, Ontario, 1952), pp. 448-49.

11. American Missionary Society, *Fourth Annual Report* (1850), p. 29.

12. *American Anti-Slavery Reporter* 4 (1856), pp. 110-13, 124-38;
Pease and Pease, *Black Utopia*, pp. 80-81, 178-79;
Benjamin Drew, *North-Side View of Slavery* (Boston, 1856), p. 312; and
Samuel Gridley Howe, *The Refugees from Slavery in Canada West: Report to the Freedmen's Inquiry Commission* (Boston, 1864), pp. 69-70. The American Freedmen's Inquiry Commission was established in 1863 to "collect testimony of various witnesses, report to the Secretary of War, and make recommendations about what was to be done with former slaves after the Civil War ended." Congressman Robert Dale Owen of Indiana was Chairman of the Commission, which also included Benjamin Drew.

13. *Provincial Freeman*, 2 May 1857.

14. *Oberlin Evangelist*, 27 May 1846;
Voice of the Fugitive, 29 January 1851; and
Drew, *North-Side View of Slavery*, pp. 334-35.

15. *Voice of the Fugitive*, 1 June, 13 August, and 22 October 1851, and 12 February 1852;
Report of the Refugees' Home Society, Held in Detroit, Michigan, August 25, 1852 (Windsor, 1852), pp. 4-5;
Drew, *North-Side View of Slavery*, pp. 341-43, 323;
Fred Landon, "Henry Bibb, A Colonizer," *Journal of Negro History* 5 (October 1920), pp. 437-47; and
Henry Bibb, *Narrative of the Life and Adventures of Henry Bibb, an American Slave, Written by Himself* (New York, 1850).

16. Drew, *North-Side View of Slavery*, pp. 327-28;
National Anti-Slavery Standard, 18 July 1857;
Voice of the Fugitive, 25 August 1852; and
Laura S. Haviland, *A Woman's Life Work* (Chicago, 1889), pp. 186-92.

17. *National Anti-Slavery Standard*, 20 January 1853; and
Samuel Ringgold Ward, *Autobiography of a Fugitive Negro: His Anti-Slavery Labours in the United States, Canada, and England* (London, 1855), pp. 126-43, 163, 205, 218, 227-28.

18. Mary Ann Shadd to George Whipple, 22 and 28 December 1852, in Mary Ann Shadd Papers, American Missionary Association Archives, New Orleans;
The Liberator, 15 October, 5 November, and 10 December 1852; and
Drew, *North-Side View of Slavery*, pp. 323-28.

19. Alexander McArthur to George Whipple, 22 December 1852, American Missionary Association Archives, New Orleans; and

The Liberator, 15 October and 10 December 1852, and 4 March 1853.

20.   *The Liberator,* 4 March, 22 April, and 15 October 1853;
Frederick Douglass' Paper, 20 May 1853, 11 August and 17 November 1854, and 26 January 1855;
American Anti-Slavery Reporter 9 (1861), pp. 18-19; and
Roger W. Hite, "Voice of a Fugitive: Henry Bibb and Ante-Bellum Black Separatism," *Journal of Black Studies* 4 (March 1974), pp. 269-84.

21.   *United States Statutes at Large,* vol. 9, pp. 462-65. The bill was approved 18 September 1850. For more on the Fugitive Slave Law of 1850, see
Stanley W. Campbell, *The Slave Catchers: Enforcement of the Fugitive Slave Law, 1850-1860* (New York, 1970); and
Marion G. McDougall, *Fugitive Slaves, 1619-1865* (Boston, 1891).

22.   Wilbur H. Siebert's statistics on the number of refugees in Canada in his "Fugitive Slaves in Canada," Siebert Papers, Ohio State Historical Society, Columbus;
Census of Canada, pp. 178-99;
Fox, ed., *Letters of William Davies,* p. 45; and
Winks, *Blacks in Canada,* pp. 484-96.

23.   *Voice of the Fugitive,* 20 May 1852;
Fred Landon, "Fugitive Slaves in Ontario," p. 6; and
Robin W. Winks, "The Canadian Negro: A Historical Assessment Part II—The Problem of Identity," *Journal of Negro History* 54 (January 1969), pp. 8-9.

24.   For more general information on the Elgin or Buxton Settlement, see
Pease and Pease, *Black Utopia,* pp. 84-108;
Idem, "Opposition to the Founding of the Elgin Settlement," *The Canadian Historical Review* 38 (September 1957), pp. 202-18;
A.M. Harris, *A Sketch of the Buxton Mission and Elgin Settlement, Raleigh, Canada West* (Birmingham, Ala., 1866);
Fred Landon, "The Buxton Settlement in Canada," *Journal of Negro History* 4 (October 1918), pp. 360-67;
William N. Sexsmith, "Some Notes on the Buxton Settlement, Raleigh, Kent County," *Kent Historical Society, Papers and Addresses* (1919), pp. 40-44; and
Walton, "Blacks in Buxton and Chatham," pp. 38-52, 89-110.
For more on King's life, the most valuable source of information is his manuscript autobiography in the King Papers, Public Archives of Canada, Ottawa, currently being edited by Jason H. Silverman and Robin W. Winks for publication by the University of Georgia Press. See also
Annie S. Jamieson, *William King, Friend and Champion of Slaves* (Toronto, 1925);
Victor Ullman, *Look to the North Star: A Life of William King* (Boston, 1969);
Pease and Pease, "William King: From Master to Servant," *Rensselaer Review of Graduate Studies* 16 (May 1959), pp. 3-10;

J.C. Hamilton, "The African in Canada: The Rev. William King and the Elgin Association," *Knox College Monthly and Presbyterian Magazine* 11 (November 1889), pp. 30-37;

William R. Gregg, *The African in North America: Their Welfare after Freedom as Effected and Influenced by the Life of William King* (Ashtabula, Ohio, 1933); and

Rev. William King, *History of the King Family Who Settled in the Woods, Near Where the lage of Delta, Ohio, Now Stands in the Year, 1834* (Delta, Ohio, 1893).

25.   "Scheme for Improving the Coloured People of Canada," "Prospectus of a Scheme for the Social and Religious Improvement of the Coloured People of Canada," Synod of Presbyterian Church of Canada to Lord Elgin, 28 August 1848, and William King to John Redpath and J. Gibb, 27 October 1848:

all in William King Papers, Public Archives of Canada, Ottawa;

Chatham *Gleaner*, 5 December 1848.

26.   William King to Clerk of the Toronto Presbytery, 21 June 1848,

William King to Rev. John Bonnar, 15 July 1849, and

King Autobiography, pp. 255-56:

all in William King Papers, Public Archives of Canada, Ottawa.

27.   Copy of Petition of District Council of the Western District to the Legislative Assembly of the Province of Canada, 19 February 1849, in William King Papers, Public Archives of Canada, Ottawa; see

Chatham *Chronicle*, 30 April 1850;

Pease and Pease, *Black Utopia*, pp. 97, 103-6; and

Idem, "Opposition to the Founding of the Elgin Settlement," p. 205.

28.   The petition was signed by approximately 20 percent of the town of Chatham's total population which was between 1,500 (according to the census of 1845) and 2,070 (according to the census of 1851). For more on population figures of Chatham, see the *Census of Canada*.

29.   "Memorial of the Inhabitants of Raleigh Township and Vicinity" (to the Presbyterian Synod at Toronto, June, 1849), in William King Papers, Public Archives of Canada, Ottawa.

30.   King Autobiography, pp. 257-64, in William King Papers, Public Archives of Canada, Ottawa;

Chatham *Chronicle*, 21 August and 4 September 1849;

Kent *Advertiser*, 20 August 1849.

31.   Kent *Advertiser*, 20 August 1849;

Chatham *Chronicle*, 21 August 1849;

Amherstburg *Courier*, 27 October 1849;

Journals of the Legislative Assembly (1840), p. 138; (1850), pp. 37, 77, 127.

Edwin Larwill was elected a member of the Vigilance Committee.

32.   Chatham *Chronicle*, 11 September 1849.

33. Chatham *Chronicle,* 4 September 1849.

34. Chatham *Chronicle,* 18 September 1849.

35. Toronto *Globe,* 13 September 1849.
    See also Pease and Pease, "Opposition to the Founding of the Elgin Settlement," pp. 209-10.

36. Chatham *Chronicle,* 18 September 1849.

37. Chatham *Chronicle,* 18 September and 6 November 1849;
    Amherstburg *Courier,* 27 October 1849;
    Journals of the Legislative Council (1850), pp. 50, 78, 187, 192-93, 195, 214;
    Journals of the Legislative Assembly (1851), pp. 82, 101; and
    Hamil, *Valley of the Lower Thames,* pp. 321-22.

38. Chatham *Chronicle,* 16 October and 6 November 1849.

39. Kent *Advertiser,* 11 April 1850.

40. Elgin Association, *Seventh Annual Report* (1856), p. 4;
    Buxton Mission, "Third Annual Report" (1852), in *Ecclesiastical and Missionary Record* 8 (1851-1852), p. 130;
    Frederick Douglass' Paper, 17 September 1852; and
    Drew, *North-Side View of Slavery,* p. 295.

41. Session Book of the Buxton Congregation (1858-1880), located at the Kent Historical Society, Chatham, Ontario; and
    King's report to the *Ecclesiastical and Missionary Record* 7 (1850-1851), pp. 131-32.

42. For more on Elgin's schools, one should consult various issues of the *Ecclesiastical and Missionary Record* which covered the Elgin Settlement on a regular basis.

43. *Frederick Douglass' Paper,* 17 September 1852;
    William King Autobiography, p. 287, in the King Papers, Public Archives of Canada, Ottawa; and
    Howe, *Refugees from Slavery in Canada West,* p. 108.

44. *Voice of the Fugitive,* 17 December 1851; and
    Journals of the Legislative Assembly (1854), p. 185.

45. *Parliamentary Debates* of 16 October 1854 in Public Archives of Canada, Ottawa (this is a clipping file included in a collection entitled "Microfilm Hansard");
    Elgin Association, *Fifth Annual Report,* 1854; and
    Chatham *Western Planet,* 31 December 1857.

46. The politician was Congressman James T. Rapier of Alabama, and the judge was Thomas W. Stringer of the circuit court of Mississippi.
    The Liberator, 24 December 1858;
    William King to J.C. Hamilton, 19 August and 23 November 1889 in the Fred Landon Collection, Regional History Collection, D.B. Weldon Library, University of Western Ontario, London;

Harris, *A Sketch of the Buxton Mission;* and

Howe, *Refugees from Slavery in Canada West,* pp. 107-10.

47. Amherstburg *Courier,* 12 January 1850; and

Howe, *Refugees from Slavery in Canada West,* p. 58.

48. Howe, *Refugees from Slavery in Canada West,* pp. 40 and 49.

49. American Freedmen's Inquiry Commission Interviews, 1863-1864, Record Group 94, rolls 199-201 of Microcopy 619,

Letters Received by the Office of the Adjutant General, Main Series, 1861-1870 in National Archives, Washington, D.C.

The above quotes may be found more conveniently, however, in

John W. Blassingame, ed., *Slave Testimony: Two Centuries of Letters, Speeches, Interviews, and Autobiographies* (Baton Rouge, 1977), pp. 394, 404, 413-14.

50. Blassingame, *Slave Testimony,* pp. 437, 443-44.

51. Windsor *Herald,* 20 October and 3 November 1855;

Ward, *Autobiography of a Fugitive Negro,* pp. 144-46, 202;

Lauriston, *Romantic Kent,* pp. 380-85;

Daniel Hill, "Negroes in Toronto," (Ph.D. dissertation, University of Toronto, 1961), pp. 125-50;

Idem, "Negroes in Toronto, 1793-1865," *Ontario History* 55 (June 1963), pp. 73-91;

Daniel Hill and Arnold Bruner, "Heritage of Overcoming: The 350th Anniversary of Blacks in Canada," *The (Toronto) Globe and Mail,* 19 August 1978, p. 10;

William H. Pease and Jane H. Pease, "Organized Negro Communities: A North American Experiment," *Journal of Negro History* 47 (January 1962), pp. 19-34; and

Fred H. Armstrong, "The Toronto Directories and the Negro Community in the Late 1840s," *Ontario History* 61 (June 1969), pp. 101-19.

Four

THE NEW EXODUS: THE DEVELOPMENT OF THE BLACK CHURCH

Apocryphal though it may be, we are told that immediately upon their safe arrival in Canada West, many of the fugitive slaves stopped their journey to savor the moment. With unrestrained religious zeal, one after another exclaimed aloud his thanks to God for delivery from oppression. Jermain W. Loguen, himself a fugitive slave, would later describe the scene: "When he put his foot on the soil, the angel of freedom touched his heart...he felt the divine hand within him, and he instinctively exclaimed, 'O Lord God, I thank thee—I am free!'" Biblical analogy lent to Canada the name of Canaan, and to the Detroit River that of the river Jordan, and when entering the province from the Underground Railroad station at Niagara Falls, the spectacular sight provided even greater inspiration. "Loud roared the waters of Niagara," declared one devout refugee, "but louder still ascended the Anthem of praise from the overflowing heart of the freeman." Like their counterparts in the United States, the fugitive slaves brought with them a strong penchant for religion. Indeed, Samuel Gridley Howe during his trip to Canada observed that "whenever a few refugees congregate together, the first thing they do in common is to provide for public worship. They have a passion for a church." Within a short time of their arrival the fugitive slaves did establish their own churches, making most worship on a segregated basis. To understand fully the nature and development of the black church in Canada West, it is essential, however, to examine first those white Canadian Christian attitudes which, through insensitivity, ambivalence, or overt racism, fostered in the eyes of the fugitives the need for a separate church.[1]

The impulse for aiding fugitive slaves varied widely among the Protestant denominations in Canada. The white Methodists, for example, never organized province-wide support for the refugees, yet neither did they completely ignore the black community. Perhaps the best available reference to the sentiments of the main body of Methodists toward blacks appeared in the columns of the *Voice of the Fugitive.* When Josiah Henson said there was "neither minister nor church in Canada which would identify themselves with their black brethren," the Methodist New Connexion Conference in Canada replied:

> We are not ashamed to call this oppressed people our brethren. Our ministers are at all times ready to conduct their religious services. We have coloured children in our sabbath schools; and our teachers have taught in their schools, and have been always ready to contribute to the erection of places of worship when they desired to have them separately. We have coloured brethren as members of our churches and we sit at the Communion together. We attend the anniversary of their West Indian Emancipation;...our denomination have stood forward on this,...contending for the universal establishment of civil and human freedom and religious equality.[2]

In contrast, another sect of the Methodist Church in Canada, the Wesleyan Methodists, remained absolutely silent and inactive about the fugitive slaves. The Canadian Wesleyans sustained their affiliation to the Methodist Episcopal Church of the northern United States, which eschewed the topic of slavery in the hope of retaining some of its border churches. The Canadian Wesleyan Methodists concurred with this policy of evasion and managed to avoid any discussion— much less action—in behalf of the fugitives. For this they were resoundingly rebuked by the black *Provincial Freeman* in an editorial: "As the role of accessory with his previous knowledge is worse than a thief, so is the Wesleyan Methodist Church in Canada as compared with the pro-slavery and heathenish Church it fellowships with in the United States.... We hope that...this Church will not allow the stigma to rest on their Wesleyan body or on a Church named after the pious man who described slavery as the son of all villanies."[3]

Unlike the Wesleyan Methodists, each local church of the Canadian Baptists, because of congregational independence, was able to choose its own position regarding the blacks. Among the Regular Baptists, the churches belonging to the Western Association of the province seemed most inclined toward assisting the refugees in both material and spiritual senses. This was significant in view of the high concentration of fugitive slaves there, but the allocation of resources was sporadic and slight. In another vicinity of dense black population—the Niagara community—the Regular Baptists at one time condemned prejudice in religious organizations as "a monstrous evil and a crying sin and one, the commission of which dishonours God by trampling on his laws." No other Canadian Baptist association would ever make similarly strong pro-black declarations.[4]

But even the small efforts of the Western and the Niagara associations went unheeded by the vast majority of white Regular Baptists. When the white Baptist Church at St. Thomas refused fellowship to several blacks, a precedent was established that recurred commonly throughout the province. Indeed, the friction between white and black Baptists in Canada West led the fugitives to contend in 1841 that "we should form ourselves into an Association because we cannot enjoy the privileges we wish as Christians with the white churches in Canada.... (and because) many of our fathers have gone down to the grave not enjoying their just privileges and rights in the Christian Churches of the same faith...let us (now) see what we can do for ourselves and our children."[5]

It had become painfully apparent to the blacks that white antipathy within the Canadian Baptist churches precluded any degree of religious equality. The Baptist record with regard to the fugitives, however, boasted one positive contribution. The Free Will Baptists of the United States actively opposed the institution of slavery and demonstrated much interest in the plight of the fugitive blacks both in Canada and the United States. Through the work of the Canada Mission, they labored to improve the physical condition and assist the education of refugee blacks in Canada. A few white Baptist congregations in Canada, such as those led by the Reverend Robert Dick of Toronto and the Reverend M. Gilmour of Peterborough, joined with the Free Will Baptists under the name of the Union Baptists, but their success in working with the black community was marginal at best.[6]

Still, the Union Baptists were more successful with the fugitive slaves than the Canadian Church of England. The rituality and solemnity, as well as the stringent educational qualifications for church assistants, completely alienated black refugees from the white Anglican church. For example, to become an Anglican, it was necessary for any candidate to know both the creed and the catechism. To become a Methodist or Baptist, it was necessary only to repent and accept Christ as one's personal saviour. The Church of England in Canada, presented less appeal to the fugitives, whose religious education remained, understandably, on a very fundamental level.[7]

In spite of its limited membership among blacks, the Church of England in Canada made conscious, thorough, organized efforts on behalf of the fugitive slaves. Concern for the refugees was inspired by some of the more prominent Anglican clergymen, such as Benjamin Cronyn and Bishop John Strachan, while the institutions of higher education within the Canadian Church of England, specifically at Huron and Trinity colleges, promoted the importance of black education.[8] The most significant contribution by the Anglican church, however, came in the work of the Colonial Church and School Society (C.C.S.S.).[9]

Organized to establish an evangelical mission among fugitive slaves in Canada West, the C.C.S.S. intended that their clergy would administer to both the spiritual and the educational development of the fugitive blacks. The clergyman selected by the C.C.S.S. to start this mission was the British-born Reverend Marmaduke Dillon,[10] who had already spent twenty years working as a missionary among blacks. Expressing strong opinions about the errors that Britain had committed in regard to blacks, particularly in the West Indies, Dillon encouragingly had concluded: "The mistake in the West Indies had been to free them without educating them."[11]

Upon his arrival in Toronto, Dillon was welcomed by Bishop John Strachan and by the future bishop of London (Canada West), Reverend Benjamin Cronyn. Other white clerics soon hailed this projected establishment of a major Christian mission, including the Reverend William King, who by now was highly respected by the black community. With this initial support, Dillon attracted more than five hundred blacks to the Sayer Street Church in Toronto in September 1854 to hear him explain the purpose of his mission.[12]

Dillon told the black assembly that his program consisted of the formation of a school in which blacks would be trained to return to Africa as missionaries. Yet this program differed markedly from the one that Dillion had described during a previous appearance before the executive committee of the C.C.S.S. At that time, he had argued that schools for black adults and children alike were imperative to provide the education necessary to help diminish racial prejudice in Canada. The records of the C.C.S.S. also fail to mention any provision that the blacks return to Africa after attending school at its mission.[13]

Perhaps a well-intentioned proposal, the missionary plan nevertheless met with no enthusiasm from the blacks. The *Provincial Freeman* correctly charged that this "missionaries for Africa scheme" was not part of the original C.C.S.S.'s objectives, but was, instead, Dillon's own creation. In anger, the *Freeman* commented,

> seldom can a school be got up by coloured people but their fatherland must be attended to—they are suddenly and all of them to become teachers and preachers and such like. We are American and cannot in common sense be supposed to have other than a common interest in Africa. We should do something else besides teach and preach and be servants.... If coloured men are to be trained to teach and preach, why not let them decide without suggestions from others. Or why may they not labour in Canada after having served their time?

The *Freeman* persisted in its assault on Dillon by asserting that the mission would only serve to stigmatize the black community by portraying refugees as incapable of helping themselves.[14]

This vituperation directed toward Dillon did not represent merely the sentiments of one indignant black editor. Within a few days of the Toronto meeting, the black fugitives in that city again met in the Sayer Street Chapel to adopt a number of resolutions in response to Dillon's program. Although expressing appreciation for the concern shown by the C.C.S.S., these resolutions stated that blacks could not support the project and would, in fact, encourage other fugitives to reject it as well.[15]

In private meetings with some of the black protesters, Dillon tried to regain their support. He claimed that his plan had been misinterpreted, denying that attendance would be restricted exclusively to blacks or that it was mandatory for blacks to become teachers in Africa. This attempt at reconcilation only caused more consternation as the *Freeman* criticized Dillon's inconsistencies as being indicative of white ambivalence and insensitivity.[16]

If Dillon expected to placate his critics and commence work immediately, he was to be quickly disappointed. Thereafter, the black community closely scrutinized his every word and deed. Unfortunately for the C.C.S.S., Dillon himself personified those white Christians who felt called upon by God to assist the fugitives but who, in actuality, had great difficulty in believing that the effort was truly worthwhile. Finding the "real negro...very ignorant," Dillon showed insincerity in purpose and cast deep doubt about his dedication to black equality.[17]

Nonetheless, Dillon determined to make his mission successful. Intimidated by the black opposition in Toronto, he moved the enterprise to London (Canada West) where it would be closer to the greatest concentration of fugitive slave settlements. The new location also had the added advantage of being the residence of Dillon's powerful ally, Benjamin Cronyn. The rector of the Canadian Church of England in London, Cronyn exerted much influence over a large group of white evangelical clergy and laity, and as such, he could easily sway public opinion toward endorsement of Dillon's plan. Changing his strategy as well as his location, Dillon sought to establish schools in London without distinction as to color. Approvingly, the *Freeman* reversed its attitude, noting with amazement:

Is this the same Dillon?... Is this the school which...would have for its object the training of Preachers and Teachers for Africa? It appears to be the same Dillon but his plans have undergone a radical change. We are now to have schools for Canadians without reference to color which will dispel ignorance in Canada as well as in Africa. Since his mission will be a means of increasing a true Gospel Clergy we shall heartily wish it God speed.[18]

At first, Dillon's mission in London seemed successful. Two interracial schools were established and, with the enthusiastic response of local parents, their classes, curriculum and staff were soon expanded. Early in 1855 a local branch of the C.C.S.S. was formed with wide support from the leading Anglicans in London. At the zenith of his career, Dillon was invited to conduct the Emancipation Day Service on 1 August 1855 for over six hundred fugitives.[19]

Within a year, however, Dillon and his mission suffered irrevocable damage. Several of the mission's teachers became ill, thereby significantly reducing the size and effectiveness of the staff. Concurrently, the mission faced increasing financial problems when funds from Canada and the United States became inadequate. Instructed by the executive committee of the C.C.S.S. to decrease the size of his faculty and budget, Dillon reacted irrationally by verbally attacking the governor general, the *Provincial Freeman*, and John Hurst, the junior master of the school. Suffering an apparent nervous breakdown, Dillon resigned in April 1856 for reasons of ill health, and his departure essentially meant the demise of the Anglican-sponsored mission.[20] A severe shortage of funds and inadequate leadership soon sounded the final death knell for the C.C.S.S. mission and with it an end to white Anglican assistance to the fugitives in Canada West.

In contrast, perhaps the strongest commitment on behalf of the fugitives came from the Free Presbyterian church. The deep schism within the Scottish Presbyterian church over the separation of church and state, which had led to the formation of the Free Kirk, transcended the forty-ninth parallel and affected the Canadian churches as well. In 1844, a minority group supporting the Free Kirk principles withdrew from the Canadian synod to form a new church, in part, because the original Presbyterian church in Canada had exhibited little concern for the fugitives. With its zeal for reform, the new Free Presbyterian church took a decidedly pro-black position. Indeed, many of the members of the Free Presbyterian church were actively involved in philanthropic and welfare projects related to the refugees, and they were noticeable among the founders of the Canadian Anti-Slavery Society.[21]

The Free Presbyterians of Canada West urged other churches to speak out against discriminatory legislation, contending that each house of worship should espouse this cause or in the future share "the responsibility of guilt involved in the effects of such legislation." Pledged to avoid Communion with all anti-black churches, the Free Presbyterians, through their monthly *Ecclesiastical and Missionary Record*, tried to convert the white community to their point of view.[22] Their major effort at assisting the fugitive slaves, however, came through their support of the Reverend William King—of his Elgin Settlement, in general; and of the Buxton Mission, in particular. The Free Presbyterian church's primary institution of higher learning—Knox College—not only accepted blacks as students but also encouraged its white graduates to participate in the education of black fugitives. Nevertheless, the blacks perceived the Presbyterians in very much the same way as they viewed the Anglicans: their services seemed too formal, too intellectual, and too inflexible. Despite the efforts of the Free Presbyterians, blacks never joined the denomination in significant numbers.[23]

Surprisingly, the Canadian Quakers never actively assisted the fugitive slaves. True, their opposition to the institution of slavery was comparable to that of their American counterparts, and they most assuredly aided fugitives during the perilous journey to Canada West via the Underground Railroad. After the fugitives arrived, though, the Canadian Quakers attempted no organized religious work and provided no financial support for the black communities, perhaps naively assuming that the worst of the refugees' troubles had passed. The Society of Friends did at one time endeavor to "collect and forward several large boxes of clothing and bedding to be distributed by agents to the most needy." Yet this effort occurred only once, scarcely enough to be noticed by the thousands of fugitives residing in Canada West.[24]

What did the white Canadian churches accomplish on behalf of the fugitive slaves? The Anti-Slavery Society of Canada acclaimed the work of the white churches for supplying some of the best teachers for blacks in Canada West, while William King applauded the generosity of white Canadians in promoting the Elgin Settlement. It is significant, however, that these were judgments made by whites about whites. The *Provincial Freeman*, the articulate organ of the fugitives, beleaguered the white Canadian churches for supporting the blacks in theory but not in reality. To the *Freeman* the position of the white churches was bewildering, incoherent, and sanctimonious. In an unusual editorial, the *Freeman* hypothesized on the reaction of an alien from another world who visited Earth and observed the actions of the white Christian churches in Canada and Africa: "He would undoubtedly be obliged to say that the Christians...are the vilest and most despicable hypocrites and pretenders under the sun.... (He would) curse the...Churches and ministers denying the...Africans the same rights, privileges, and franchises which are now and have been extended to the ancestors and co-relatives of these people in the foreign lands to which American and Canadian Missionaries are sent."

In the end, the passivity and minimal acceptance by white Canadian Christians of black Christian worshippers forced the fugitives to look elsewhere for religious solace: toward the creation of their own churches.[25] The refugees, extremely sensitive to the issue of slavery, wished to avoid further association with white Canadian churches that retained ties with American ones. The issue pertained, not only to the origins of the mother churches in the United States, but also to the fact that those denominations fostered the continuation of slavery. The Canadian Wesleyan Methodists, the Regular Baptists, and the Presbyterian Synod all conspicuously avoided the issue of emancipating the slaves, and the fugitives in Canada West condemned these churches for their silence. Resolving to secede from the white denominations, one black association proclaimed that baptism by ministers whose Canadian church shared fellowship with pro-slavery churches "be not considered lawful bible baptism... nor shall such ministers be considered as the children of God so as to be permitted to approach our communion, believing that he who will sell his brother or sister for gold or silver today is unfit to baptize tomorrow."[26]

The character and nature of white worship services in Canada also convinced the black community of the need for their own separate churches. Most of the fugitives practiced fundamental Protestantism, and as such, flocked to the Methodist and Baptist denominations. The Methodist emphasis on emotional catharsis in their camp meetings, along with their ministry to rural people, struck a familiar chord in the hearts of refugee blacks. As one fugitive slave aptly surmised, it was as close to "a religion...(as we) could understand." But the fugitives expected and demanded a highly emotional service more consistently than any white Christian denomination could provide. The Reverend Dr. Blackman, an Anglican clergyman, observing a revival meeting of fugitives in Hamilton, with great amazement remarked, "I could not believe it possible that such actions and gestures and shrieks and cries as I saw and heard could pass under the name of religion."[27] Indicative of the white response to black religious practices, Blackman's statement revealed the incompatibility of integrated worship; the style of white and black services differed so blatantly that white clergy simply felt too uncomfortable with black members of their congregations.

On the other hand, fugitive slaves in Canada West wanted preachers who could speak to them in a language with which they could identify. The *Provincial Freeman* castigated the white Methodist and Baptist churches for neglecting the fugitives, and leaving the missionary duties to the denominations less popular among them. In an editorial entitled "The Way to Do Colored Canadians Good," the *Freeman* chastised the Canadian preachers saying that they "should have been selected from the religious denominations, TO WHICH THE PEOPLE BELONGED.... We thank our Presbyterian and Congregational friends for what they intended to do for us. They meant well! But we must admonish our Baptist and Methodist friends, that they are sadly in fault, since they neglected their duty, and done but little or nothing for us, when they have been earnestly entreated to do something; nor are our 'Free Mission Baptist' friends, even to be excused, in this case."[28]

The clergy of the white Canadian churches were, in addition, simply unprepared to accept fugitives as bishops, rectors, deacons, or in any other similar religious post, having always considered the black refugees as intellectually less adept and as doctrinally unsound. A considerable and ever-increasing gap existed between white clergymen and black worshippers, and without satisfactory white preachers, the fugitives actively sought black religious leadership.

When the fugitives did create separate churches, most of their religious activity centered around fundamentalist Methodist and Baptist churches. Eventually every black community in Canada West of any significance established either one or both of these churches, clearly reflecting the preeminence of these two denominations in the United States, where almost one-fourth of the entire Methodist and Baptist membership was black. The revivalist character of these two denominations held particular appeal for the refugee blacks, as emphasis was placed on the individual experience of conversion, thereby personalizing religion and allowing a basic understanding of Christianity. Not expected to repeat complex catechisms in the Methodist or Baptist churches, members of these denominations appeared more egalitarian than others to the blacks, who were devoted to the religious beliefs to which they were accustomed when they arrived in Canada. The Methodist and Baptist churches continued, then, to play an important role in the refugee communities. As a black writer to the *Provincial Freeman* summarized: "I suppose by this time you will have concluded that we are all Methodists and Baptists, or that this is the extent of our religious diversions. It is pretty much the case, I assure you, to which I am quite agreed they should be limited."[29]

One of the earliest black churches in Canada was the African Methodist Episcopal (A.M.E.) church, created in late 1828. Dissatisfied with white services, fugitive slaves had earlier that year sent a petition to the General Conference of the A.M.E. church, and acting on its request for missionaries, the New York Conference, under whose jurisdiction Canada remained, sent several missionaries to Canada West. By the end of the year, the General Conference of the A.M.E. church reported, with pleasure, that four missions in the province—at Malden, Gambia, Niagara, and Fort Erie—were flourishing.[30]

Though the missionaries sent from the New York Conference provided leadership and moral support to the black Canadians, they were, nevertheless, incapable of supplying financial assistance. The missionaries in Canada merely received "public prayer and supplication to Almighty God for the spread of the Gospel." Still, the missionaries met with a receptive black community, and by 1839 the A.M.E. church had expanded to include congregations in Toronto,

Hamilton, and Brantford.[31]

The rapid growth of the A.M.E. church in Canada the following year necessitated its organization into a distinct, separate conference—the Upper Canada Conference—with a black membership of almost three hundred. When the second session of the Canadian Conference of the A.M.E. church convened in St. Catharines in 1841, its membership had increased by another two-thirds, to approximately five hundred. Similarly, the number of black preachers in Canada West rose to fourteen, which prompted the Reverend George Weiss of Toronto encouragingly to inform the New York Conference of "the prosperity of the churches under his pastoral care."[32]

The A.M.E. church in Canada grew even more during the mass exodus of fugitive slaves from the United States after 1850. New churches were established in a number of Canadian cities, and existing churches were expanded to accommodate new members. By 1852, the *Voice of the Fugitive* reported the presence of eighteen flourishing A.M.E. churches in the province, and within three years the total membership approached some two thousand.[33]

So auspicious was the A.M.E. church in Canada that a petition was submitted at a meeting of the Canadian Conference in 1854, calling for complete separation from the A.M.E. church in America. The petition read in part:

> Whereas, we the members of the Canada Annual Conference of the African Methodist Episcopal Church. . .see the great disadvantages under which we labour by not having a discipline in conformity with the laws of the province in which we live; therefore, be it Resolved that it is our indispensable duty to have a Book of Discipline in accordance with the laws of Her Most Generous Majesty, under whose scepter we enjoy our rights as men; and that we do hereby petition the General Conference to set us apart as a separate body.

A.M.E. church members in Canada West, embarrassed at the relationship with the American mother church, wanted to demonstrate their loyalty to the British Crown by conforming to provincial law. They had no desire to create another church but rather to alter the A.M.E. Book of Discipline to concur with the laws of Canada West. The General Conference of the A.M.E. church in the United States approved this petition, and the first successful black church in Canada had matured sufficiently to gain independence from its American mother church. Willis Nazrey, a former bishop of the Canadian A.M.E. church, was named the first bishop of the newly renamed British Methodist Episcopal Church. The selection was a sound one, for Nazrey had been in Canada for several years and was already well versed in the fugitives' problems. Under his leadership, the

B.M.E. church grew impressively, so that by 1864 it could boast over sixty preachers and 3,000 members.[34] The separation had caused no strife, and the Methodist Episcopal denomination continued to retain a major position among blacks in Canada West.

The most important church in the black community in Canada West, however, was the Baptist church. In contrast to the A.M.E. church, the creation of the black Baptist church in Canada did not result from missionary activity on the part of a mother church in the United States. Rather, the first black Baptist churches developed spontaneously in various locations. Indeed, believing "that God by his Providence had led them to the 'Promised Land' and thus like the Israelites of old while building their homes, they also built their tabernacle," the black Baptist "congregations" held services wherever they could until log or frame churches were completed.[35]

Founded in Colchester in 1821, the earliest formally organized black Baptist church was administered by Elder William Wilks, the first ordained fugitive in the province. Black Baptist churches were then established in Toronto, Gosfield, Hamilton, St. Thomas, St. Catharines, and Amherstburg, and their numbers grew from forty-seven members and seven churches in 1840 to over one thousand members in twenty churches by the eve of the American Civil War.[36]

During their early years, some of these churches claimed titular affiliation with the regular white Baptist churches in the province. For example, the black church at Colchester belonged to the Western Baptist Association, and its minister, Elder Wilks, had been ordained by two white Baptist ministers. By the 1840s, however, many fugitives thought it best to separate from the white churches and unite into their own association because of "the blind-folding of the Regular Baptist churches of Canada" to their spiritual and material needs. There were simply too many examples, the black refugees believed, where "persons of color who gave evidence of being born again. . . were told that it was against the rule of that church to admit to its fellowship any person or persons of color." The fugitives even went so far as to send representatives to the Western Association of white Baptist churches to discuss their grievances. But, they were not warmly received. According to one black delegate, the white Canadian Baptists, "refusing to hear council, or suffer us so much as to pray or speak in their church,. . . drove us away."[37] Increasingly more blacks felt uncomfortable as well with the white Baptist service and ministers, and actively sought a religious organization that would better serve the newly arrived fugitives.

Initially, the organizational meeting of the black Baptist Association, held at Amherstburg in 1841, attracted representatives from only three churches; within a few years, emissaries from sixteen churches attended. Much of the leadership in this association originated with the Amherstburg church and its pastor, Elder

Anthony Binga. His powerful influence earned Binga the title, "father of the black Baptists," while the Amherstburg church became designated the "mother church."[38] The Amherstburg Baptist Association condemned the reluctance of white churches to oppose discrimination in their congregations and took a stronger and more public stand on other salient racial issues. Consequently, member churches of the association were prohibited from affiliating with people or churches that discriminated against fugitives.

One white church organization with which they could work closely, however, was the American Baptist Free Mission Society, an antislavery organization dedicated to aiding slaves wherever they migrated. The Free Mission Society, anxious to work in Canada West, so desired its activities to be in concert with the Amherstburg Baptist Association that it made the Amherstburg Association its auxiliary in 1849. Well-intentioned, this cooperative arrangement between the two groups was short-lived. Unfortunately, the activities of the white Free Mission Society antagonized many black Baptists who, in turn, accused the Free Mission agents of "teaching a strange religion." It became increasingly apparent to the black community that white men could neither understand nor appreciate their needs.[39]

When a number of churches severed their connections with the Free Mission Society, a deep schism developed in the Amherstburg Association. In response, the churches at Dawn, Mt. Pleasant, and Chatham formed their own dissenting association, the Canadian Anti-Slavery Baptist Association. Refusing to acquiesce, these churches chose to maintain their relationship with the Free Mission Society and soon added to their membership the churches at Elgin, Colchester, London, and Toronto.[40]

This division profoundly and detrimentally effected the fugitive slave community. Using the split in the black church to reinforce their negative stereotypes about the fugitives, white Canadians declared that if blacks could not coexist with one another, they certainly could not be expected to live in harmony with whites. Black Baptist leaders recognized the potential damage to their reputation, and responded by calling for a meeting in Amherstburg in 1857 to reconcile their differences. The result was the creation of the Amherstburg Regular Baptist Association, and the impetus provided by this union led not only to an increase in baptisms but in new church members as well. The Amherstburg Regular Baptist Association established a number of black Baptist churches that furnished thousands of fugitives with as satisfactory a religious life as they could find. It provided food and clothing to the destitute, thereby aiding blacks in the acclimation to their new homeland. And it even assisted the fugitive in finding a job; in cases when the refugee became a farmer, the association helped him acquire agricultural equipment.[41]

The Amherstburg Association churches, though, were too small and poor to have a minister in each pulpit, so consequently a traveling black preacher administered to the needs of several churches within his assigned district. Horace H. Hawkins, the first minister to be so appointed, accepted monthly one Sunday's offering from each church to defray his expenses. Hawkins and his successors labored under such difficult conditions that adequate attention to the spiritual needs of the fugitives was almost precluded. Indicative of the extent and type of the work performed by the black preachers was the report submitted by Israel Campbell to the Association: "I have travelled 2,500 miles, preached 100 sermons, visited 212 families, attended 24 prayer meetings, 6 church meetings and administered the Lord's Supper 6 times, attended 1 covenant meeting and baptized 13 persons."[42]

This notwithstanding, the Amherstburg Regular Baptist Association did indeed serve the fugitive slave community more completely than any other religious institution in Canada. Yet in addition to spiritual and material well-being, black churches in general expressed intense concern for the religious education of their people. Social-welfare programs and weekly sermons were augmented by the establishment of Sabbath schools, in part because many Canadian Christians, white and black alike, felt that secular academic work was an incomplete education. In fact, one black church popularized the maxim, "Intellect neglected can be restored, but a soul once in ruin, nothing human can restore."[43]

Sadly, for many children of destitute fugitives, the Sabbath School represented their only education. With this in mind, the A.M.E. church in Canada, by 1852, operated 5 schools with 29 teachers and 250 students while the newly organized British Methodist Episcopal church (black) reported a few years later that in their Sabbath Schools, 126 teachers were teaching approximately 900 students. Additionally, the Methodist churches established some twelve libraries containing more than 2,100 volumes for use by the black community.[44]

The Amherstburg Baptist Association similarly dedicated itself to the success of Sabbath Schools. As early as 1842, the association implored its membership to establish Sunday Schools and Bible classes "for the benefit of the rising generation and for [its] edification." By 1860, almost every church in the association had a Sabbath School, with the purview of these schools increasing annually.[45]

Basically, the Sabbath Schools of both the black Baptist and Methodist churches taught fundamental reading and writing. A majority of the fugitives availed themselves of this rare opportunity, for the simple reason that they wanted to be able to read and understand the Bible. It was this intense desire to read the Scriptures, then, that provided the greatest incentive for school attendance among Canadian blacks; with such a willing and receptive audience, the Sabbath Schools flourished. The work of the Sabbath Schools did not end there, however. Once the fugitive slaves acquired enough skill to read the Bible, the black churches sought to provide further reading materials. And persistent attempts to secure books for the Sabbath School libraries from American and British church societies met with a generous response. For example, in 1864, the London (England) Sunday School Association alone sent more than thirty-six hundred volumes to the black Methodists in Canada for use in their Sabbath Schools.[46]

Undeniably, the black churches in Canada expended a great deal of time and money organizing educational programs within their own facilities, but they were also interested in fostering more extensive educational programs. The early A.M.E. Conferences discussed at length the comprehensive educational needs of the fugitives and in 1837 they resolved, "that as education is the only sure means of creating in the mind those noble feelings...of piety, virtue, and temperance ...we, therefore, recommend all our preachers to enjoin undeviating attention to its promotion and earnestly request all to neglect no opportunity of advancing it." The inaugural issue of the A.M.E. church magazine, published a few years later, cajoled the individual churches to assist the fugitives in obtaining a liberal education and implored its ministers to strongly endorse and encourage educational achievement. Likewise, the B.M.E. Committee on Education reflected this sentiment: "We believe it to be the imperative duty of both Ministers and Laity...to labor earnestly...in the preaching of the Gospel and in promoting the sacred cause of education."[47] Calls for the improvement and mass utilization of educational facilities also echoed throughout the minutes of the Amherstburg Baptist Association. Believing that the churches had a major responsibility in fostering these attitudes "Father" Binga, the spiritual and administrative leader of the association, wrote to its members linking together intellectual and spiritual development: "If all our churches would live up to their high privileges and exert a holy influence, it would disarm our enemies, overthrow prejudice and sectarianism and do more good than nice deliberations, or loud contentions against the errors and follies of the world.... It would rouse an interest in education, for where a people feel a deep interest in spiritual things, there is likely to be an interest in intellectual pursuits."[48]

Yet to accomplish successfully all these ambitious educational goals, it was imperative to have an enlightened and educated black clerical leadership. According to the white Canadians, however, such leadership never materialized. An annual report of the white Canadian Mission stated that in many black settlements, the fugitives had "pious and faithful but illiterate preachers of color." Perhaps better reflecting the popular white sentiments John Scoble, manager of the Dawn Settlement, wrote in a lengthy harangue that

> those who set themselves up as instructors...should at least be able to read and understand what they read.... Many of the colored preachers in W. Canada are woefully ignorant, thoroughly illiterate, and much wanting in the reputation of good manners and a holy life.... The class of which I speak, glory in their ignorance, and are never satisfied without they can, by their preachments, drive their hearers, as ignorant oftentimes as themselves, into a fever of wild excitement. It is sad to hear the things which are said.... I hope for a better state of things when education shall be more generally diffused among them, and the sacred verities of religion shall be better understood.

Examination of the Colonial Church and School Society Reports indicates that their missionaries, too, did not hold the black church leadership in high esteem. An 1854 paper published by the society charged that "the colored preachers, with some few exceptions, are uneducated and incompetent... scarcely able to read." Another example of white dissatisfaction with the black clergy appeared in a story on fugitive blacks in Canada published in the *Christian Watchman.* Unequivocally, the author maintained, the churches established among the black refugees paled in comparison with even the black churches in the American South, "which were composed principally of slaves."[49]

In response, the black community attempted to improve the reputation of their clergy. To exercise some degree of control over the caliber of black preachers, it was suggested that candidates for the clergy must receive the endorsement of a minimum of two churches as to their abilities, character, and education. At least one Canadian black individual seemed destined for approval in this manner. The powerful Anglican bishop of Toronto, Dr. John Strachan, considered young Peter Gallego of such exemplary moral character and tolerable education that he sponsored him for admittance "into Holy Orders" by directing his study of theology. Strachan stated that "should I find him sufficiently qualified in learning and seriously impressed with proper views of religion," he would enthusiastically support Gallego's entrance to the clergy.[50] Inexplicably, Gallego's potential career as a minister must have been circumvented for no further information about him exists. Had Gallego succeeded, it is probable that other young blacks would have aspired to and achieved prominent clergy status. But such was not the case, and whites continued unabated in their criticism of what they perceived as incapable and inadequate black church leadership.

To exacerbate the situation, Canadian blacks themselves recognized that the weakest and most illiterate individuals were serving as pastors of their churches. The articulate Samuel Ringgold Ward, writing of his visit to the Toronto Bethel church (A.M.E.) described the "disgusting, abusive, indecent language and the threatening gestures" of one Mr. Taylor, the minister. "Our religious leaders do us more harm than good," lamented Ward. "Our conferences impose upon us by sending such Elders as Taylor, and a meeting such as he holds is a downright disgrace, a religious burlesque, a profanation of the Sabbath, a perfect nuisance."[51] Soon other members of the black churches became cognizant of the need to improve the education of their clergy. The A.M.E. church passed resolutions supporting more education not only for its parishoners but also for its ministers as well. Confronting the issue directly the A.M.E. church magazine recommended that "literary institutions should be selected by our Conferences, to which those of our young men whom we shall hereafter choose as candidates for the ministry may be sent that they may be prepared for the work." In concluding, the article suggested that Canadian blacks additionally advocate their ministerial candidates through training at such white institutions of higher education as the University of Toronto.[52]

Concerned about the reputation of their clergy, the Amherstburg Association called for a convention of all black Baptist churches and ministers in Canada West to discuss the necessity for formal training of its clergy. All those in attendance at this meeting were asked "to take into consideration the propriety of establishing an institution of education among yourselves where young men might be instructed for work of the ministry and also to deliberate on other important subjects pertaining to the moral improvement and intellectual elevation of our people." Out of this request came the collective effort of the Amherstburg Association and the Free Will Baptists to create the British-American Institute as a potential university for fugitives in Canada.[53] As discussed previously, this noble goal never reached fruition; still the very attempt demonstrated the recognized importance of an educated clergy to the black Baptists.

Given their shortcomings, then, did the black churches and clergy successfully administer to their congregations? Obviously not, according to the Colonial Church and School Society which felt that the white churches could better handle the religious needs of the fugitives. So, too, did John Scoble of the Dawn Settlement. Attacking those black preachers who encouraged the refugees to withhold their confidence from whites and remain in segregated churches, Scoble lamented "the feeling which has been created...(that) prevents the improvement of the colored population which would undoubtedly result from contact with persons more cultivated than themselves and who might be helpful to them in many ways." Most likely, Scoble naively and erroneously assumed that he had both humanitarian concern and the fugitives' best interests in mind. The majority of the black community thought otherwise, however, perceiving Scoble's statements as patronizing and condescending platitudes.[54] They argued, instead, that despite the degree of education and competence of their clergy, a separate black church was necessary. To them, the overbearing attitudes and unsatisfactory performance of the white Canadian Christians simply demanded this. For example, John Holmes, a fugitive slave residing in London (Canada West), attempted once to persuade his friends to attend a white church, but he found that the white Canadians "spoke a different language." Holmes was also dissuaded by what he perceived to be a paternalistic and domineering disposition on the part of the white Christians. Many fugitives like Holmes found this attitude to be as distasteful to them as flagrant segregation and discrimination. In its own way, then, white patronage could be just as stifling to the black personality and identity as blatant racism.[55]

Consequently, many fugitives deeply and sincerely believed that a separate black church played an indispensible role in the development of their self-confidence and independence. The exodus from the established white churches forced the fugitives to rely upon their own resources, whatever their merit, and it compelled them to create and refine their own church government and religious doctrine. They learned fiscal responsibility by administering church finances, and through the practice of self-help, the black churches in turn passed the concept on to the fugitives. One black clergyman determined that the black church had provided the fugitive with "an independence of character which he could neither hope for nor attain unto, if he had remained as the ecclesiastical vassal of his white brethren." Another echoed this sentiment, stating that "the (black) church has set before (the fugitive) an open door which no man can shut; has opened for him an avenue which no man can close; and has put him on a line of march for the front by which he may, if he will, reach the acme of human usefulness." A third poignantly believed that the black church was "the source from which the (fugitive)...received his truest and most efficient leaders.... (It) gave the (fugitive) an object lesson on the importance of self-reliance which he could not by any other means have learned so soon."[56]

If other opportunities in Canadian society were closed to them, the black church became the fugitives' school, college, and municipal government. In fact, it has been said that it "held in common unity more (blacks) than any other organization, and it has had more influence in moulding the thought and life of the black people than any other single agency." And as long as the fugitive blacks were treated as second-class citizens by white Canadian society, their church would continue to supply solace and comfort. Notwithstanding the barrage of white criticism, a separate black church meant one form of freedom and identity to which, despite the pitfalls of the secular world, the black refugee could always retreat. The black church, more than anything else, provided the fugitives in Canada West with the hope that they could soon sing, with conviction, the words of an old hymn, "Shout the glad tidings o'er Egypt's dark sea; Jehovah has triumphed, his people are free!"[57]

NOTES

1. J.W. Loguen, *The Rev. J.W. Loguen, as a Slave and as a Freeman* (Syracuse, 1859), p. 335;
    Sarah E. Bradford, *Scenes in the Life of Harriet Tubman* (New York, 1869), p. 52;
    Howe, *Refugees from Slavery in Canada West,* p. 89; and
    Donald G. Simpson, "Negroes in Ontario from Early Times to 1870" (Ph.D. dissertation, University of Western Ontario, 1971), pp. 36-40.
    For more on the general nature of Canadian churches and the fugitive slave, see
    William H. Elgee, *The Social Teachings of the Canadian Church: Protestant, the Early Period, before 1850* (Toronto, 1964);
    Fred Landon, *Western Ontario and the American Frontier* (Toronto, 1964), pp. 170-80; and
    John S. Moir, *Church and State in Canada West* (Toronto, 1959).
2. Toronto *Globe,* 15 June 1852; and
    Voice of the Fugitive, 23 September 1852.
    The Methodist New Connexion was the Canadian equivalent of the American True Wesleyans, and was vehemently opposed to the institution of slavery.
3. *Provincial Freeman,* 6 June 1857.
    Under the influence of Egerton Ryerson, superintendent of Education in Canada West for many years and a Wesleyan Methodist, this religious sect would eventually take a more favorable attitude toward the fugitive slave.
4. Murray, "Canada and the Anglo-American Anti-Slavery Movement," pp. 242-45, 257-62; and
    Niagara Baptist Association, *Minutes of the Thirty-Seventh Anniversary Meeting* (June 1856), p. 6, located in the Baptist Historical Collection, McMaster Divinity College, Hamilton, Ontario.
5. Amherstburg Baptist Association, *Minutes* (1841), located in the Baptist Historical Collection, McMaster Divinity College, Hamilton, Ontario.
    On the general history of black Baptists in Canada see
    Dorothy Shadd Shreve, *Pathfinders of Liberty and Truth: A Century with the Amherstburg Regular Missionary Baptist Association* (n.p., 1940);
    Wilfred Sheffield, "Background and Development of Negro Baptists in Ontario" (B.D. thesis, McMaster University, 1952);

James W. Johanson, "The Amherstburg Baptist Association, 1841-1861, including a Survey of the Civil War Period," unpublished ms. in the Canadian Baptist Archives, McMaster Divinity College, Hamilton, Ontario;

James K. Lewis, "Religious Life of Fugitive Slaves and the Rise of Coloured Baptists, 1820-1865, in What is Now Known as Ontario" (B.D. thesis, McMaster University, 1965), and

"Religious Nature of the Early Negro Migration to Canada and the Amherstburg Baptist Association," *Ontario History* 58 (June 1966), pp. 117-32.

Much of my account of the Baptist church in Canada and its relationship to the fugitive slave draws heavily on these sources.

6. Elgee, *Social Teachings of the Canadian Church*, pp. 173-75; and *Canadian Baptist Magazine* 1 (1838), p. 205; 4 (1841), pp. 239-43.

7. Harry Richardson, *Dark Glory* (New York, 1947), p. 6; Moir, *Church and State in Canada West*, pp. 25, 54, 61.

8. Benjamin Cronyn was the bishop of London, Canada West. Bishop John Strachan was the leading Anglican clergyman whose diocese included all of Canada West from 1839 until 1867.

9. The impetus behind this major attempt to assist fugitive slaves was undoubtedly the United Kingdom. Its efforts were directed through an organization which had been functioning in British North America for some years in assisting immigrants from the British Isles. The Society was established in 1841 as the Newfoundland School Society, but in 1851 it united with the Colonial Church and School Society. In 1861 the body became the Colonial and Continental Church Society. For more on the history of this organization, see

J.I. Cooper, "The Mission to the Fugitive Slaves at London," *Ontario History* 46 (Spring 1954), pp. 133-39.

10. Dillon had served in Canada and the West Indies as an officer in the 89th Regiment and subsequently had taken Holy Orders and served as a missionary in Antigua and Dominica.

11. Colonial Church and School Society, Mission to the Free Colored Population in Canada, *Occasional Paper*, no. 4 (December 1854), p. 5. See also the *Minutes of the Colonial and Continental Church Society*, microfilm reels A-23 and A-24, in the Public Archives of Canada, Ottawa.

12. John Strachan to M.M. Dillon, September, n.d., and October, n.d., 1854, in Letter Book of Bishop John Strachan, 1839-1868, in the Strachan Papers, Ontario Provincial Archives, Toronto.

13. Colonial Church and School Society, Mission to the Free Colored Population in Canada, *Occasional Paper*, no. 4 (December 1854), pp. 3-11, 15.

14. *Provincial Freeman*, 23 September 1854.

15. Ibid., 27 and 28 September 1854; and

Cooper, "The Mission to the Fugitive Slaves at London," pp. 133-39.

16. *Provincial Freeman,* 26 September 1854.

17. Dillon's private letters indicate that he perceived the fugitives to be inherently inferior; they also indicate his anger and disdain for those who disagreed with his viewpoint. See the M.M. Dillon Papers, Record Group 7, G. 20, vol. 59, in the Public Archives of Canada, Ottawa.

18. *Provincial Freeman,* 25 November 1854.

19. Dillon Papers, Public Archives of Canada, Ottawa; and
Colonial Church and School Society, *Annual Report* (1855).

20. Cooper, "The Mission to the Fugitive Slaves at London," pp. 137-39; and
Colonial Church and School Society, *Annual Report* (1855).

21. The Free Presbyterian founders included the Reverend William McClure and Dr. Michael Willis. For more on the Anti-Slavery Society of Canada, see
I.C. Pemberton, "The Anti-Slavery Society of Canada" (Ph.D. dissertation, University of Toronto, 1967);
Winks, " 'A Sacred Animosity'," pp. 301-42; and the following articles by
Fred Landon, "Anti-Slavery Society of Canada" (1919), pp. 33-40;
"Abolitionist Interest in Upper Canada," pp. 165-72;
"Anti-Slavery Society of Canada" (1956), pp. 125-31; and
"The Canadian Anti-Slavery Group Before the Civil War," *University Magazine* 18 (December 1918), pp. 540-47.

22. Anti-Slavery Society of Canada, *Second Annual Report* (1853), p. 10;
Moir, *Church and State in Canada West,* pp. 7-8, 22, 54, 90, 137, 185; and
Elgee, *Social Teachings of the Canadian Church,* pp. 173-75.

23. Thomas Henning, *Slavery in the Churches, Religious Societies, etc., A Review:... with Prefatory Remarks by J.E. Linton* (n.p., n.d.), pp. 3-9;
Simpson, "Blacks in Ontario," pp. 47-49; and
Murray, "Canada and the Anglo-American Anti-Slavery Movement," pp. 239-40, 250-53, 476-79.

24. Levi Coffin, *Reminiscences of Levi Coffin* (Cincinnati, 1876), pp. 252-53; and
Arthur G. Dorland, *A History of the Society of Friends in Canada* (Toronto, 1927), pp. 275-84.

25. *Provincial Freeman,* 29 April 1854. For more on the development and significance of the "black church" in general, see
Carter G. Woodson, *The History of the Negro Church* (Washington, D.C., 1921);
Benjamin E. Mays and Joseph W. Nicholson, *The Negro's Church* (New York, 1933);
Joseph R. Washington, Jr., *Black Religion: The Negro and Christianity in the United States* (Boston, 1964);
Gary T. Marx, "Religion: Opiate or Inspiration of Civil Rights Militancy among Negroes," *American Sociological Review* 32 (February 1967), pp. 64-72; and

Albert Raboteau, *Slave Religion: The "Invisible Institution" in the Antebellum South* (New York, 1978).

26. Amherstburg Baptist Association, *Minutes* (1853), in the Baptist Historical Collection, McMaster Divinity College, Hamilton, Ontario.

27. Colonial Church and School Society, *Report of the Mission to the Fugitive Slaves in Canada* (London, 1860), p. 54; and
Richardson, *Dark Glory*, p. 6.

28. *Provincial Freeman*, 10 November 1855.

29. *Provincial Freeman*, 6 May 1854; and
Raboteau, *Slave Religion*, pp. 130-33.

30. Daniel Payne, *History of the African Methodist Episcopal Church* (Nashville, 1891), p. 57.

31. Ibid., p. 117; and
S.J.C. Edwards, *From Slavery to a Bishopric or the Life of Bishop Walter Hawkins* (London, 1891), pp. 1-25.

32. Payne, *History of the A.M.E. Church*, pp. 128-29, 135, 154; and
Edwards, *From Slavery to a Bishopric*, pp. 35-50.

33. The A.M.E. congregations were located in Amherstburg, Windsor, Colchester, Elgin, Chatham, Dawn, London, Norwich, Simcoe, Queens Bush, Hamilton, Niagara Falls, Drummondville, North Grand River, Dunnville, St. Catharines, Toronto, and Oro. See *Voice of the Fugitive*, 10 July and 12 August 1852.

34. Payne, *History of the A.M.E. Church*, p. 322;
Minutes of the Second General Conference of the B.M.E. Church (Chatham, 1864), p. 19;
George A. Singleton, *The Romance of African Methodism* (New York, 1952), p. 108; and
Daniel A. Payne, *The Semi-Centenary and the Retrospection of the African Methodist Episcopal Church in the United States of America* (Baltimore, 1866), p. 106.

35. Lewis, "Religious Life of the Fugitive Slaves," p. 26. See also note 5 supra.

36. Lewis, "Religious Life of the Fugitive Slaves," p. 27;
Johanson, "The Amherstburg Baptist Association," pp. 3-6; and
Amherstburg Baptist Association, *Minutes* (1856), pp. 7, 12, 20, 33, 145, 171, in the Baptist Historical Collection, McMaster Divinity College, Hamilton, Ontario.

37. *Provincial Freeman*, 6 December 1856;
Shreve, *Pathfinders of Truth and Liberty*, p. 12.

38. Lewis, "Religious Nature of Early Negro Migration," p. 122;
Shreve, *Pathfinders of Truth and Liberty*, pp. 4-5, 16-17; and
Johanson, "The Amherstburg Baptist Association," pp. 1-10.

39. Amherstburg Baptist Association, *Minutes* (1856), pp. 5, 6, 32-33, 44-49, 68, 78,

85, 99, 116, 124-27, 133, 143-47, 169-71, McMaster Divinity College, Hamilton, Ontario;

Amherstburg Baptist Church *Minutes*, 30 April 1853, in the private possession of Mr. Alvin McCurdy, Amherstburg, Ontario.

40.   Amherstburg Baptist Association, *Minutes* (1856), pp. 184-85, 188, 191, 195, 197, 206, 221, 224, 238, 252, 275, McMaster Divinity College, Hamilton, Ontario; and Johanson, "The Amherstburg Baptist Association," pp. 6-38.

41.   Lewis, "The Religious Nature of Early Negro Migration," pp. 130-31, and Idem, "Religious Life of the Fugitive Slaves," pp. 68-88.

42.   Ibid.;

Sheffield, "Background and Development of Negro Baptists," pp. 25-40;

Shreve, *Pathfinders of Truth and Liberty*, pp. 4-5, 16-17, 20-25;

Amherstburg Baptist Association, *Minutes* (1856), pp. 160-70, McMaster Divinity College, Hamilton, Ontario; and

Amherstburg Baptist Church Minutes, 9 February 1856 in the private possession of Mr. Alvin McCurdy, Amherstburg, Ontario.

43.   Minute Book of the Sandwich Baptist Church in the Baptist Historical Collection, McMaster Divinity College, Hamilton, Ontario;

Public Prayer for Civil Rulers and the Slavery Question Being a Contrast Between the Apologists for Slavery in the United States and the Ministers of Religion in Great Britain and Her Colonies (n.p., 1851). This pamphlet was written by an anonymous correspondent of the (Toronto) *Ecclesiastical and Missionary Record.* See also

Elgee, *The Social Teachings of the Canadian Church*, pp. 173-75; and

Hill, "Negroes in Toronto," pp. 73-91.

44.   *Voice of the Fugitive*, 10 July and 12 August 1852; and

Minutes of the Third Annual Conference of the B.M.E. Church (Toronto, 1858), 11 September 1858, p. 3.

45.   Amherstburg Baptist Association, *Minutes* (1842), pp. 10-20, McMaster Divinity College, Hamilton, Ontario; and

Shreve, *Pathfinders of Truth and Liberty*, pp. 23-24.

46.   *Minutes of the Seventh Session of the Annual Conference of the B.M.E. Church* (Hamilton, C.W., 1863), June 1863, p. 10; and

Carter G. Woodson, *The Education of the Negro Prior to 1861* (Washington, D.C., 1916), p. 221.

47.   *Minutes of the Fourth Annual Conference of the B.M.E. Church* (Chatham, C.W., 1859), August 1859, p. 10;

Elgee, *The Social Teachings of the Canadian Church*, pp. 173-75; and

Payne, *History of the A.M.E. Church*, p. 115.

48.   Anthony Binga to the members of the Amherstburg Baptist Association, 1847, in

the Amherstburg Baptist Association Papers, McMaster Divinity College, Hamilton, Ontario.

49. Canada Mission, *Seventh Annual Report* (1844), p. 5;
     Scoble in the *Anti-Slavery Reporter* as quoted in the *Voice of the Fugitive,* 20 May 1852;
     Colonial Church and School Society Mission to the Free Colored Population in Canada, *Occasional Paper,* no. 1 (February 1854), p. 6; and
     Christian Watchman quoted in the *Provincial Freeman,* 24 November 1855.

50. Amherstburg Baptist Association, *Minutes* (1851), pp. 30-40, McMaster Divinity College, Hamilton, Ontario; and
     John Strachan to the Society for Promoting the Gosepl in Foreign Parts, 28 April 1840 in the Strachan Papers, Ontario Provincial Archives, Toronto.

51. *Voice of the Fugitive,* 17 December 1851.

52. Payne, *History of the A.M.E. Church,* p. 150.

53. Amherstburg Baptist Association, *Minutes* (1849), pp. 119-35, McMaster Divinity College, Hamilton, Ontario.

54. *Voice of the Fugitive,* 20 May 1852; and
     Colonial Church and School Society Mission to the Free Colored Population in Canada, *Occasional Paper,* no. 1 (February 1854).
     Although not enamored with Scoble themselves, two significant black leaders did agree with him in theory. Samuel Ringgold Ward consistently argued that separate black churches were not necessary. Mary Ann Shadd, editor of the *Provincial Freeman,* wrote that "the character of the exclusive [black] church in Canada tends to perpetuate ignorance, both of their true position as British subjects, and of the Christian religion in its purity." See the *Voice of the Fugitive,* 8 October 1851, and Mary Ann Shadd, *A Plea for Emigration or Notes on Canada West...* (Detroit, 1852), p. 18.

55. Drew, *A North-Side View of Slavery,* p. 121.

56. Payne, *History of the A.M.E. Church,* p. 12; and
     Hood, *One Hundred Years,* pp. 17, 21.

57. Richardson, *Dark Glory,* p. xi; and
     Raboteau, *Slave Religion,* p. 319.

Five

A WRITTEN RESPONSE: THE DEVELOPMENT OF A BLACK PRESS

From the black perspective, the white Canadian church provided little or no solace. Indeed, black discontent with the white church prompted the fugitives to create their own separate churches wherein they could worship free from prejudice. Yet the antipathy which the refugees met in the white church was subtle when compared to the enmity they experienced in the white press. As a vehicle of public opinion, newspapers were quickly employed by Canadian whites for catharsis; that is, in lieu of an illegal physical attack, it was far easier and more convenient—not to mention, legal—to launch a written assault upon the black fugitives. Letters, editorials, and advertisements all revealed a blatant and burgeoning negrophobia on the part of white Canadians. The more readily apparent the fugitives became in Canadian society, the more intense and vehement the anti-black sentiment became in the white press.

As strangers in a new land, the runaway American slaves found they had little recourse at the outset but to accept whatever abuse they received. With few friends in the white press, the fugitive slaves could expect, at best, ambivalence, and at worst, vicious racist propaganda. Having endured sufficient levels of anti-black vituperation, the blacks took matters into their own hands in the early 1850s with the founding of an independent and vocal black press. Designed primarily as an outlet for black expression and self-improvement, the fugitive-slave press provided refuge blacks with a source of news, identity, and strength.

Their experience with the white churches fresh in their minds, the blacks in Canada maintained an attitude of intense skepticism about white motivations and concerns, in general, and those of the white press, in particular. Even white editors who considered themselves pro-black were viewed as potential enemies by blacks. The white editor of the Windsor *Herald* stated that anything short of complete and unequivocal support of black causes was, according to the blacks, tantamount to racism. He elaborated:

> If a man expresses his opinions fairly on any question affecting the colored people, and, at the same time, does not coincide with every notion entertained by themselves, he is liable to draw down on himself a load of abuse and opprobrious epithets. It may be remembered that a few months ago, the *Herald* suggested that a white man, owning property, had a right to choose his neighbors when selling a portion of it. This was caused by colored bids having been refused at a sale of village lots at one particular locality in Windsor, but nothing was said which could be construed into hostility to the people themselves. Notwithstanding this the *Herald* gave great offence to most of the colored residents.[1]

Blacks responded by labeling the *Herald* as insensitive to their plight and needs; and the situation only became exacerbated. The *Herald's* explanation unfortunately served to publicize the divergent points of view and resolved nothing.

Because of the negative black reaction to the Windsor *Herald*, many newspapers chose to avoid any comment on the black fugitives for fear that such statements might be misconstrued. Others, however, took the opposite response, and disregarding black opinion, removed any ambivalence from their racial opinions. For example, late in 1851 the white Toronto *Colonist* observed the contemporary scene and anticipated the migration of huge numbers of blacks into Canada. Proposing to discourage this influx by the enactment of a poll tax, the *Colonist* stated, "We fear that they are coming rather too fast for the good of the Province. People may talk about the horrors of slavery as much as they choose; but fugitive slaves are by no means a desirable class of immigrants for Canada, especially when they come in large numbers."

The editor of the *Colonist* continued by defending his paper's antislavery position while concurrently declaring the institution suitable for blacks. The *Colonist* chastised the United States for its treatment of blacks but was itself incapable of disguising its own racism. In an editorial reminiscent of the black codes in the northern United States, the *Colonist* asserted:

> Already, we have a far greater number of negroes in the Province than the good of the country requires; and we would suggest the propriety of levying a poll-tax on all (fugitives) who may come to us in the future. Such a tax must, at present, be paid by emigrants arriving in this country from

all parts of the British dominions, and we see no just reason why we should use the negroes better than our own countrymen.... Patriotism induces us to proclaim against having our country overrun by blacks, many of whom are woefully depraved by their former mode of life.[2]

The *Colonist,* in its attack upon the black fugitives, was soon joined by the *Canada Oak,* published in Sandwich, Canada West. The *Canada Oak* consistently published editorials demeaning the black personality in general and accentuating the detrimental and destructive effect of blacks on Canadian society. Derogatory and condemnatory remarks, published in the editorial columns under the pseudonym "W.C.," described blacks as ignorant and imperious, while the topic of racial amalgamation and miscegenation inspired the most racist comments. One W.C. editorial, designed to discourage integration, referred to the fugitive slave as a "sensual animal out to defile the fragile flower of white womanhood," and warned that blacks must be kept at a safe and significant distance. W.C. criticized the presumptuousness of some blacks in adopting the titles Reverend or Esquire and concluded that the fugitives "added nothing to Canadian society."[3]

The actual identity of W.C. remained undiscovered, though his editorials encouraged much anger within the black community. Blacks attempted to respond to W.C.'s racial slurs with rebuttals and counterattacks of their own. According to one newspaper account, W.C. was forced to concede that black enmity made him "a target to be shot at by negroes."[4] But without a strong and independent black press to dissuade them, other W.C.s pursued similar tactics. The Hamilton *Spectator* at once criticized both the fugitives and the white Canadians who supported them. The *Spectator* questioned the validity of Canadian white philanthropy toward the blacks, and in so doing, revealed its true perception of the fugitives. The *Spectator* asked, "Are begging and crime, idleness and dissipation in Canada so preferable to food and employment in the South, even with the occasional lash of the task master, that the [fugitive] slave is benefitted by a transfer from the cotton field to the Gaols and Penitentiary of this Province?" The *Spectator* rarely missed an opportunity to attack pro-black activity in Canada as a "waste of time," and frequently declared that since the institution of slavery did not legally exist within Canadian borders, blacks should have no complaints. In this regard, the *Spectator* saw no need for whites to concern themselves with the fugitives and run the risk of angering slaveholders in the United States.[5]

The fugitives were assailed in this manner from virtually every white newspaper in Canada West. Even the pro-black Toronto *Globe* occasionally printed anti-black sentiments. Under the editorship of George Brown,[6] the *Globe* firmly opposed discriminatory treatment of blacks; yet anti-black letters still appeared. One frequent contributor—"Plain Sense"—vehemently opposed black migration into the province and declared it to be an "undeniable fact...that there is an antipathy physical and moral between the races and well- or ill-grounded it is not to be subdued." Warning that Canadian assistance to fugitive slaves would only antagonize American slave owners, Plain Sense cautioned that were it not for the protection of Great Britain, Canada would have been invaded by the United States "in consequence of the organized seduction of black slaves by a neighbour with whom that country is at peace." Although Plain Sense's arguments never went unanswered by Brown in the *Globe*, it nonetheless must have been quite unnerving for blacks to read defamatory language in a newspaper considered unequivocally pro-black.[7]

In 1850, Edwin Larwill, the white racist demagogue who had fought to raise public and governmental opposition to the settlement of blacks at Buxton, Canada West, assumed the editorship of the Chatham *Journal*. Within little time Larwill used the *Journal* for his anti-black vituperation. Although he signed only one anti-black editorial, his responsibility for much of the newspaper's prejudicial content was obvious. While referring to white Canadians, Larwill wrote that he was "speaking now of human beings, the link between the celestial and the terrestrial and not of negroes who connected the orangoutang [sic] with the monkey." Larwill's journalism was also characterized by some rather intriguing and creative reporting. For example, he noted that "fifty-three lunatics had been placed in the Provincial Asylum, under the following circumstances...the owners of these negroes had caused them to be sent North, landed under the care of keepers on the Upper Canada shore and then left free to be provided for by the People of Canada." Larwill's suggested solution to this problem: a return to the United States "of all negro, or colored male or female, quadroon, mulatto, samboes, half-breeds or mules, mongrels or conglomerates in the Penitentiary, Lunatic Asylum or other public institutions."[8]

Larwill's diatribes received the outspoken support of Colonel John Prince, a white lawyer from Sandwich. Formerly considered a friend of the fugitives, Prince in the 1850s inexplicably reversed his public position. Though this change of opinion has been attributed to the marked increase in the number of blacks in his vicinity in the 1850s, a more likely explanation concerns the dismissal of two Canadian magistrates for allowing a fugitive slave to be improperly extradited to the United States. Prince considered this dismissal to be a form of nineteenth-century reverse discrimination and insisted that the two magistrates be reinstated. When they were not, Prince redirected his hostility toward the blacks.[9]

In one newspaper article, Prince described the fugitives as "extremely demoralized, repaying with ingratitude, with pilfering, theft, and other vices and crimes, the kindness they have received at (white) hands." He also proposed that the black refugees be "kept apart" and be prohibited from "tainting the atmosphere and corrupting white society." Toward this end Prince recommended that the blacks be relocated and a "colony of them be founded in the Manitoulin Islands, or some other place."[10]

When the black community attempted to answer Prince's attack, the white attorney again used the forum of the press to respond. Prince backhandedly conceded that some fugitives were "respectable enough in their way" but went on to say that they "perform the inferior duties belonging to their station intolerably well." He suggested that whites accepted the presence of blacks only because of a dearth of white servants, and therefore thought of black domestics as a necessary evil. In his opinion, however, blacks were "the greatest curse ever inflicted upon the two magnificent counties" in which he resided and worked. Prince concluded his invective by observing that he had never seen a black man do "an honest weeks' work." Instead, he believed that blacks were "rogues and thieves, and a graceless, worthless, thriftless lying set of vagabonds. This is my very plain and simple description of the darkies as a body, and it would be endorsed by all the western white men, with very few exceptions."[11] Obviously jaded, Prince's appraisal of the prevailing attitudes, nevertheless, held much truth. Prejudiced whites in Canada West had found the fugitives a readily accessible target and exploited every opportunity to attack them in the press.

Black rebuttals appeared infrequently in the white newspapers. One black immigrant, George Sunter, managed to defend the fugitives' position in a letter to the Brantford *Expositor.* He declared:

> Because you suppose us weak and ignorant, and because we are friendless and oppressed, therefore you meanly give us additional kicks. You deny us the opportunities of improvement, and then reproach us with our degradation.... You reproach us with our poverty; we bring no wealth to the province, forsooth! We bring what is better, a test of your morals, an occasion for the exercise of that *justice,* the meaning of which you have well nigh forgot, and for a reinstatement of those principles of *liberty* which you would betray and banish.

But, by and large, such black appeals for justice went unheeded in the white Canadian press. Anti-black statements continued unabated, and the white readership quickly endorsed the opinions of prejudiced reporters and editors. As justifiable black dissatisfaction toward the white press increased in fervor, the blacks themselves assumed the initiative through the creation of a vocal and viable black Canadian press.[12]

The creation of this black press in Canada was not without precedent, however. The black editors in British North America used as models their predecessors in the United States. In 1827, in New York City, John Russworm had founded the first American black newspaper, *Freedom's Journal.* The first American black to receive a college degree, Russworm had graduated from Bowdoin College in 1828 and pioneered in the field of Afro-American journalism. Although his career as a journalist was short-lived, owing to the prejudice of the day, he opened the occupation to other black Americans. *Freedom's Journal* was soon followed by the *Weekly Advocate,* edited by the Reverend Sam Cornish; the *Colored American,* administered by Phillip Bell; and one of the most significant nineteenth-century black newspapers, the *North Star,* established by Frederick Douglass.[13]

Emulating his counterparts in the United States, fugitive slave Henry Bibb established the first black newspaper in Canada, the *Voice of the Fugitive,* in 1851. Born a slave in Kentucky in 1815, Bibb had seen the members of his family sold, one by one. Consequently, quite early in life, he determined to be free and became such an incorrigible slave that he was sold to six different masters after attempting to escape an equal number of times. Finally, in 1842, Bibb successfully escaped to Detroit. For the next six years, he traveled from Michigan to Pennsylvania lecturing most effectively for the antislavery cause. In 1849, he furthered that cause with the publication of one of the most reliable slave autobiographies, *Narrative of the Life and Adventures of Henry Bibb, An American Slave.* The following year, when Congress passed the Fugitive Slave Act, Bibb joined many of his fellow fugitives in crossing the border into Canada West. He and his wife, Mary, settled in Chatham where they quickly assumed the leadership of the black community. Besides establishing the bimonthly *Voice of the Fugitive,* the Bibbs founded a day school, participated in the building of a Methodist church, and assisted in the creation of educational, temperance, and antislavery societies, as well as a society devoted to welcoming and aiding newly arrived fugitive slaves.[14]

Without doubt, though, Bibb's greatest accomplishment was the establishment of the *Voice of the Fugitive.*[15] By the year 1852 the newspaper had already acquired an international character with agents in Michigan, Ohio, Pennsylvania, New York, and New Hampshire. Such notable blacks as J.W. Loguen and Martin Delany served as Bibb's agents in Syracuse and Pittsburgh respectively. At the end of its first year of circulation the newspaper could claim eleven hundred subscribers.[16]

In the inaugural issue of the *Voice of the Fugitive,* Bibb clearly set forth the aims of his paper: "We shall advocate. . .the cause of human liberty in the true meaning of the term," he wrote. "We shall advocate the immediate and unconditional abolition of chattel slavery everywhere...we shall advocate the cause of temperance and moral reform...(and) the cause of education shall have a prominent space in our columns." Bibb proposed an agricultural career for the fugitive slaves as the "most certain road to independence and self-respect." Perhaps most significantly, he asserted that his newspaper would fill the void that had long existed for the fugitives in Canada: "We intend this to be a mouthpiece for the refugees in Canada.... We mean to speak out our sentiments as free men upon all subjects that come within our sphere, and if others differ with us...all we shall ask shall be the toleration of opinion and free discussion which is the refutation of error and the bulwark of liberty. We shall make no compromise with wrong."[17]

Bibb responded immediately to the derogatory accounts of the fugitives that appeared in the white Canadian newspapers. Castigating W.C. as a "poor, weak thing destitute of principle or argument," Bibb warned his fellow fugitives that W.C. represented a more fundamental and dangerous mentality permeating white Canadian society. Rather than a mere individual, W.C. represented an outlook "that the colored men are not to inhabit the same country—to be taught in the same schools, or to worship God in churches with whites." Bibb blamed the attitude of W.C. and other similar whites for the bitter "pill made up by old Dr. Slavery," and likened the concomitant prejudice in Canada West to a reptile. In graphic terms he described this allegorical anti-black snake as "biting and poisoning every one that he can without being seen." In an effort to reassure the fugitives in the province, however, Bibb informed the black community, "We understand (prejudice) well, and shall endeavor to keep our eye upon the slimy reptile."[18]

Bibb's newspaper, for the most part, was true to its initial editorial policy statement. The *Voice of the Fugitive* covered in depth the activities of the Underground Railroad, providing the black community with lists of newly arrived fugitive slaves. Bibb also devoted significant coverage to the temperance, religious, and educational activities of Canadian blacks. Further, he published items gleaned from American newspapers concerning abolition, slavery, and colonization. In his editorials Bibb consistently encouraged American blacks to move to Canada West where collectively they could oppose white Canadian prejudice and build a better life.

With this in mind, Bibb called for a convention of black people to convene in Toronto in early September 1851. The central theme of this meeting was "the future of the black race on the North American Continent." To stimulate interest, Bibb also published an agenda for the meeting that included such topics as black abandonment of demeaning jobs, the means by which to become landowners, and how to become self-sufficient farmers. Discussion also would be held concerning the suggested colonization of blacks in Africa, which Bibb considered "prejudicial against color and pro-slavery." In yet another aspect, Bibb urged the refugee blacks to consider ways to support only those governments that would ensure their freedom. Finally, recognizing his own importance and contribution to Canadian blacks, Bibb also cajoled the fugitives in Canada West to take "proper steps for sustaining such presses only as will faithfully vindicate (their) rights."[19]

When the North American Colored Convention met in Toronto on 9 September, the fifty black delegates in attendance passed a number of resolutions regarding the improvement of black life in Canada. The black representatives also passed condemnatory measures on the American Colonization Society and the Fugitive Slave Law of 1850. Perhaps the most important resolution, though, concerned the founding of a distinct agricultural "league of colored people," a theme that Bibb would relentlessly advocate in the *Voice of the Fugitive.* Unlike the black assimilationists of his day, Bibb believed that the cause of black equality could best be served by separating from the mainstream of white Canadian society. He thus publicized this agricultural league "for the protection of the (fugitives') common rights...and for their social, political, and moral elevation." He proposed that the league purchase land in Canada and in the West Indies to promote the development of agriculture among blacks. For funding, the executive committee of the North American and West Indian League would sell certificates of stock.[20]

Bibb strove for black acceptance of this agricultural league through a series of editorials in the *Voice of the Fugitive.* He admonished his fellow blacks that "the eyes of the civilized world are looking down upon us to see whether we can take care of ourselves or not." Should the black refugees fail to adopt this organization, Bibb wrote, "We would prove ourselves incapable of self-government (and) would bring down reproach and disgrace upon the whole race with which we are connected.... (It) would be used as an argument against (us)." Thus, to prevent dependence upon white Canadians, and to remove the stigma of financial failure already evidenced in the several organized black communities in Canada West, Bibb foresaw that the fugitives had to formulate an independent economic base. "The remedy for (prejudice)," Bibb editorialized, "is in the hands of the colored population of North America...which we shall hereafter endeavor to show, by bringing free labor cotton, sugar and rice into competition with slave-grown products. This we can apply most effectually by a systematic, well-directed agricultural and commmercial organization."[21]

Despite Bibb's impassioned editorials in the *Voice of the Fugitive,* the idea of a separate commercial association for fugitives was anathema to a majority of blacks. Many fugitives in Canada West aspired to be accepted by the white

Canadian community, and hence, Bibb's concept of separatism appeared counterproductive to them. Instead, they supported the black assimilationists and integrationists in the province who exhorted them to prevail as equal partners in Canadian society. Disagreement also arose within the black separatist community itself. The more militant fugitives perceived Bibb's plans as utopian dreams rather than practical solutions to the real problems of discrimination and prejudice facing Canadian blacks. Perhaps most destructive to his cause, in late 1853 Bibb's printing office was destroyed by fire, a setback from which he never fully recovered. Certain that arson was the cause, Bibb nonetheless continued to publish a less effective single-page version of the *Voice of the Fugitive.* By this time, however, his separatist philosophies had become seriously undermined by the appearance of a more prominent and widely read black newspaper, the *Provincial Freeman.* Until his death in August 1854, at the age of thirty-nine, Bibb would be plagued by the competition of Canada's second black newspaper.

Staunchly assimilationist in tenor, the first issue of the *Provincial Freeman* appeared in March 1853. Its Committee of Publication then took approximately one year to ascertain the degree of support in Canada West for another black newspaper. Once its supporters were convinced of the black need and desire for an alternative to Bibb's *Voice of the Fugitive,* the publication of the *Provincial Freeman* became a weekly event, beginning early in 1854 in Toronto. The notable fugitive slave, Samuel Ringgold Ward, was designated the editor, but the "Black Daniel Webster" spent most of his time traveling extensively through Britain, raising funds for various black causes. At no time did Ward act as editor; he merely lent his name to the paper to generate interest and subscriptions. The real editor, who promoted the *Freeman's* motto of "Self-Reliance Is the Fine Road to Independence," was the remarkable Mary Ann Shadd.

Born in Wilmington, Delaware, in 1823, to a prominent free black family Mary Ann Shadd was educated in West Chester, Pennsylvania, by the Society of Friends. She returned to Delaware in 1840, where she opened a school for black children who prior to that time had received no public education. After the city of Wilmington legally endorsed the education of its free blacks, Shadd left to assume other teaching posts in New Jersey, New York, and Pennsylvania. In 1849 she wrote a pamphlet entitled "Hints to the Colored People of the North," in which she underscored the importance of black self-sufficiency. Like so many others, Shadd decided to reside in Canada, after the passage of the Fugitive Slave Law of 1850 made it difficult for blacks—fugitive slaves and free alike—to live in the North. In 1852 she published the pamphlet *Notes of Canada West,* which invited more blacks to emigrate to Canada from the United States; in spite of the prejudice she herself found in her new home of Windsor, where white Canadians were "hostile, the result of preconceived notions on the one hand, and of caste (segregated) institutions on the other." She established a school open to both black and white pupils with the support of the American Missionary Association, became a member of the executive committee of the Windsor Anti-Slavery Society, and promoted the *Provincial Freeman* on a lecture tour after its introductory issue.[22]

Like Bibb's *Voice of the Fugitive* and other black newspapers in the United States, the *Provincial Freeman* had as its primary goal the "elevation of the Colored People." To assist the fugitives in achieving this ambition, the *Freeman* advocated "the cause of Temperance in the strictest and most radical interpretation of that word." "The religious influence of this Journal," though Protestant in principle, was nonsectarian, as the editor announced the intention to include varied religious information. Shadd further declared that the *Freeman* would be a straightforward and outspoken antislavery paper covering "the news of the day, the state of the markets, foreign and domestic intelligence." She also pronounced the *Freeman* to be apolitical, noting that "as a free, untrammeled journal, it will, from time to time, take note of what is done in Parliament and elsewhere, and make free comments thereon wielding what influence it may have, on the side of the great principles of (black) Progress."[23]

Attacking Bibb's separatist agricultural league, Shadd and the *Provincial Freeman* opposed *any* institution that tended to remove the fugitive from the mainstream of white Canadian society. Instead of endorsing the segregation of blacks, Shadd advocated the elimination of separate schools, churches, and communities, suggesting, "Were not scatteration a better idea?" This attitude prompted one white critic to state that Shadd and the majority of black refugees "are seeking for an amalgamation with the whites. Whatever they may say to the contrary this is their end.... This is the object of their organ the 'Provincial Freeman.'" Perhaps the difference in viewpoint between Bibb's separatism and Shadd's assimilation was more subtly expressed by the very titles of their respective journals. On the one hand, the *Voice of the Fugitive,* by terming the blacks as actual fugitives, implied the temporary relocation of blacks in Canada West; also implicit in the title is the belief that the runaways continued to think of the United States as home. On the other hand, the *Provincial Freeman* obviously used Canada West as the point of reference, imparting the feeling of a more permanent move. As such, Shadd's editorial opinion promoted the integration of free blacks in "a fair comparison with all other classes" into Canadian society. In its columns then, the *Freeman* frequently urged its readers to contribute "by their energy and industry, to the weal of their adopted country."[24]

In conjunction with this assimilationist policy, Shadd and the *Freeman* urged the fugitive slaves to achieve financial independence in Canada West. The newspaper's motto of self-reliance was Shadd's personal motto as well, one that she stressed repeatedly in the five years of the *Freeman*'s existence. To her, the best means available to help "the refugees from the southern plantations" was to emphasize "measures for such improvement, as shall make them independent, self-sustaining laborers" within the given social structure. Their success in this endeavor would thereby prove "the fitness of the slaves for freedom...and the perfect capability of the negro to live and to advance under the same government and upon terms of political and social and equality with the anglo-saxon race or any other of the one great human family." The attainment of autonomy thus would benefit the fugitives not only personally but socially as well. According to Shadd, the fugitives would be more readily accepted in Canada West on the basis of that financial independence; it also would aid the cause of abolition by acting as an example to American slaveholders. Thus, the fugitives' progress in the province "would be a triumphant rebuke to those who once held them as chattels, and to those who hold that the slave requires to be prepared for freedom, for they would exhibit the spectacle of a people just escaped from a galling yoke competing as free men, successfully and honorably with other labour."[25]

Not surprisingly, Shadd and the *Provincial Freeman* condemned every black man and organization which upheld the practice of begging. Among those criticized by Shadd was Israel Lewis, who had besought funds on behalf of the refugees at Wilberforce. In addition, the *Freeman* criticized Bibb's and the *Voice of the Fugitive*'s support of the Refugee Home Society: first, because the Home Society was another separatist, segregationist organization; and second because it survived in large part by sending begging agents abroad. To solicit funds in that mendicant way for the Refugee Home Society infuriated Shadd, who censured all its begging agents for setting blacks "before the world as a class of improvident, thriftless and imbecile paupers."[26]

The *Provincial Freeman* also played a major role in revealing the corruption occurring in another black community, the Dawn Institute, under the leadership of Josiah Henson and John Scoble. As another manifestation of the begging system, Dawn and its governing body, the British-American Institute, collected vast sums of contributions intended to aid the black refugees in Canada West. Yet, as Shadd boldly questioned, "What happened to the thousands of dollars that were raised for the Dawn Community?" The *Freeman* demanded to know how the buildings there "were allowed to fall into such dreadful ruin" in view of the amount of money that the managers had received. By publicly requesting to see the Dawn Institute's annual reports and to audit its accounts, the *Freeman* helped to expose the fraudulence of Henson's and Scoble's begging schemes.

Furthermore, Henson stood accused by one of Dawn's own trustees, James C. Brown, of obtaining money under false pretense. In Shadd's journal, Brown declared that the contributions that Henson had gathered in England were importuned for debts which had already been paid.[27] Thus, Shadd and the *Freeman*'s coverage of Dawn's mismanagement expedited its end.

But the *Provincial Freeman* reserved its most vituperative attacks concerning the begging issue for Hiram Wilson. The white missionary who had assisted the black communities of Wilberforce and Dawn, Wilson had consistently stressed the refugee's need for clothing and provisions. He made frequent trips to the United States to secure these necessities. Wilson did not, however, keep accurate records on the items or monies collected. In one typical example, he traveled to Boston in January 1854, where the newspaper presented his case for the fugitives in Canada West. As a result, contributions poured in from throughout the lower New England states of Connecticut, Rhode Island, and Massachusetts. While the entire value of the donations remains undisclosed, Wilson himself admitted that it was enough to pay his own debts and those of his aid society in St. Catharines.

Shadd's response to Wilson's activities was one of indignation. In November 1855, she lashed out at Wilson, claiming that his house, fine furnishings, and valuable real estate were "proof that no missionary field is more profitable than that of the fugitive negroes in Canada!" By the next Spring, the *Freeman*'s criticism of Wilson was even more unrestrained. The journal accused Wilson of donating most of the contributed clothing to those blacks who supported him and not giving it to those who needed it most—the newly arrived destitute fugitives. It charged him with refusing to reimburse black families who, under his instructions, boarded sickly refugees. It claimed that he made certain that visitors could not ascertain the truth about his begging system because he then implicated others and was virtually threatening to those "who *intended* to tell them the facts." Wilson termed his entreaties for donations the "skimming of some of the cream," and the *Provincial Freeman* queried: "Will the cream be absorbed as soon this year as last while a fine dwelling is hastening toward completion...and a family living luxuriously? Verily, the field of missionary labor in St. Catharines should be a tempting one to gentlemen...I wonder it does not tempt some other enterprising (beggars), one or two more might make a comfortable living."[28] According to the *Freeman*, the worst aspect of Wilson's begging was that it fostered black dependence upon whites, that insidious state which the paper repudiated.

Along with the accusations specifically launched against Hiram Wilson, the black newspaper that represented most fugitives launched a broad attack on begging in general. Whether black or white, impostors often left Canada West to solicit funds which never reached the fugitives. The fair distribution of clothing caused much strife in the province, and was recognized even by Henry Bibb as "a 'bone of contention' in Canada among the refugees." The *Provincial Freeman* resented this image of black indigence being presented to white Canadians and others. The association of the fugitive slaves with importunate begging merely increased the racial distance between blacks and whites in the province, and Shadd took it upon herself and the *Freeman* to warn philanthropists on both sides of the border that "BEGGARS are wending their way from Canada to the States in unprecedented numbers." She cautioned donors to beware of the scoundrels' "annual peregrinations," noting that "bees gather honey in the summer, but beggars harvest in the winter." The editor implored all those who read the *Provincial Freeman* to make their opinion on the subject known: "Speak through papers *not in the begging interest,* to the generous donors whose pockets are being relieved of gold, and whose generosity is thus abused by the horde of long-faced pretenders of piety and brotherly regard for the 'poor colored man,' who make incessant appeals to help this 'mission' or that other 'institution.' "[29] Shadd, then, believed that this was one way to engender white Canadian respect for the fugitives.

If black economic independence and the condemnation of beggars did not succeed in destroying racial prejudice in Canada West, Shadd presented a final means to achieve equality—legal action. Through the *Provincial Freeman,* she advised all blacks in the province to insist on fair treatment, even if it meant being "manhandled." In such a case, one could sue for redress and most likely would win. This optimism toward the impartiality of Canadian law echoed for years throughout the *Freeman*'s columns. And while this legal neutrality generally held true in the province, the *Freeman* exposed discrimination in at least one town. The *Freeman* reported, "It is notorious that colored citizens of St. Catharines cannot hope for protection nor justice in that town. Their rights, as taxpayers, are not recognized by the Administration of British law." As a result, many fugitives left that particular community. Similarly, complaints were registered regarding judicial decisions against blacks in the towns of Windsor and Chatham.[30] Shadd failed to realize, however, that while British law protected black rights, it did not legislate equality. Thus, blacks could appeal to the courts when threatened by the removal of their rights, but not before. The fugitives could seek legal redress only after the endurance of much bigotry.

Indeed, Shadd's journal was intimately acquainted with the prejudice aimed at blacks in Canada West. The *Freeman* scathingly reported numerous cases of prejudice, for wherever discrimination occurred, Shadd wanted to publicize it. In one article, the *Freeman* described Wardsville, a town near London, as "just as contemptible a little place in the bush, as disgraces Canada anywhere." The town was singled out for condemnation because of its "very uncertain sort of

Canadians." Shadd advised fugitive slaves to avoid that area and others like it or experience "lessons in colorphobia."[31]

Blacks could avoid specific places, but they could not escape the discrimination that spread throughout the province. Shadd saw that prejudice was pervasive enough to affect them whether they tried to buy land, attend church, or send their children to school.[32] It was evident in politics as well. In 1855, Shadd reported that in the town of Essex, "the Reformers are with the fewest exceptions enemies of the colored people, of the most contemptible kind." Even Canadian abolitionists came under fire from the *Provincial Freeman.* Shadd criticized "this disgusting, repulsive surveillance, this despotic, dictatorial, snobbish air of superiority of white people over the fugitives, by Canadian *anti-slavery people.*" Further, the *Freeman* repeatedly wrote of Canadians who verbally endorsed antislavery but who never attended meetings, gave contributions, or assisted the fugitives in any tangible way.[33] The black press itself came very close to stating that verbal opposition to slavery was not tantamount to a belief in racial equality.

The *Freeman* struck at the heart of anti-black sentiment in an outstanding editorial on 31 October 1855. In it, Mary Ann Shadd wondered why blacks should be subject to the "peculiar detestation" of white Canadians. She noted the biblical precedent for leaving a land ruled by tyrants, saying, "We had as well find fault with the children of Jacob, for leaving Egypt, as the *colored Americans* for leaving the hell of the continent and the piety of demons!'" Perhaps her most telling analogy was with the historical precedent set by the Puritans. She chided:

> But ye *hollow-hearted* folks of the Province of Canada! Do you hate the *Puritan Family* of the neighbouring States as ye do this *Family of Sorrow* who is settled among you? Why not? One is a 'Fugitive' from Europe, and the other is a 'Fugitive' from *Democratic* America!... Both are fugitives from oppression, only one is from the 'Old World' and the other from the 'New' and there is but this difference between them:—that of their dress:—one wears a *white* skin and the other wears a *black* one! Tell us, ye 'wise-sages' the difference intrinsically between a *white fugitive* and a *black one!*[34]

With powerful editorials such as that, the *Provincial Freeman* inspired the fugitive slaves in Canada West to persevere against racial discrimination.

While the *Provincial Freeman* admirably represented the assimilationist views of most refugees in the province, it had difficulty obtaining the three thousand subscriptions needed if it was to continue publication. In 1856 the newspaper ceased printing for several months as a Toronto businessman sued for the payment due to shareholders. Publication resumed, but with many of its subscribers in arrears, the financial state of the *Freeman* worsened. Shadd's husband started selling lamps and "fluid for the same" to supplement the family's personal income. A widespread depression during the late 1850s hastened the paper's financial demise. The last extant issue was dated 6 September 1857, but copies appeared sporadically until 1859.[35]

In the aftermath of the *Provincial Freeman*, Shadd remained in Canada as a teacher at an American Missionary Association-supported school. She continued her journalistic talents, however, by helping Osborne P. Anderson, one of John Brown's assistants, prepare his reminiscences, entitled *A Voice from Harpers Ferry* (1861), for publication. With the outbreak of the American Civil War, Shadd returned to the United States to work for a short time as a schoolteacher in Michigan. In August 1863, Governor Oliver P. Morton of Indiana appointed her as a recruiting officer in charge of enlisting black volunteers into the Union army. At war's end, Shadd moved to Washington, D.C., where she became the principal of a public school and also wrote for Frederick Douglass's *New National Era* and John W. Cromwell's *People's Advocate*. A suffragist, she joined the National Women's Suffrage Association and returned to Canada briefly in 1881 to help organize a woman's rights rally. Intermittently, Shadd pursued a law degree at Howard University, graduating in 1883. She died in Washington, D.C., in 1893, four months short of her seventieth birthday.

Several other black-oriented newspapers appeared in Canada West during the late 1850s and early 1860s. J.J.E. Linton, a Presbyterian abolitionist, published numerous pamphlets on fellowship and then issued a collection of these articles in a newspaper called the *Voice of the Bondsman*. Apparently Linton was one of the few antislavery whites of whom the fugitives unqualifiedly approved. Even the *Provincial Freeman* praised Linton's efforts, acknowledging that "Mr. Linton stands confessedly at the head of British philanthropists in these Provinces. His labours are herculean.... He exposes to Christian gaze, in Europe and America, the machinations of the slavery *religionists* in Canada, and that, too, at an enormous expense of time and pecuniary means."[36] There were, however, only two issues of the *Voice of the Bondsman*, perhaps because of Linton's ill health or his lack of interest in a newspaper of such limited scope.

In 1860, the Reverend A.R. Green of the British Methodist Episcopal Church founded *The True Royalist and Weekly Intelligencer*, intending it to emphasize the British loyalties of B.M.E. worshippers; but it lasted for ten editions and then perished. Similarly, early in 1865, the *Missionary Messenger* was established by the B.M.E. Church. The Reverend Josephus O'Banyoun of Chatham acted as editor, and received the support of prominent Bishop Willis Nazrey. Unfortunately, the paper again limited its reports to those concerning church resolutions and activities.[37]

In spite of the weaknesses of the black press, the two major black newspapers, the *Voice of the Fugitive* and the *Provincial Freeman* contributed much to the lives of the black refugees in Canada West. They provided a vehicle for the catharsis of blacks, much as the white press did for its readers. By allowing the resentment, bitterness, and disappointment of blacks to appear in print, the wrath that might otherwise have manifested itself in the form of physical outrage or violence was averted. As spokesman for the fugitives, the two papers expressed black aspirations for equality in an articulate and compelling way. Beyond that, the black press served as a platform for the secular exhortation of both races. The *Provincial Freeman*, in particular, used its columns to encourage blacks to move toward independence, and to rebuke whites for bigotry. It called on black and white Canadians alike to weave a new social fabric characterized by egalitarianism, and it constantly chastised those whose efforts fell below its expectations. In its cathartic and exhortative capacities, the black press was quite effective.

In addition, the black press successfully administered to the fugitives' desire for news about black events. It covered the social activities of blacks throughout the province, from bazaars to dances. Included in its columns were detailed accounts of fish dinners, the Queen's birthday, and Emancipation Day celebrations, fire-company parades, school commencements, and of course, church functions. Both the *Voice of the Fugitive* and the *Provincial Freeman* made a particular point of recording local improvements, high moral standards, and widespread abstinence from alcoholic beverages. These reports were especially important because they promoted a positive self-image among the fugitives, and helped to negate the destructive effects of pejorative white publicity. The black press thereby engendered a sense of racial pride that was crucial to the well-being of the refugees in Canada West. As one black bishop of the African Episcopal Church explained, the black press cultivated "in every man a personal pride, in every home a family pride, in every man a race pride."[38] Thus, the black newspaper provided a source of cultural identity for the thousands of fugitive slaves in the province.

Ironically, by acting as the mouthpiece for blacks, the black press in Canada West ultimately destroyed itself. Its parochial outlook appealed exclusively to blacks; therefore, white subscriptions were virtually nonexistent. Although the *Voice of the Fugitive* and the *Provincial Freeman* were organized, managed, and written by blacks, they received only sporadic and limited support from the very people they hoped to help. Many fugitive blacks simply had too little education to read, and still more wished to avoid the stigma of associating with an all-black newspaper. After all, one way to learn how to assimilate in this new white society was to read established white journals. Though Henry Bibb and Mary Ann Shadd served their communities well, they nevertheless failed to educate their public on the importance of maintaining a black press. In the end, their newspapers provided only a temporary solace in an enduringly hostile land.

NOTES

1. Windsor *Herald*, 11 June 1856. For more general information on the development of a black press, see
    I. Garland Penn, *The Afro-American Press and Its Editors* (Springfield, Mass., 1891);
    Frederick G. Detweiler, *The Negro Press in the United States* (Chicago, 1922);
    Maxwell R. Brooks, "A Sociological Interpretation of the Negro Newspaper" (M.A. thesis, Ohio State University, 1937);
    Canada Ethnic Press Federation, *Fact File* (Winnipeg, 1963);
    Edith G. Firth, ed., *Early Toronto Newspapers, 1793-1867* (Toronto, 1961); and
    James J. Talman, "The Newspaper Press of Canada West, 1850-1860," *Transactions of the Royal Society of Canada*, 2d Series, 33 (1939), pp. 117-131; and
    Idem, "The Newspaper Press of Upper Canada," *The Canadian Historical Review* 19 (March 1938), pp. 65-73.
2. Toronto *Colonist*, 27 April 1855;
    Toronto *Globe*, 25 September 1851;
    Jason H. Silverman, " 'We Shall Be Heard!': The Development of the Fugitive Slave Press in Canada," *The Canadian Historical Review* 65 (March 1984), pp. 54-69.
3. No copies of the *Canada Oak* have been discovered; many of "W.C." 's editorials, however, were reprinted in the columns of the *Voice of the Fugitive* in late 1852.
4. *Voice of the Fugitive*, 2 December 1852.
5. The Hamilton *Spectator* as quoted in the Toronto *Globe*, 22 March 1853 and 12 April 1851.
6. The Toronto *Globe* was unequaled in its defense of black rights and stood out as the leading reform journal in Canada. Emigrants from Scotland, Peter Brown and his son George established the newspaper in 1844 as an outgrowth of the Presbyterian journal, the Toronto *Banner*. George Brown was a member of the Elgin Association and of the Canadian Anti-Slavery Society, and both organizations found much support in his columns. The *Globe* condemned acts of violence directed at the fugitives and considered discrimination "a disgraceful abberation (sic) from British justice." For more on this topic, see
    J.M.S. Careless, *Brown of the Globe* (Toronto, 1959); and
    John Lewis, *George Brown* (Toronto, 1907).
7. Toronto *Globe*, 25 September 1851, 1 May 1852, and 22 March 1853.

8. Larwill's editorials quoted in the Toronto *Globe*, 29 December 1854 and 13 May 1856;
   Provincial Freeman, 12 May 1855;
   Liberator, 29 August 1856.

9. For more on the Canadian policy regarding extradition, see
   Silverman, "Kentucky, Canada, and Extradition," pp. 50-60.
   For more on the dismissal of the magistrates and Prince's reaction, see
   Murray, "Canada and the Anglo-American Anti-Slavery Movement," pp. 310-15, 532-35.

10. Prince's remarks reprinted in the *Liberator*, 31 July 1857. Manitoulin Island is a possession of Ontario's in Lake Huron. It is the world's largest island in a lake.

11. Prince's remarks are from the Toronto *Colonist* as reprinted in the *Liberator*, 7 August 1857.

12. Brantford *Expositor*, 10 June 1859.

13. For more on this topic, see
    Penn, *Afro-American Press*; and
    Detweiler, *Negro Press in the United States.*

14. For more on Bibb's life, see his autobiography, *Narrative of the Life and Adventures of Henry Bibb*, conveniently reprinted in Gilbert Osofsky, *Puttin' On Ole Massa: The Slave Narratives of Henry Bibb, William Wells Brown, and Solomon Northup* (New York, 1969). See also
    Landon, "Henry Bibb," pp. 437-47;
    Hite, "Voice of a Fugitive," pp. 269-84;
    Hilda Hill, "Henry Bibb, The Colonizer," *Negro History Bulletin* 4 (April 1941), p. 148; and
    Alvin McCurdy, "Henry Walton Bibb," *Negro History Bulletin* 21 (October 1958), pp. 19-21.

15. The original run of the *Voice of the Fugitive* from 1 January 1851 to 16 December 1852 can be found in the Burton Historical Collection of the Detroit Public Library.

16. Simpson, "Blacks In Ontario," pp. 170-75;
    Hite, "Voice of a Fugitive," pp. 269-73; and
    Winks, *Blacks in Canada*, pp. 395-98.

17. *Voice of the Fugitive*, 1 January 1851.
    For more on Bibb's advocacy of agriculture as a vocation for fugitive slaves, see
    Fred Landon, "Agriculture Among the Negro Refugees in Upper Canada," *Journal of Negro History* 21 (July 1936), pp. 304-12.

18. *Voice of the Fugitive*, 7 October 1852.

19. Ibid., 16 July 1851.

20. Ibid., 24 September 1851; and
    Hite, " Voice of a Fugitive," pp. 275-79.

See also Hite's doctoral dissertation, "The Search for an Alternative: The Rhetoric of Black Separatism, 1850-1860" (University of Oregon, 1971).

21. *Voice of the Fugitive*, 13 November and 3 December 1851.

This idea did not originate with Bibb. The American Quakers adopted a very similar theory during the years 1826-1856 when they launched a propaganda campaign to dissuade foreign nations from purchasing slave-grown or manufactured goods. For more on this topic, see

R.K. Nuermberger, *The Free Produce Movement* (Durham, N.C., 1942).

22. *Provincial Freeman*, 8 December 1855.

For more on Mary Ann Shadd's life, see the Mary Ann Shadd Cary Papers, American Missionary Association Archives, New Orleans;

"Mary Ann Shadd Cary, 1823-1893: The Foremost Colored Canadian Pioneer," unpublished manuscript in the Mary Ann Shadd Cary Papers, Moorland-Spingarn Research Center, Howard University, Washington, D.C.;

"Life Sketch of Mary Ann Shadd Cary," unpublished manuscript in the Mary Ann Shadd Cary Papers, Public Archives of Canada, Ottawa;

Mary Ann Shadd Cary Letters, Ontario Provincial Archives, Toronto;

Clifton H. Johnson, "Mary Ann Shadd: Crusader for the Freedom of Man," *The Crisis: A Record of the Darker Races* 78 (April/May 1971), pp. 89-90;

Hallie Q. Brown, *Homespun Heroines and Other Women of Distinction* (Xenia, Ohio, 1926), pp. 92-96;

Harold B. Hancock, "Mary Ann Shadd: Negro Editor, Educator, and Lawyer," *Delaware History* 15 (April 1973), pp. 187-94;

Sylvia G.L. Dannett, *Profiles of American Negro Womanhood, 1619-1900* (Philadelphia, 1964), vol. 1., pp. 151-57;

Jim Bearden and Linda Jean Butler, *Shadd: The Life and Times of Mary Ann Shadd Cary* (Toronto, 1977); and

Jason H. Silverman, "Mary Ann Shadd and The Search of Equality," in *Black Leaders of the Nineteenth Century*, eds. August Meier and Leon Litwack (Urbana, Ill., forthcoming).

23. *Provincial Freeman*, 25 March 1854.

For an interesting article on this newspaper's history, see

Alexander L. Murray, "*The Provincial Freeman:* A New Source for the History of the Negro in Canada and the United States," *Journal of Negro History* 44 (April 1959), pp. 123-35, and its shortened version in *Ontario History* 51 (April 1959), pp. 25-31.

24. M.M. Dillon to [?], 23 September 1854, in the Dillon Papers, Record Group 7, vol. 59, Public Archives of Canada, Ottawa;

Provincial Freeman, 25 March 1854; and

Voice of the Fugitive, 26 February 1852.

Shadd apparently chose to name her journal after the Garrisonian antislavery newspaper with which her family in Philadelphia was familiar, the *Pennsylvania Freeman.*

25. *Provincial Freeman,* 25 March 1854.
26. *Liberator,* 15 October 1852. For more on the Refugee Home Society see
    Pease and Pease, *Black Utopia,* pp. 109-22;
    Drew, *North-Side View of Slavery,* pp. 327-43;
    Haviland, *A Woman's Life Work,* pp. 190-200;
    Peter Carlesimo, "The Refugee Home Society: Its Origin, Operation, and Results, 1851-1876" (M.A. thesis, University of Windsor, 1973); and
    Mary Ann Shadd Cary Papers, American Missionary Association Archives, New Orleans.
27. *Provincial Freeman,* 25 August and 4 November 1854, 12 May and 20 October 1855.
    For more on Henson, Scoble, and Dawn, see
    Pease and Pease, *Black Utopia,* pp. 63-83;
    Winks, *Blacks in Canada,* pp. 178-81, 195-204;
    Winks' introduction to Henson's autobiography in *Four Fugitive Slave Narratives;* and the
    Robin W. Winks Collection on Blacks in Canada, Schomburg Center for Research in Black Culture, New York City.
28. *Liberator,* 10 February and 19 May 1854;
    Provincial Freeman, 3 November 1855, 5 April, 10 May, and 17 May 1856; and
    Hiram Wilson Letters, American Missionary Association Archives, New Orleans.
29. *Voice of the Fugitive,* 12 February and 11 March 1852; and
    Provincial Freeman, 14 April 1855, 27 December 1856.
    The *Provincial Freeman* editorial of 27 December 1856 was signed MASC, denoting the married name of Mary Ann Shadd Cary. The wedding between Mary Ann Shadd and George Cary, a Toronto barber, occurred on 3 January 1856. The editor continued to use her maiden name during lecture tours.
30. *Provincial Freeman,* 24 June 1854, 15 September, 29 September, and 3 November 1855.
31. *Provincial Freeman,* 14 April 1854.
32. Jason H. Silverman and Donna J. Gillie, " 'The Pursuit of Knowledge Under Difficulties': Education and the Fugitive Slave in Canada," *Ontario History* 74 (June 1982), pp. 95-112;
    Daniel G. Hill, *The Freedom Seekers: Blacks in Early Canada* (Agincourt, Ont., 1981), pp. 126-61;
    Robin W. Winks, "Negro School Segregation in Ontario and Nova Scotia," *The Canadian Historical Review* 50 (June 1969), pp. 164-91.
33. *Provincial Freeman,* 8 December 1855, 24 May, 21 June, and 26 July 1856, and 20

June 1857.

34. *Provincial Freeman*, 31 October 1855.

35. *Provincial Freeman*, 20 September 1857;
Mary Ann Shadd Cary Papers, Public Archives of Canada, Ottawa; and
Murray, *"The Provincial Freeman,"* pp. 123-35.
The B.M.E. Annual Conference referred to a notice placed in the *Provincial Freeman* in August 1859.

36. *Provincial Freeman*, 7 February 1857;
John J.E. Linton, *Slavery Question, Report of New York General Association, 26 August 1855* (Stratford, C.W., 1855);
Thomas Henning, *Slavery in the Churches, Religious Societies, etc., A Review: With Prefatory Remarks by J.E. Linton* (n.p., n.d.).

37. The only two extant copies of the *True Royalist* are located at Fort Malden National Historic Park, Amherstburg, Ontario. See also
Ninth Annual Conference of the B.M.E. Church (1865), p. 4.

38. Penn, *Afro-American Press*, p. 11.

Six

"THE PURSUIT OF KNOWLEDGE UNDER DIFFICULTIES": EDUCATION AND THE FUGITIVE SLAVES

Legal constraints severely restricted black education in the United States prior to the Civil War. Southern whites, fearful that enlightenment might lead to slave revolt, succeeded in making the education of blacks illegal in all the slave holding states except Kentucky. A Virginia state representative aptly summarized Southern white sentiment when he remarked, "We have as far as possible closed every avenue by which light may enter their minds. If we could extinguish the capacity to see the light our work would be completed." Anxious slave owners, then, endeavored to keep their chattel as ignorant as possible about life outside the plantation. Although a few whites disregarded the law and clandestinely taught their slaves to read, the proportion of literate blacks in the American South was estimated at only 2 percent in the 1840s and at approximately 5 percent in 1860. Similarly, free blacks in some Northern states, such as Ohio, were denied access to public schools, while in Pennsylvania, Massachusetts, and New York, blacks were compelled to attend separate and inferior schools. Northern whites feared that educational opportunity would encourage black immigration, antagonize Southerners, hurt public education, and result in violence.[1]

Because of the proscriptions on black education in the United States, the vast majority of fugitive slaves who fled to Canada West in the 1840s and 1850s were illiterate. Thus, they eagerly looked to education as "one of the most important measures connected with the destiny of our race." This fervor was later attested to by one black who declared, "Few who were not right in the midst of the scenes can form any exact idea of the intense desire which the people of my race showed for education. . . . Few were too young, and none too old, to make the attempt to learn."

To the fugitive slaves, education became one way to demonstrate intellectual parity with whites and thereby to undermine the racist allegations of American slaveowners. By proving their ability to learn, the fugitive slaves hoped to refute all those who belittled black capabilities in general. Education would also enable blacks in Canada West to hold better jobs, to understand provincial laws, to exercise intelligently their right to vote, and to command the respect "of our most inveterate enemies."[2] If the fugitive slaves could succeed in Canada West, they believed, it would act as a glowing example to all who belittled black capabilities in general.

With this in mind, many general conventions were called by and for blacks in Canada, all extolling, among other things, the value of an education as a means of improving their condition. At the 1853 Amherstburg, Canada West, Convention for the Improvement of Blacks in Canada, the advisory committee on education recommended that all blacks "accept the earliest opportunity of sending their children to schools whereby they may obtain a fortune that none can take away from them." Considered priceless, education seemed to be an attainable goal for the otherwise destitute refugees. The Committee on Education concluded its report by typically directing the fugitives to place their children in "any and all of the white schools accessible to them: thereby striking at the unchristian negro hate among us, and extending the social link that should bind humanity together."[3]

Despite their eagerness to learn, however, most of the black refugees in Canada West, with the exception of those attending school at the Elgin Settlement, were to be denied the fulfillment of their ambition. Certainly destitution itself prevented many blacks from attending the available common schools in the province. Under the Common School Act of 1816, any village or township could determine whether or not it wanted to establish a school. If twenty students enrolled, the government of Upper Canada would provide twenty-five pounds toward a teacher's salary; though funds to construct the school were raised locally and administrative decisions were made by locally elected trustees.[4] This cost, however, prevented even some white Canadian children from attending school, not to mention the many more needy blacks.

But the more insidious and pervasive deterrent to black attendance in common schools[5] was inaccessibility caused by "negro hate" in the province. Put simply, white Canadian opposition limited the educational opportunities open to the fugitive slaves almost as successfully as similar opposition did in the northern United States. Governed by locally elected white trustees, school boards across the southwestern portion of the province, where most refugees resided, either excluded black children from white common schools or relegated them to inferior separate schools. Consequently, school segregation in Canada West became established even before the Fugitive Slave Law of 1850 propelled thousands of blacks north of the forty-ninth parallel. This latter influx served only to intensify the prejudice and publicize the discrimination. In the end, black/white relations in education during the years 1840-1860 closely resembled the racial environment that many fugitives hoped, and believed, they had escaped.

Indeed, the first manifestation of black discontent with the school system of Upper Canada appeared as early as 1828. In that year, some two hundred fugitive slaves gathered at Ancaster, located midway between Brantford and Hamilton, to protest the lack of educational opportunities for blacks. In a petition sent to Sir Peregrine Maitland, the lieutenant governor of the province, the aggrieved refugees stated in part: "(We) duly appreciate the excellent constitution of the Province, and anxiously desire to enjoy more fully the many privileges it confers, and from which (we) are...in a great measure excluded. One of the many, and perhaps the greatest disadvantage under which (we) labour, is the want of means of educating (our) children—which desirable object we fondly cherish the hopes of being able to accomplish...with all its happy consequences."[6] This determination to see their children admitted to common schools met, however, with no success. Lieutenant Governor Maitland, under the influence of clergyman and educator John Strachan, apparently directed his energies instead toward the creation of a system of monitorial schools in the province.[7] Maitland also participated in Strachan's attempt to reform provincial education through the institution of a centralized General Board of Education. Together their interest lay more in the promotion of education for the general population than in the problems of the small percentage of that population who happened to be black.

There were no further indications of black dissatisfaction with the public school system until the 1840s. On the contrary, there was even an instance when blacks succeeded in establishing and maintaining a school superior to that of their white counterparts. In the small community of Brantford on the banks of the Grand River, the white Canadian trustees had voted to prevent black children from attending the common school. As a response to this discrimination, the black community in 1837 opened its own school. The quality of instruction at this black school so exceeded the level of the white school, however, that white children began to request admission there. Unfortunately little more is known about this remarkable situation, except that the white trustees reversed their decision, and children of both races attended classes together when the two schools consolidated.[8]

But the situation in Brantford was unique. Particularly after 1841, it was standard to deny blacks accessibility to white common schools, and consequently, black fugitives were obliged to create their own. The Act of Union in 1840 legally endorsed the concept of separate schools, though albeit not in a racial context. In its authorization of separate facilities, the provincial legislature intended to sanction Roman Catholic or other denominational schools. Yet white Canadians interpreted the law loosely and used it to justify black segregation in education.

When the Reverend Isaac Rice, a white Presbyterian missionary, arrived in Amherstburg in 1838, he established a private "first class school, where the white children. . . and the colored children, should be admitted on an equal footing, so as to do away if possible with the growing prejudice existing amongst them." Despite Rice's efforts, however, only whites attended the common school, and only blacks attended his school. In January 1846, the missionary forwarded a complaint from the black fugitives to the superintendent of schools for Canada West, Egerton Ryerson. In the letter, the blacks quoted the trustees and white citizens of Amherstburg as saying that they would rather "cut their children's heads off and throw them into the road Ditch" than have the two races study together. The fugitives further explained how the whites had claimed that their school was private, when in fact it was a public school, actually receiving public funds, which the black school did not. Worse for the children, the white trustees had instructed the teacher "not to let the colored children come to school," and she subsequently "turned them out doors." The blacks had set their grievance before the town superintendent of schools, Robert Peden, but suspected that he would not act favorably on their behalf. Rice included a short addendum wherein he reported privately that Peden suggested the fugitives sue for redress. The missionary, placed awkwardly between black and white factions, concluded by saying "any counsel from you (Ryerson) in the above case will be gratefully received."[9]

One month later, Peden wrote to Ryerson. In his letter, he acknowledged the validity of the fugitives' grievance, but attributed the difficulty to the widespread racial animosity in Amherstburg. He declared: "The prejudice in this part of the country is exceedingly strong against the coloured people, and the general proportion of the white people are opposed to the admission of coloured children into schools along with whites. To prevent as much as possible the injury to the coloured race arising from this prejudice, I designated District No. 3 in town principally for them."[10] Apparently, Peden had provided an alternative for blacks: the creation of a separate common school. He suggested this solution after unsuccessfully attempting to withhold government funds from the all-white school. Informed by the Town Council that he had no such authority, Peden looked for another way to assist the fugitives and could only suggest a separate school. At this point, though, according to Peden, the blacks became obstinate and "seemed bent on having their children on the same footing with the whites."[11]

Superintendent Ryerson responded with no positive suggestion for the blacks at Amherstburg. He informed them that "the exclusion of your children from the school was at variance with the letter and spirit of the Law, and the espousal of that exclusion is at variance with the principles and spirit of British Institutions." Yet an apology was all Ryerson offered. Because Peden had recently changed his residence and thereby resigned his position, the refugees relied on Isaac Rice for help. Years later, Mary Ann Shadd would criticize Rice's role in the dilemma. In the *Provincial Freeman,* she asserted that "before Rice and his co-adjusters came hereabouts the children were in the same schools...but the missionaries recommended schools...for the fugitives, and hence the separations, prejudices, distrust, etc."[12] Without other recourse, the blacks at Amherstburg remained barred from the common schools.

To the east of Amherstburg, the towns of Sandwich, Chatham, and London extended the same form of discrimination toward the fugitive slaves. Only one school for blacks existed in the Sandwich area during the 1840s and in 1846, the black residents complained about this in a petition sent to the Sandwich Municipal Council. The situation, however, was not rectified. In Chatham, an early attempt by the fugitive slaves to form a school failed because of lack of funds. In 1840 a separate black school opened, but it was substandard. Chatham school officials, meanwhile, planned to build three additional schools, with one location set aside for black children. The new facility—described in 1851 as a dilapidated log building—improved the quality of black education negligibly at best. Moreover, the two common schools in London seemed even worse, due to "the prejudice of the whites. Many of the whites object to having their children sit in the same forms with the colored pupils; and some of the lower classes will not send their children to schools where the blacks are admitted." A few black children attempted to obtain the education to which they were entitled, but were refused admittance by the teachers, or were made to feel so unwelcome that they quickly left. According to the London branch of an Anglican Bible Society, prejudice deprived the children of fugitive slaves of practically all educational benefits. The society sadly observed: "If any Coloured child enters a school, the white children are withdrawn, the teachers are painfully obliged to decline, and the Coloured people, while they acutely feel the anomaly of their painful position, yield to an injustice which they are too weak to redress." London's own school system effectively denied the education of blacks until it opened a separate school for them in 1849.[13]

The easternmost example of prejudice in education prior to 1850 occurred in Hamilton. Although no permanent building had been constructed, and classes were held in various locations during the school year, the fugitives nevertheless believed their children should receive public instruction. Yet black children were excluded from attending public classes. In 1843, the fugitives appealed for redress to Hamilton's Board of Police, which also acted as the public school trustees. Granted no satisfaction from that quarter, the blacks petitioned Lord Elgin, the governor general, to rectify the matter. Their entreaty lamented the lack of cooperation from the Board of Police and indicated deep disappointment in encountering so much discrimination in the province as they "thought that there was not a man to be known by his color under the British flag, and we left the United States because we were in hopes that prejudice was not in this land." The fugitives attested to the degree of that prejudice when they charged that bricks were thrown at them, and they were "called nigger when we go out in the street." All they sought, they concluded, was justice.[14]

Upon receipt of this petition, the Reverend Robert Murray of the governor general's office immediately requested more information from the Hamilton Board of Police. George S. Tiffany, the president of the board, responded several weeks later and attributed the exclusion of the twenty school-aged black children to the "strong prejudice existing amongst the lower orders of whites against the coloured people." Tiffany went on to assert that, according to the teachers and others most acquainted with "the extent of this prejudice," the parents of the white children would withdraw their children if blacks gained admission. But Tiffany faced an awkward question when Murray inquired as to what measures "the Board of Police have adopted or would recommend to be adopted to afford these children the means of education." In response, the very body that had previously denied the rights of black children reversed its opinion, in all likelihood because of the implications in the letter from the governor general's office. Representing the opinion of the entire Board of Police, Tiffany magnanimously declared that "whatever may be the state of feeling at present with respect to the admission of the coloured children into the same school with the whites, it would not be advisable to yield to it, but that the law ought to be enforced without distinction of colour."[15] The intervention of the higher officials meant that children of fugitive slaves could finally attend the common schools in Hamilton, at least on a temporary basis.

While most blacks in the province fought to enter their children in the public schools where they would study alongside white children, some chose to place them in the voluntarily segregated schools at Wilberforce or Dawn. This may have occurred, in part, because of a sense of inadequacy on the part of the fugitive slaves. With no prior schooling, many of the adult blacks professed an inability to do the normal work required by the Education Department. To those with some schooling, the unfamiliar curriculum of the province—based on a combination of the educational programs of Massachusetts, New York, Britain, and Ireland— discouraged participation. And there were those fugitive slaves who, preferring the British-American Institute at Dawn, expressed the desire to learn a trade or vocation, rather than classical Latin or Greek. A number of refugees also tended to be suspicious of white teachers. John Francis, a fugitive living in the Queen's Bush, expressed black fears that a white could not properly teach the evils of slavery or the way to elevate the black race. He personally intended to instruct local black children "about slavery, and get books to show them what we have been through, and fit them for a good example."[16] Keeping to themselves, then, seemed the only way for blacks to exert and maintain control over the selection of subjects and teachers. Unfortunately, the schools at Wilberforce and Dawn existed for merely a few years each, not nearly long enough to educate the fugitive slaves or their children.

Even before the Fugitive Slave Law of 1850 significantly increased the number of blacks migrating to Canada, few blacks were able to realize their dream of obtaining an education. Those who succeeded did so in inferior facilities separate from whites, or in the half-dozen private schools operated under the auspices of the various missions. Often, however, black schools closed "for want of teachers and the means of supporting them," leaving the fugitives with no educational opportunity. White missionary Hiram Wilson and others encouraged blacks to ignore white prejudice and enroll in the public schools. If denied admission, "they have but to make known to the Governor and Council their aggrievances and stand up like men to their legal and constitutional rights." Such advice may have been motivated by good intentions, and indeed it succeeded in the case of Hamilton's black residents. But generally the destitute, inexperienced refugees hesitated to "remonstrate and petition," as the procedure was too time-consuming and perplexing.[17]

By the mid-1840s, approximately 2,600 schools in Canada West served the needs of some 97,000 students. Five years later, 151,891 out of 259,258 school-aged children were enrolled in public schools.[18] Though no separate reports specify the number of black pupils in either case, the figures do serve to illustrate why discrimination toward a small minority received so little attention. The dramatic increase in the overall number of total students can be attributed largely to the efforts of the new superintendent of schools for Canada West, Egerton Ryerson.

Born in 1803, Ryerson attended grammar school in Upper Canada and remained to teach there. In 1825 he became a Methodist minister, later to assume the editorship of the Methodist newspaper, the *Christian Guardian*. In 1833, he gained prominence after successfully negotiating the union of the Methodist Episcopal Church of Upper Canada with the British Wesleyan Conference of Lower Canada. Maintaining his interest in education, however, he solicited funds for the establishment of the Upper Canada Academy, which ultimately became Victoria College. Ryerson acted as its first president, and soon after, through political connections, was awarded the post of assistant superintendent of schools. His promotion to superintendent in 1844 prompted a trip abroad to study the educational systems of more than twenty countries. Returning with a proposal to make education in Canada West universal, free, practical, and compulsory, Ryerson emphasized that every child should be educated in order to ``fit him to be an honest and useful member of the community'' and to prevail over ``the evils of want and poverty.'' Thus, in Ryerson's view, education would serve both social and individual ends.[19]

Toward this goal, Ryerson drafted the Common School Act of 1846 and quickly began to implement such reforms as the creation of a strong central authority over educational matters. He also presented a plan to tax property for school funds, but this aspect did not reach fruition until 1850. Of Ryerson's primary reform measures, the Common School Act of 1850 represented the greatest potential for the promotion of education in the black community as school boards were finally granted the option to levy property assessment taxes for educational support. Unfortunately for the fugitive slaves, the Common School Act of 1850 authorized separate schools not only for religious denominations but for ``Coloured People'' as well. The applicable clause stated that any group of five black families could request separate facilities as Ryerson intended to allow the fugitive slaves the privilege of choice whether to attend schools with or without white students.

Ironically, the Common School Act of 1850 effectively reinforced and legally entrenched a system of segregated schools for blacks in Canada West. For example, black children in Simcoe were turned away from the public school later that same year, ``for the sole reason that they differed in Colour from the great body of other pupils.'' The fugitive slaves paid the required school tax, and expected to be able to set up a separate school; but lacking the funds for construction, they found it necessary to request financial support from the Municipal Council. Because the council offered no assistance, the refugees contacted Ryerson for advice. The superintendent reiterated the pertinent clause of the School Act, and clearly explained that the establishment of a black separate school ``is a matter of choice with themselves. If they do not choose to establish a separate school, they have the same right, of access, for their children to the Common School as the Parents of any other children.'' Ryerson regretted the ``deplorable calamity'' of the black children's exclusion, and suggested the fugitives prosecute for damages from the school trustees.[20] No immediate compensation was available, and perhaps because of the complicated litigation involved, the black residents of Simcoe declined Ryerson's advice. Although the fugitive slaves agreed to a segregated school in accordance with the law, lack of money prevented its construction, and white Canadian prejudice precluded black attendance at the common school. As a result, the black children of Simcoe received no education at all.

A different situation existed in Amherstburg where a black separate school was established in 1851, not at the request of the fugitive slaves but rather by the white trustees of the common school system. Boston journalist and abolitionist

Benjamin Drew graphically described the inferior quality of the black school, which contained neither blackboard nor chairs. Uncomfortable benches sufficed for seats, and "miserably tattered" readers served as books. "A very little bad ink" from two nearly empty inkstands had to be stretched for use by the entire class of thirty pupils. Drew concluded: "The whole interior is comfortless and repulsive.... The whole school adds one more dreary chapter to 'the pursuit of knowledge under difficulties.' " A separate board of trustees never existed to administer the black separate school and despite complaints from blacks, the trustees deemed the separate school "sufficient for the wants of the colored people."[21] Instead of providing the fugitive slaves with an alternative, Ryerson's Common School Act of 1850 inadvertently allowed the white trustees in Amherstburg to force the blacks into a segregated school.

The case of *Hill v. Camden* clarified the interpretation of the Common School Act. In 1852, Dennis Hill of Dawn Mills informed Ryerson of his unsuccessful attempt to enroll his children in the local public school. According to Hill, the white trustees "say that I am a black man and that it would be presumtion [sic] in me to contend for my son to go to school among white children." Hill protested that the nearest separate school was more than four miles away, and that as a taxpayer on three hundred acres, "to be debarred from my rights of school privilege for no other crime than that my skin is a few shades darker than some of my neighbours, I do think it unfair." Consistent with his advice to the Simcoe petitioners, Ryerson replied that Hill should prosecute or at least apply for an injunction. Finally accepting that the law could be abused by prejudiced whites, Ryerson acknowledged that "it is *mean* beyond expression, as well as unjust, for the Trustees and other supporters of the school to levy and receive taxes from you, for the education of their own children, and then refuse admission to yours."

Hill waited until the next year, when his second child reached school age, and formally demanded entry for both. The trustees again refused to permit the black children access to the public school, and then unlike his predecessors, Hill heeded Ryerson's advice and prosecuted. In a most significant decision, the chief justice of Canada West, John Beverly Robinson, clearly pronounced that "the separate schools for coloured people were authorized...out of deference to the prejudices of the white population." Robinson explained the white Canadians' fear that their children would suffer from the bad morals and habits exemplified by black children. He elaborated: "It can hardly be supposed that the legislature authorized such separate schools under the idea that it would be more beneficial or agreeable to the coloured people." In addition, the chief justice asserted that once a separate school had been established, a black child had no choice but to attend that particular school, regardless of its quality or distance.[22] This decision in essence sanctioned educational segregation throughout the province. Notwithstanding the intention or spirit of the law, the highest provincial court had ruled that black children could be willfully excluded in virtually any public school district.

Despite Robinson's position, George Washington, another black plaintiff, instituted legal proceedings in 1855 when his son, he charged, was denied admission to the common school in Charlotteville, "owing to his colour." In fact, the white trustees had attempted to segregate black children in the area by gerrymandering the geographical boundaries of the school district; yet they established no separate school. With Ryerson's encouragement, Washington took legal action against the trustees. At the initial trial, the lawsuit was dismissed for lack of sufficient evidence, but a higher court set aside this ruling "leaving each party to pay his own costs," and enabling Washington to prosecute again. A second trial rendered the verdict that the black child should be admitted, but it was not until the third trial that Washington obtained an award for damages. Unaccountably, the white trustees owned no property commensurate in value to the court costs, and because they could not be held individually responsible, it appeared that Washington would have to assume the court fees. Washington's attorney, J.G. Hanton, contacted Ryerson explaining that "the plaintiff has a small farm acquired by his industry and sober habits, which he will be under the necessity of sacrificing if he cannot get assistance" in paying the trial costs. Nevertheless, Washington had to sell his farm to defray the expenses.

Thus, the case of *Washington v. Trustees of Charlotteville* had two significant repercussions. On the one hand, it proved that the fugitive slaves could win in a clear case of discrimination. Chief Justice Robinson pointed out that as no separate school existed, the redistricting prevented the black child from attending school entirely. The court decided that "colored people are not to be excluded from the ordinary common schools, if there be no separate school established and in operation for their use."[23] On the other hand, the moral victory was hollow, for the black man who had shown enough courage to prosecute ultimately lost his property. Having observed the outcome, Washington's fellow blacks recognized the futility of fighting segregation in the courts.

If the fugitive slaves hesitated to prosecute, they still registered vehement objections with Canada West's superintendent of education. In January 1856, William P. Newman lobbied Ryerson on behalf of the blacks of Dresden, who were forced to send their children to a separate school approximately eight miles away. Newman queried, "Is the *spirit* of the law, to meet the convenience of families or to satisfy the *prejudice* against color?" Ryerson responded through his secretary, George Hodgins, who wrote that the intent of the law was to provide separate schools, "If the persons for whom they are intended *wish* to have them; not otherwise." Hodgins affirmed, however, that Dresden's school officials could indeed refuse to admit black children at the closest common school because another school had been made available to them.[24] Once again, as Chief Justice Robinson ruled in the case of *Hill v. Camden,* the black children had to attend the stipulated school, albeit segregated, inferior, and distant.

White Canadians complained to Ryerson as well about the ambiguity of the Common School Act. In June 1857, members of the board of school trustees in St. Catharines directed one James G. Currie to contact Ryerson for clarification of their rights. Currie prefaced his questions with a brief explanation of the situation: "Owing to the large number of coloured persons residing here, and the strong prejudice that exists in the minds of many of the whites, against allowing their children to attend the schools which coloured children are admitted to, we have lately had a good deal of trouble with our schools." In a case similar to that at Dresden, the school board wished to know if it had the right to compel blacks to enroll in one segregated school. Ryerson replied that the trustees had the authority to decide "the number, the kind and description" of schools in their district, but he also emphasized that "the Board have therefore unlimited power to determine the objects of each school and who shall and who shall not attend."[25] In other words, the superintendent gave wide discretionary power to the white common school trustees. St. Catharines, admittedly rampant with negrophobia, could now establish any kind of school that the community felt best met its social conditions. Ryerson appeared to have reversed his position about black choice in favor of white choice.

Meanwhile, a different set of circumstances led to protests from both blacks and whites in Malden Township. In 1855, the blacks there had agreed to the establishment of a separate school, to be supported by local taxes and by government matching funds. Notwithstanding this agreement, the black school failed to receive its legal share of government funds. Claiming that "their means are not sufficient to keep the school in operation if denied the Government apportionment," the black trustees in August 1856 petitioned Ryerson for their rightful aid. A second petition sent six months later and signed by forty black residents of Malden Township complained of their "being set apart from, and shut out from the schools in our neighborhood." It repeated the request for money, emphasizing their school's privation. The white trustees, however, viewed the situation differently, and in a letter to Ryerson, charged that the fugitive slaves "have numbers and means enough to keep up a school themselves if they would act right." The white Canadians conceded that a mixed school would not be tolerated, and asked how to "prevent them from coming to our school... [and] pushing themselves on us."[26] Ryerson suggested that the matter be resolved by the courts, but no such action occurred. Instead, the black school operated without government funds for another year, and once it closed, the black children in Malden Township had access to no public school at all.

Where public common schools prohibited blacks entirely, the fugitive slaves often sent their children to private schools. Such was initially true in Windsor, where Mary Ann Shadd established a school in 1851 for all children who wished to attend. A staunch opponent of segregated institutions, Shadd emphasized the accessibility of her school to children of both races. Inadequate financial support from parents, however, forced her to appeal to the American Missionary Association for assistance from which she received $125 annually until 1853. During that spring Shadd closed her school as a result of "a regular and well executed series of attacks" on her image by Henry Bibb, who sharply disagreed with her financial handling of the school. With its collapse went the best opportunity of education for Windsor's black children.[27]

That blacks were relegated to the lowest priority in the educational systems became readily apparent in Windsor in 1854 when the community decided to construct three new public schools, one each "for Protestant, Catholic and colored pupils respectively." No action ensued on the facility for black students until 1858, when the school board rented a "coop," just 16 feet by 24 feet, for all forty-five black children. Shortly thereafter, in January 1859, the white trustees tabled the request of fugitive slave Clayborn Harris to admit his son to the Protestant common school. In response, Harris contacted a London, Canada West, attorney, William Horton, about the legalities of the exclusion. Harris explained that he had personally spoken with all the school trustees, who unanimously denied black rights to attend. Harris then tried to enroll a few black children in classes, but the teachers peremptorily refused to admit them. Reflecting black opinion, Harris stated that the fugitives would acquiesce and attend a separate primary school in exchange for the assurance that their children would have access to public higher education. But "the idea of us asking for a separate school when it will debar us from all the higher branches of literature," Harris wrote, "we think would be like cutting off our noses to spite our faces." Further, Harris viewed the segregation in Windsor as indicative of a larger principle, asserting

> that we feel forced to examine fully into this matter, as a people, for if it is admitted in this village to set our children out of school, the children that lives (sic)...where there are not sufficient numbers to establish a separate school...will be excluded in those sections just as much as in the village.... But for a few of us to yield to a prejudice in towns at the destruction of the rights of our people around us would not be doing to others what we would have them do to us.
>
> The question that we wish settled is, Shall the trustees use the government money to support a prejudice of one class of Her Majesty's subjects against another?

Supporting Harris's action, a committee of Windsor blacks followed his letter with another of the same sentiment to Ryerson. They cited that similar problems occurred in nearby Sandwich, and that if the "hydra headed monster" of prejudice be allowed to grow, blacks would soon be denied all benefits to which they were entitled. Ryerson replied that "it is very undesirable that such a prejudice should be entertained," but conceded that the white officials could legally prevent the black children from attending the Protestant common school as long as other facilities existed. The latter stipulation, however, did not come to fruition there until 1862, when a separate schoolhouse was at long last completed for the black children of Windsor.[28]

The separate school that had been established in Chatham in 1851 under the auspices of the white school trustees still remained inadequate by the end of the decade. James E. Grant, the teacher there, notified the *Voice of the Fugitive* that the number of pupils increased steadily until the school was overcrowded. During the winter he sent "some 15 small scholars to my house for instruction by my wife." In addition to its insufficient room, the black separate school lacked supplies. Nonetheless, the fugitive slaves registered little significant opposition to the separate school until in 1859 a white man, one Mr. Nichol, was designated to be its teacher. This appointment of Nichol precipitated much hostility in the black community. The local newspaper, the Chatham *Planet,* castigated the school trustees, noting that if Roman Catholics could specify a teacher of their creed, blacks should have the same right. One trustee publicly defended the action in a letter to the *Planet,* explaining that of three applicants for the position in the black school, the white teacher had the best qualifications. Nichol had "a first class letter 'A' certificate," while the other two, who were black, had second-class teaching certificates. Further, the trustee claimed that those who supported Nichol had requested, " 'Give us the best teacher, whether he be white, black or grey.' " The fugitive slaves denied ever endorsing Nichol, and contended that his support came from out-of-town whites. The angry black taxpayers maintained that they were "only waiting for a colored man holding a first class certificate" before demanding the teacher's replacement; yet the opportunity never arose.[29]

The racial tension in Chatham increased in 1861 when at the petitioning of several black families, a second segregated school was established. Rather than defending the boundaries of the black school districts in conventional geographical terms, however, Chatham's school officials drew district lines according to the presence or absence of blacks. Thus all black children in Chatham, regardless of where they lived, attended a segregated school. One disgruntled black resident, William Simmons, took legal action against the Corporation of the Township of Chatham for excluding his children from a nearby white common school. The Court of the Queen's Bench then ruled that the attempt to gerrymander the school districts was clearly illegal. The court's opinion quashed the fluctuating arrangement because it did "not give to the school section any limits that can be said to be known at any point of time."[30] Simmons won the court battle, but the majority of black children still continued to attend the inferior segregated schools as before.

At about the same time, Superintendent Ryerson received new objections from dissatisfied whites at Harwick, located outside of Chatham. In that township, seven black children were enrolled in the common school, resulting in the withdrawal of approximately fifty white students by their hostile parents. Duncan Campbell, who had been a school trustee for ten years, resigned in disgust at these activities. He assumed the responsibility of informing Ryerson that because Harwich's black residents owned no property, they did not pay taxes toward the support of public education. Regarding the blacks, Campbell self-righteously suggested that "there should be some provision made that the white people would not be compelled to admit them to their schools, *and that the Government would pay* the expense of their schools where they have no property of their own that can be rated." Campbell proposed that Ryerson submit an amendment to the current session of Parliament to resolve this grievance, appealing to Ryerson's advocacy of universal education by emphasizing the senselessness of teaching seven or eight pupils when some fifty or sixty stayed away. In a final plea Campbell asked, *"What are we to do?"* Interestingly, Campbell never inquired about creating a separate school for blacks. Perhaps he realized from his decade of experience as a school trustee that it would be illegal to do so, with too few black families living in Harwich to qualify for the establishment of a separate facility.

Ryerson had little time to reply to Campbell's correspondence before another Harwich school trustee, C.T. Sifton, sent him a letter. On behalf of the school board, Sifton presented a novel approach to the problem of school segregation. Because whites refused to consider a racially integrated school, he suggested "that a building be erected connecting with our present school house so that the one teacher could teach both colored and white children." Sifton inquired if such an arrangement, where the whites prevented blacks from being taught in the same room, was justifiable.[31] Without waiting for Ryerson's advice, however, the community commenced construction of a completely new building for white children, while making no provision for the blacks. The hostile local environment simply forced the Harwich blacks to seek education elsewhere, presumably at the Chatham separate school some one and a half miles away.

Yet it remained for the most intense dispute over educational segregation to transpire in London. A separate school had been established for blacks in 1849; but most black children attended classes at the Anglican Colonial Church and School

Society's mission. After the mission's demise in 1856, some black children enrolled in the common schools. By 1862, though, the white school trustees proposed and approved plans to institute a policy of racial exclusion in common schools throughout the city. This change in attitude was recorded in the minutes of the schoolboard record wherein a number of reasons were given to justify segregation. First, the whites of London generally believed that "the negro differs so essentially from the Caucasian race in organic structure, in the effects of climate influences, or both, that any close or intimate relations with them are not desirable." The repugnance manifested by white adults was transmitted to their children. Consequently, the white officials observed in the schools, "a bandying of offensive epithets, embittered acrimonious feelings and juvenile quarrels. In these petty disputes the parents frequently take part, complaints are made. . . that their children have been insulted; and, by the colored parents, that theirs have been harshly and perhaps unjustly treated." Such incidents, it was concluded, could be avoided by segregation. Second, the school board felt compelled to note the "effluvium" emitted by black children during the summer, which highly offended white children and teachers alike. Separation, it was maintained, would solve that problem as well. Finally, the school board's investigating committee reported on the want of sympathy between white teachers and black students. This estrangement led to jealousy on the part of blacks, which might turn into future enmity. The committee concluded: "When educated apart, they will not be educated for evil; they will not have some of the worst passions of the human heart called daily into play and thus strengthened by exercise; they will have no taunts and insults to remember; and when they enter life as men, they will be enabled to meet their white fellow-citizens without a single acrimonious feeling, arising from the recollections of wrongs suffered or injuries retaliated."[32]

A retort to these points quickly came from "Diogenes," a member of Toronto's black community. Diogenes accused the white trustees and teachers of London of thwarting the progress of Canadian education by their relapse into negrophobia. He cited numerous cases in Toronto where quite cordial relations existed both among the scholars and between the teachers and black students, and he invited the London officials to visit Toronto to observe the lack of hostility. As to the so-called "effluvium," he replied that the children must have been trained to sniff, "like the bloodhounds down South 'in Dixie' " by their prejudiced parents. He continued:

> And as to the teachers, they must have extraordinary organs of scent to enable them to distinguish which of their scholars it is from whom the "disagreeable effluvium arises," without a personal scenting of each one separately. If they can, I, for one, would advise our city fathers to employ

them to scent out the "pig nuisance" that is so much complained of in our city, for it is certainly an occupation more suited to them than common school teaching.

Turning to the alleged envy in integrated schools, the black representative offered the story of an animal trainer who put different types of wild animals together when young. The animals grew up as friends and thereafter remained so. Diogenes thought this a useful lesson for the London school officials, and he concluded by declaring that the black community would seek redress through the legislature to arrest the power of white school trustees to impose separate schools on black children. "Not only so," he asserted, "but we will agitate the subject for the purpose of getting those already established, abolished."[33] Perhaps because of this direct public confrontation, or perhaps because the number of black students had started visibly to decline, the London school board never fully practiced segregation.

By this time, then, there was much confusion and ambiguity over the rights of whites to segregate blacks and/or over the right of all to public education. In 1862, Ryerson offered an explanation in which he delineated two marked interpretations. He contended that "it is within the power of school trustees in cities and towns to make a distinction between colors...but in country places... it is at the option of the colored people to have separate schools or not."[34] Originally the advocate of black freedom to choose, Ryerson realized that to belabor this point would be to jeopardize his reforms in the provincial schools. He, therefore, was willing to bend the intent of the law on separate schools whichever way was necessary to protect the educational system as a whole.

Regardless of Ryerson's rationalization, the courts continued to see litigation on the matter. In 1864, Chief Justice William Henry Draper ruled in the case of *Stewart v. Sandwich East* that blacks indeed had the privilege of admission to the nearest common school when their own separate school ceased functioning. In other words, the creation of a separate school for blacks suspended but did not annul their right to attend white common schools, a moral victory for blacks at the least. Seven years later, Justice Joseph Curran Morrison of the Court of Queen's Bench in the case of *Re Hutchison v. St. Catharines* found that the town's establishment of a separate school for blacks prior to the Common School Act of 1850 was illegal. The black plaintiff again won the case, but ultimately gained nothing when his child was forced to remain in the same separate school. The white trustees prevented the Hutchison child from gaining access to the common school by claiming that the school was filled to capacity. Similarly, in *Dunn v. Windsor* (1885), the court ruled that blacks could be prohibited from transferring from a separate school to a white common school, giving as grounds the lack of space to accommodate the black child at the white school.[35] Despite the previous rulings upholding black rights to an equal education, white Canadian trustees used this "pupil placement" maneuver as still another means to keep blacks segregated. More than anything, the judicial decisions in Canada West contributed confusion rather than clarification to the subject of school segregation.

Essentially, then, segregated schools developed wherever a large fugitive-slave population resided in Canada West. The larger the number of blacks, the more intense was the white prejudice. In Amherstburg, Windsor, Sandwich, and Malden in Essex County, which lay closest to the American border, racial animosity occurred most frequently. It appeared almost as often in Chatham, Harwich, and Dresden in Kent County, the next district to the east. Both counties harbored many blacks after passage of the Fugitive Slave Law of 1850. Yet 1850 cannot be viewed exclusively as a watershed in the history of race relations in Canada West. The discrimination and hostility directed toward blacks there existed in a nascent state prior to the passage of the Fugitive Slave Law. The sheer increase in the black population brought on by this act served only to aggravate and augment Canadian negrophobia. In turn, the new concentration of refugees prompted vehement anti-black sentiment on the part of white Canadians that translated into discrimination in education. Bigotry became manifested in the schools because, as Samuel Gridley Howe observed, "Each party begins to see that the democratic tendency of the common school is to prevent or weaken castes while the inevitable tendency of the separate schools is to create and strengthen them."[36] White Canadian segregationists covertly expressed the desire to exclude fugitive slaves from their society, or at least to ensure that blacks remained confined to its lower levels.

And to some extent, the fugitive slaves themselves assured white success in the endeavor to practice segregation. So believed several prominent blacks, among them *Provincial Freeman* editor Mary Ann Shadd. In her pamphlet, *Notes on Canada West,* she chastised those fugitives who docilely accepted separate schools for their children. She berated them for extending "the line of separation ...between them and the whites," and for actively perpetuating "prejudices originating in slavery and as strong and objectionable in their manifestations as those entertained by whites toward them." Rather than breaking down racial barriers, such behavior entrenched them.

Shadd's advocacy of integration in the schools was echoed even by her perpetual adversary, Henry Bibb. When Bibb learned that several black families had submitted a petition for a separate school in Windsor, he indignantly denied its validity. He railed that the request "was not made by the intellectual portion of the colored population, but by a lot of ignoramuses who were made tools of (by whites) and who knew not what they were doing." The black bishop of the British Methodist Episcopal Church, William Nazrey, concurred with Shadd and Bibb as well. He preached fervently against separate schools, exclaiming "I will speak against them while I live," and prevailed upon other ministers to do likewise. Nazrey explained that, to his way of thinking, "If we expect to keep up with this fast age we must educate our children, and there is no better way to do this than to make good use of the rights and privileges as they are laid down by British law and measured out by British Institutions—that all men are free and equal irrespective of hue or clime; and therefore, all have a right to public schools, the high as well as the low."[37]

White abolitionists also criticized fugitive slaves for agreeing to place their children in separate schools. In 1856, Benjamin Drew observed the state of black education in Sandwich, and noted that "here, as in many other parts of the province, the colored people, by accepting of that provision of the law, which allows them separate schools, fail of securing the best education for their children." He feared that the quality of the separate black schools would always be inferior and would prevent the fugitive slaves from reaching their full potential. Drew warned that "unless separate schools are abolished...the progress of the colored people in education will be very much retarded in the greater part of the province." Several years later, Samuel Gridley Howe expressed grave concern, also, over the request by a few fugitives for separate facilities. In Howe's opinion, this enabled whites to point to these examples as indicative of black opinion as a whole. The establishment of a few separate schools promised a future of "compulsory *caste* schools" for all blacks in Canada West. When Archibald McKellar, cofounder of the Teachers' Association of Canada West, spoke at its convention in Toronto in 1864, he chided black segregationists as well, and prodded the delegates into endorsing a resolution opposing separate schools.[38]

Both black and white critics of segregated schools, however, may have been blinded by their idealism to the reality of prejudice in Canada West. White Canadians controlled the educational system, and in most cases, they tacitly assumed that segregation embodied the only course acceptable to both races. In any event, whites actually needed no justification because, as the majority, they easily overruled the desires of the fugitive-slave minority. The provincial courts handed down inconsistent decisions, some supporting the rights of blacks, others denying them. Thus, to the refugees who so desperately wanted their children to be educated, separate schooling often seemed the most feasible solution.

Segregated schools in the province did provide a start toward the education of fugitive slaves. Undeniably, these separate schools often lacked necessary supplies, talented teachers, and adequate room. And one black parent in Hamilton even complained that the children left school "knowing but little more about the grammar of their language, than a horse does about handling a musket." But despite the problems involved in seeking an education in Canada West, the fugitive slaves retained their compelling desire to learn. This alone accounts for the perseverance, the litigation, and the general agitation of blacks over schooling. The mere possibility of obtaining an education gave them hope in the face of a rising tide of Canadian white prejudice, for they truly believed that "as soon as we become educated we will become great."[39]

NOTES

1. *Liberator*, 14 December 1855;

    Thomas L. Webber, *Deep Like the Rivers: Education in the Slave Quarter Community, 1831-1865* (New York, 1978), pp. 27-33, 131-38;

    Eugene D. Genovese, *Roll, Jordan, Roll: The World the Slaves Made* (New York, 1974), pp. 50-51, 563;

    Woodson, *Education of the Negro*, pp. 177, 307-35;

    Bibb, *Narrative of the Life and Adventures of Henry Bibb*, pp. 101-2;

    Litwack, *North of Slavery*, pp. 113-16;

    Franklin, *From Slavery to Freedom*, pp. 202-3, 228-29; and

    Herbert Aptheker, ed., *A Documentary History of the Negro People in the United States* (New York, 1951), pp. 19-20.

2. W.E.B.DuBois, *Black Reconstruction in America, 1860-1880* (Cleveland, 1962), pp. 641-42; and

    Minutes and Proceedings of the General Convention for the Improvement of the Colored Inhabitants of Canada (Windsor, 1853), p. 19.

3. *Minutes and Proceedings of the General Convention for the Improvement of the Colored Inhabitants of Canada*, p. 19.

4. J. Donald Wilson, Robert M. Stamp, and Louis-Philippe Audet, eds., *Canadian Education: A History* (Scarborough, Ontario, 1970), pp. 200-10.

5. Nondenominational "Common Schools" were created by the Common School Act of 1816 and were meant to educate children of the "middling and poorer classes." Canadian education was defined by the District Public (Grammar) School Act of 1807. This legislation provided for the establishment of a grammar school in each of the eight districts of the province. The government allotted an impressive £100 to teachers of grammar schools. The expense of tuition, books, and often board and lodging, meant that these district or grammar schools cost almost as much as sending a child to the United States for an education. Only the "sons of gentlemen" could afford to attend the grammar schools. See

    Wilson, Stamp, and Audet, *Canadian Education*, pp. 190-95; and

    J. George Hodgins, ed., *Documentary History of Education in Upper Canada: From the Passing of the Constitutional Act of 1791 to the Close of Rev. Dr. Ryerson's*

Administration of the Education Department in 1876 (28 vols., Toronto, 1894-1910), 1, p. 77.

6. "Petition of Colored People Presented at Ancaster, Upper Canada, July 25, 1828," *Journal of Negro History* 15 (January 1930), pp. 115-16; and

    "Interesting Notes on Great Britain and Canada with Respect to the Negro," *Journal of Negro History* 13 (April 1928), p. 194.

    The petition originally appeared in the Ancaster *Gazette* and subsequently was published in the Kingston *Gazette and Religious Advocate,* 25 July 1828.

7. Monitorial Schools, or "National Schools," were biased toward teaching the Church of England's doctrine. Maitland supported this plan because it would counteract American influences. It would exclude American teachers and books, "which are studiously composed with a view to instilling principles into the pupil's mind unfriendly to our form of government." Strachan supported it because of its Anglican bias. The system was unpopular and subsequently failed.

    Peregrine Maitland to Lord Bathurst, 4 January 1821, in Colonial Office Records, 42 Series, vol. 436, pp. 3-4; and

    John Strachan to J.S. Sinclair, 23 May 1840, in the Strachan Papers: both located in the Public Archives of Canada, Ottawa. See also

    Wilson, Stamp, and Audet, *Canadian Education,* pp. 204-5.

    For more on Strachan's life, see

    J.D. Purdy, "John Strachan and Education in Canada, 1800-1851" (Ph.D. dissertation, University of Toronto, 1962);

    J.L.H. Henderson, *John Strachan* (Toronto, 1969); and

    A.N. Bethune, *Memoir of the Right Reverend John Strachan* (Toronto, 1870).

8. Winks, "Negro School Segregation in Ontario and Nova Scotia," pp. 169-71;

    Idem, *Blacks in Canada,* pp. 365-73; and

    Silverman and Gillie, " 'The Pursuit of Knowledge Under Difficulties,' " pp. 95-112.

9. Isaac Rice to Egerton Ryerson, 23 January 1846, in the Ryerson Papers, Ontario Provincial Archives, Toronto;

    J. Dougall, "The Laying of the Cornerstone of Windsor Central School," unpublished manuscript dated November 1871, located at Fort Malden National Historic Park, Amherstburg, Ontario.

10. Robert Peden to Egerton Ryerson, 23 February 1846, in the Ryerson Papers, Ontario Provincial Archives, Toronto.

11. Ibid.

12. Egerton Ryerson to Isaac Rice and Robert Peden, 5 March 1846, in the Ryerson Papers, Ontario Provincial Archives, Toronto; and

    Provincial Freeman, 12 December 1855.

    Shadd's assertion may have been true because according to one historian, there was "no knowledge of colored schools or churches until 1838." See

Lewis, "The Religious Life of the Fugitive Slaves," p. 54.

13. W.H. Draper to Egerton Ryerson, 5 April 1847, in the Ryerson Papers, Ontario Provincial Archives, Toronto;
     Minutes of the 21st Session of the Municipal Council of the Western District Committee on Schools (1846), p. 3;
     Chatham *Journal,* 9 January 1849;
     Chatham *Gleaner,* 18 January 1848; and
     Drew, *North-Side View of Slavery,* p. 147.

14. Petition from Hamilton, Canada West, 15 October 1843, in the Ryerson Papers, Ontario Provincial Archives, Toronto; and
     L.T. Spaulding, *History and Romance of Education (Hamilton) 1816-1950* (Hamilton, 1951), p. 224.

15. Robert Peden to George Tiffany, 19 October 1843 and reply from Tiffany, 9 November 1843; both in the Ryerson Papers, Ontario Provincial Archives, Toronto; and
     J. George Hodgins, ed., *Historical and Other Papers and Documents Illustrative of the Educational System of Ontario, 1853-1868* (28 vols., Toronto, 1911), III, pp. 108-11, and *Documentary History,* IV, pp. 312-13.

16. Drew, *North-Side View of Slavery,* p. 197; and
     H.H. Spencer, "To Nestle in the British Lion's Mane: A History of Canadian Black Education, 1850-1870" (Ph.D. dissertation, Northwestern University, 1970), pp. 60-80.

17. Canada Mission, *Seventh Annual Report* (1844), pp. 4-6.

18. *Annual Report of the Normal, Model and Common Schools in Upper Canada, for the Year 1850: With an Appendix* (Toronto, 1851), pp. 70, 74-75, 182.

19. Egerton Ryerson, *Report on a System of Public Elementary Instruction for Upper Canada* (Montreal, 1847), p. 7.
     Ryerson's proposals reflected the changes occurring in education throughout Europe and the United States in the middle of the nineteenth century. One historian of education analyzed the contemporary currents as four intertwining elements: total commitment to education, social comprehensiveness, the association of education with technological and social change, and government action. Ryerson merely applied these principles to his own locale. For more on this topic see
     William Boyd, *The History of Western Education* (London, 1966).
     For more on Ryerson, see
     Sylvia Carlton, "Egerton Ryerson and Education in Ontario, 1844-1877" (Ph.D. dissertation, University of Pennsylvania, 1950);
     Nathaniel Burwash, *Egerton Ryerson* (Toronto, 1910);
     Charles B. Sissons, *Egerton Ryerson, His Life and Letters* (Toronto, 1937);

John H. Putnam, *Egerton Ryerson and Education in Upper Canada* (Toronto, 1912); and

Clara E. Thompson, *Ryerson of Upper Canada* (Toronto, 1969).

20. Petition from Simcoe, Canada West, 12 December 1851, and Ryerson's reply, 17 December 1851: both in the Ryerson Papers, Ontario Provincial Archives, Toronto; Charles E. Phillips, *The Development of Education in Canada* (Toronto, 1957), p. 369; and

    Petition of Allan Dorsey and other black inhabitants of Simcoe, 1850, in the Regional History Collection, D.B. Weldon Library, University of Western Ontario, London.

21. Minutes and Reports of the Amherstburg Board of Education Trustees, in the private possession of Mr. Alvin McCurdy, Amherstburg, Ontario; and

    Drew, *North-Side View of Slavery*, p. 245.

22. Dennis Hill to Egerton Ryerson, 22 November 1852, and Ryerson's reply, 30 November 1852: both in the Ryerson Papers, Ontario Provincial Archives, Toronto; H.W. Arthurs, "Civil Liberties—Public Schools—Segregation of Negro Students," *The Canadian Bar Review* 41 (September 1963), pp. 453-57; and

    Hill, *Freedom Seekers*, pp. 148-56.

23. S.G. Hanton to Egerton Ryerson, 25 May 1855, in the Ryerson Papers, Ontario Provincial Archives, Toronto;

    Francis G. Carter, ed., *Judicial Decisions on Denominational Schools* (Toronto, 1962), pp. 151-52; and

    Winks's "Notes on School Segregation in Canada," in his collection at Schomburg Center for Research in Black Culture, New York City.

24. William P. Newman to Egerton Ryerson, 13 January 1856;

    J. George Hodgins (Ryerson's secretary) to William Newman, 15 January 1856: both in the Ryerson Papers, Ontario Provincial Archives, Toronto.

    For more on related topics see the J. George Hodgins Papers, Ontario Provincial Archives, Toronto.

25. James G. Currie to Egerton Ryerson, 4 June 1857, and Ryerson's reply, 16 June 1857: both in the Ryerson Papers, Ontario Provincial Archives, Toronto;

    James W. St. Walker, *A History of Blacks in Canada: A Study Guide for Teachers and Students* (Hull, Quebec, 1980), pp. 109-15.

26. Thomas Buckner, Samuel Campbell, and Lewis Graynor to Egerton Ryerson, 9 August 1856;

    James Wright and others to Egerton Ryerson, 26 February 1857;

    Samuel Atkin and others to Egerton Ryerson, 29 December 1856:

    all three documents in the Ryerson Papers, Ontario Provincial Archives, Toronto.

27. *Voice of the Fugitive*, 29 January 1852;

    Miscellaneous Papers Relating to Teaching in Canada in the Mary Ann Shadd Cary

Papers, Moorland-Spingarn Research Center, Howard University, Washington, D.C.

28. Clayborn Harris to William Horton, 15 February 1859;
William Horton to Egerton Ryerson, 16 February 1859;
A.R. Green, Thomas Jones, and Clayborn Harris to Egerton Ryerson, 2 March 1859,
and Ryerson's replies, 21 February 1859 and 9 March 1859:
all in the Ryerson Papers, Ontario Provincial Archives, Toronto.

29. *Voice of the Fugitive,* 25 April 1851;
Chatham *Planet,* 29 December 1859 and 21 and 28 January 1860; and
Carol Jenson, "History of the Negro Community in Essex County, 1850-1860" (M.A.
thesis, University of Windsor, 1966), pp. 22-66.

30. The complete text for *In the Matter of Simmons and the Corporation of the
Township of Chatham* appears in *Queen's Bench,* vol. 21, 1862, pp. 75-79; and
Harriet Chatters, "Negro Education in Kent County" (M.A. thesis, Howard University, 1956), pp. 23-32.

31. Duncan Campbell to Egerton Ryerson, 14 March 1862; and
C.T. Sifton to Egerton Ryerson, 17 March 1862: both in the Ryerson Papers, Ontario
Provincial Archives, Toronto.

32. London Board of Education, *Minutes,* 4 December 1862;
Toronto *Leader,* 12 December 1862;
Howe, *Refugees from Slavery in Canada West,* p. 88; and
Alison L. Prentice and Susan E. Houston, eds., *Family, School, and Society in
Nineteenth-Century Canada* (Toronto, 1975), pp. 233-36.

33. Toronto *Globe,* 3 January 1863.

34. Howe, *Refugees from Slavery in Canada West,* p. 44.

35. The complete text of *In Re George Stewart and the Trustees of School Section No.
8 of the Township of Sandwich East, in the County of Essex* appears in *Queen's
Bench,* vol. 23, 1864, pp. 634-38;
In Re Hutchison and the Board of School Trustees of St. Catharines appears in
Queen's Bench, vol. 31, 1872, pp. 274-79; and
Dunn v. the Board of Education of the Town of Windsor appears in the *Ontario
Reports,* 6 (Toronto, 1885), pp. 455-56. See also
Carter, *Judicial Decisions on Denominational Schools,* pp. 118, 135-38, 149-52;
and
Arthurs, "Civil Liberties," pp. 455-56.

36. Howe, *Refugees from Slavery in Canada West,* p. 43.

37. Mary Ann Shadd, *A Plea for Emigration or Notes on Canada West. . . ,* p. 33;
Voice of the Fugitive, 1 January 1852; and
Minutes of the Third General Conference of the B.M.E. Church (Hamilton, 1868),
p. 9.

38. Drew, *North-Side View of Slavery,* pp. 224-26;

Howe, *Refugees from Slavery in Canada West*, pp. 50-54; and Edwin C. Guillet, *In the Course of Education: Centennial History of the Ontario Educational Association, 1861-1960* (Toronto, 1960), p. 31.

39.   Paola Brown, *Address on Slavery* (Hamilton, 1851); and *Provincial Freeman*, 6 May 1854.

Seven

THE IRONIC RETURN

By the end of the 1850s, Canada West harbored approximately 40,000 fugitive slaves. The number of blacks migrating into the province before 1830 increased steadily until, by 1850, it had become overwhelming. The vast majority of these refugees settled in the southwestern portion of the province, in the counties of Essex and Kent; and in the cities of Amherstburg, Windsor, Sandwich, Chatham, and Colchester, blacks comprised almost a quarter of the population. Yet, according to the white Canadian residents of these towns, all the fugitives had contributed to the communities were such chronic problems as illiteracy, indigence, and unemployment. During the thirty years of fugitive slave migration, white Canadians had witnessed the failure of black settlements at Oro, Dawn, and Wilberforce, the lack of harmonious black leadership, and two abortive attempts to maintain a black newspaper. Even William King's Elgin Settlement did not successfully wean blacks from dependence to autonomy. To these whites, the fugitives vividly presented "an unfavourable contrast with the hardy white laborer, who soon becomes acclimated, and by his physical energies exchanges poverty for independence." The rapid concentration of American blacks and their vexatious problems in a relatively small area resulted in the rapid growth of negrophobia in Canada West. As early as October 1843, the astute social critic, Dr. Thomas Rolph, had recognized that:

> It is only since your numbers have so greatly augmented, in this beautiful section of Canada, that all the farmers . . . have united together in firm resolve never again to give employment to a coloured man; it is only since your

151

> numbers have so increased, that Nelson Hacket was secreted in a dungeon to be given over to his master, and that Mr. Gallego was thrust out of a public steam-boat, a public stage coach, and a public tavern; . . . it is only in the Niagara District, in the vicinity of St. Catharine's, and in this western section of the province where your numbers abound, that such fearful extent of prejudice exists.[1]

Once anti-black sentiment took firm hold in Canada West, it became virtually impossible to eradicate. Most Canadians in the southwestern part of the province were willing to acknowledge the fugitives' right and need to immigrate, but were not willing to accept them on an equal basis with whites. "A white man who should admit a coloured person to his table, or allow his children to sit beside a coloured child in school would by so doing exclude himself and his family from the society of white persons," wrote one white Canadian official. "A feeling so universal, so inveterate, cannot be ignored." Social taboos and local prejudices engendered the segregation of blacks, particularly in the schools. Assuming the vanguard in the white refusal to sell land to fugitive slaves, the Canada Land Company reinforced the social and economic proscriptions on black mobility. At its worst, white Canadian prejudice, like its American counterpart, was founded on the pervading fear of miscegenation. To uproot the "inbred feeling of repugnance in the breast of almost every white person at hybridism, which must to some extent be the result of a commingling of the races" was compared, by one contemporary, with the uselessness of "trying to turn a stream against its head."[2] By the late 1850s, whites had irrevocably relegated blacks to a distinctly inferior caste.

Nevertheless, the fugitive slaves intensely sought to refute all implications of second-class citizenship. They exercised their right to vote whenever permitted, and they constantly agitated for equal educational opportunities. They appealed to the conscience of Canadians by asking in the words of one editorial,

> Is it right, is it according to the principles of freedom, is it in unison with the character of Britons, that, while the colored people are trying to elevate themselves in the scale of humanity. . . a few obscure men in the community should try to pick flaws in the laws, and hunt up decisions to deprive us of our . . . privileges; and that newspapers, which should be the palladium of freedom and good order, should stoop so low as to stir up the prejudices of the white population against the colored?[3]

While the fugitives occasionally won legal battles, ultimately they never gained what was most precious to them, social equality. Most attended separate schools and, dissatisfied with white Canadian churches, established separate black churches. The more segregation occurred, the wider the psychological distance grew between the unwelcome exiles and their uneasy white hosts.

In an almost desperate attempt to obtain control over their own destinies, the fugitives formed black cultural societies. The Dumas Literary Institute in Chatham, for example, brought in guest lecturers to speak on subjects of general interest to the blacks, while the Chatham Literary Society provided a forum for the talents of young blacks in the field of public speaking, writing, and music. Henry Bibb sponsored the Windsor Temperance Society while his wife organized a Mutual Improvement Society for the town's black women. Other black cultural societies included the Young Men's Education and Temperance Society in Amherstburg, and the Young Men's Excelsior Literary Association in Toronto. The Moral and Mental Improvement Society (African), also in Toronto, had "for its object the improvement of its members by means of essays and debates." As Harvey Jackson, a fugitive slave living in Simcoe, explained, "It is not enough for us to merely read, write and cipher in the common rudiments. We must dip . . . into the fine arts and sciences. We must become painters and sculptors and architects. In short, (we must be) scientific and it must be by our own exertions. . . . 'For knowledge is power.'" In 1859, the refugees established the Association for the Education and Elevation of the Coloured People of Canada, to promote educational opportunities for young blacks. Too, many black communities in Canada West supported their own bands and orchestras.[4]

By far the most important black cultural event occurred annually on Emancipation Day. This anniversary brought together all blacks in the province for a day of celebration and thanksgiving. There were parades, speeches, church services, military balls, fireworks, and banquets in every fugitive slave settlement. Preparations took several months, especially in Toronto and Hamilton where hundreds of blacks gathered for Emancipation Day festivities. Silk banners, special silk and satin dresses, and dinner tables that "fairly groaned under the weight of roast beef and fowls and pies and pastry of all kinds" characterized this black social occasion.[5] Significantly, it enabled the refugees to exhibit their awareness of the historical importance of Britain's abolition of slavery, and to lobby vocally for emancipation in the United States. More immediately, it provided the fugitives with a sorely needed respite from the difficulties of their daily lives, and provided a source of racial pride and consolation. For at least one day each year the fugitive slaves in Canada West experienced cultural unity and identity.

The blacks also established benevolent societies to facilitate the adjustment to Canadian society. The Provincial Union Association, founded in 1854, aimed not only to eliminate slavery in the United States but to promote racial harmony among Canadian citizens, to support the *Provincial Freeman,* and to encourage black efforts in literature, science, and the mechanical arts. The black Victorian

Reform Benevolent Society developed an insurance program that protected members in the event of sickness. Benefits included long-term indemnity, or interment in the case of death. The British Methodist Episcopal Itinerant Benefits Association financially supported sick and retired ministers of that church; and, black Freemason Lodges operated in Canada West. "To Africa is the world indebted for its knowledge of the mysteries of Ancient Freemasonry," wrote fugitive Martin Delany. The fugitives, then, thought of Freemasonry as more than a benevolent society to improve community life: it supplied one the primary sources of racial pride for blacks in the province. Another secret society, the Oddfellows, encouraged the fugitives to "obtain an honest livelihood, to be faithful to our Queen and country, to avoid turbulent measures, and to submit with reverence to the decisions of a Legislative Authority."[6] This, too, provided the fugitives with a means for expressing their identity.

The self-help orgnization with the largest number of members, however, was the True Band Society. Formed in 1854 by a group of the "most intelligent and enterprising colored people of Amherstburg," the first True Band had as one of its primary goals the elimination of begging by and for blacks. Open to both men and women, the True Band Society intended for members to be concerned with one anothers' welfare, to the extent of actively pursuing such plans "as may be for their mutual advantage." Other objectives included the improvement of schools and the ending of discrimination in education. The True Band proposed to unite all churches into one body that would disregard minor theological differences in favor of the recognition of basic similarities. The Society also urged its members to refer disputes to an in-house committee rather than airing them in public. And to help remove the widely held view that blacks depended on whites for survival, each branch was to "raise such funds among themselves as may be necessary for the poor, the sick, and the destitute fugitive newly arrived." Its ultimate purpose, though, was to prepare the refugees to be good Canadian citizens who would wisely use their political power. By 1856, fourteen chapters of the True Band Society flourished in the southwestern portion of the province.[7]

Nevertheless, black cultural and benevolent societies performed a limited function. In general, the aid societies helped the refugees feel better about themselves and their possibilities for the future. But the innumerable resolutions for improvement proved to be mere exercises in exhortation. Despite their many noble aims, these organizations failed to influence appreciably the lifestyles of the fugitive slaves. Certainly there was no tangible decrease of white Canadian prejudice, nor did the material lot of the fugitive slaves improve. With the onset of economic depression throughout the provinces in 1857, the usefulness of black societies turned primarily to providing for the poor.

Meanwhile, white Canadians became distracted and less concerned with the threat of racial amalgamation and the ruin of their society by blacks from within when they perceived an imperialist threat from without. When South Carolina led the first wave of southern states out of the Union in December 1860 and January 1861, residents of the Canadas anxiously awaited the inaugural address of the newly elected President. Though somewhat reassured by Lincoln's good sense and calm recognition of the gravity of the crisis, Canadians were deeply troubled over the appointment of William H. Seward as Secretary of State. Seward had long espoused annexation of the Canadas by the United States, and it was feared that he was not above arousing a foreign war in order to divert a domestic one. Exacerbating the situation all the more, the New York *Herald* nationalistically stated that the United States should annex the Canadas, and could do so with little hostility. The myopic Canadians would be "enlarged and expanded by . . . the energy of the people of the free States," declared the *Herald*, "who being cut off from a Southern field of enterprise, must . . . expand northward and westward. Such is the degree of manifest destiny, and such the programme of William H. Seward."[8] With such rhetoric, the possibility of invasion appeared very real to the wary white Canadians.

Such fears created consternation in the fugitive slave communities of Canada West, as well. In the event of a Southern victory, the Canadian extradition policy might be reversed to allow for the forcible return of blacks to slavery. Blacks in Canada also questioned the safety of relatives living in the United States. Just as worrisome to the refugees, perhaps, was the shifting public opinion in Canada. Most British North Americans supported abolition, so blacks logically assumed that they would support the North. After all, the publication in 1852 of Harriet Beecher Stowe's wildly popular *Uncle Tom's Cabin* had received a tremendously favorable response in Canada, prompting many to vow that "slavery must be destroyed." But when white Canadians realized that the moral issue of emancipation was less important to Lincoln than preservation of the Union, their endorsement of the North faded. Indeed, several major Canadian newspapers explicitly defended the Southern cause of independence. Many Canadian conservatives and liberals alike revised their thinking to sympathize with the South, spurred on by the number of American Southerners who vacationed or lived in Canada, particularly in St. Catharines.[9] When Queen Victoria proclaimed in May 1861, the strict neutrality of the Canadian provinces, the black community breathed a collective sigh of relief.

While white Canadian sentiment vacillated, most of the refugees wished to contribute their services to the war effort of the North. Like their American brethren, they attempted to enlist in the Union army, but were rejected early in the war, as Lincoln feared that the arming of blacks would alienate and frighten a large number of whites. When the Toronto *Globe* reported that blacks who "reached the

Union armies were being returned to their master," the attempts to enlist ceased.[10]

In January 1863, Lincoln's Emancipation Proclamation went into effect. If he had taken this action eighteen months earlier, white Canadians might have rallied much support for the North. Now it was considered hypocritical, and had little influence upon white Canadians. The fugitives, however, obviously saw this as an extremely important change in United States policy. It allowed nostalgic refugees to consider returning, but because blacks still could not enlist and no program to assist emancipated slaves had not yet been created, it did not lure them immediately homeward.

In late summer 1863, Lincoln initiated the action that would commence drawing the fugitive slaves out of Canada West. He declared in August that blacks could join the Union army and the refugees responded with alacrity and enthusiasm. Upon receiving the news, the Elgin Settlement held a town meeting where forty men immediately volunteered to fight; eventually at least seventy enlisted from that town alone. Hundreds of blacks traveled across the border to the closest recruiting station, in Detroit. The committee in charge of raising a black regiment in Massachusetts successfully sought recruits from the neighboring province. Fugitives Martin R. Delany and Mary Ann Shadd returned to the States to become recruiting agents, enlisting many blacks in Michigan, Illinois, and Indiana. Another young black who had once belonged to William King became the recruiting sergeant for the First Michigan Colored Infantry, enlisting fugitives throughout the southwestern portion of Canada West. Josiah Henson urged all able-bodied refugees to join the Northern army and even advanced money to those who joined. Concerned that young black enlistees might not receive the bounty to which they were entitled, Henson actually escorted them to and from the recruiting station. If the fugitives needed prodding, the black British Methodist Episcopal Churches offered it. At their annual conference in 1863 they resolved, "that we are in favour of colored men, in compliance with the request of the Federal Government, shouldering arms and marching to the battle-field to put down the ungodly man-stealers, who, in this war, have no rights which coloured men are bound to respect.... May the God of battles bless the right and crush the wrong!"[11]

The fugitive slaves also received, in 1863, a vivid reminder of their fragile status in Canada West. Across the river in Detroit, a major race riot ensued where two blacks were killed, more than twenty seriously injured, and some two hundred left homeless by the burning and razing of their houses. Fugitive slaves visiting from nearby Windsor were attacked and pursued across the border by angry whites who, in the process, killed one of the blacks. To the shock and dismay of the black community, local white Canadians and militiamen never came to the aid of their black fellow countrymen, refusing to get involved in the racial dispute.[12] This proved once again that the fugitives in the provinces could claim only strict legal rights through the courts in their new home. Even in the fundamental matter of personal protection, blacks received inferior treatment from white Canadians.

Following this incident, Samuel Gridley Howe made his investigation of the condition of the refugees in Canada West. His report to the Freedmen's Inquiry Commission may have indeed influenced Lincoln's plan for the future of emancipated slaves in the United States for in his conclusion, Howe observed that blacks should not be placed in segregated communities, nor should they reside in large numbers in one locality. Both circumstances, he believed, led to the white prejudice in Canada West and hence the fugitives made "less progress than where they form a small part of the local population." Howe proposed that the best communities maintain a ratio of one thousand blacks to fifteen or twenty thousand whites. This decreased the likelihood of racial animosity but allowed blacks to "imitate the best features of white civilization, and (to) improve rapidly." Perceptively, during his tour Howe noted that Canadian prejudice was "manifested with the same intensity, as in the United States," yet he offered no solution save for the above. He did, however, emphasize that

> the lesson taught by this and other emigration is, that the negro does best when let alone, and that we must beware of all attempts to prolong his servitude, even under the pretext of taking care of him. The white man has tried taking care of the negro, by slavery, by apprenticeship, by colonization, and has failed disastrously in all; now let the negro try to take care of himself. For . . . all the suffering and misery which his people may suffer in their efforts for self-guidance and support will be held cheap, if they bring about emancipation from the control of the white.[13]

Howe left the fugitives with the impression that the United States government cared about the plight of freed slaves and Lincoln reinforced this with the establishment in March 1865 of the Freedmen's Bureau and the Freedmen's Hospital. When the war ended one month later, the return of the fugitive slaves southward began in earnest.

The blacks left Canada West for many reasons. Just as white prejudice and limited freedom originally propelled them from the United States, Canadian prejudice stimulated them to return home. Perhaps Henry Bibb had described it best in an editorial in the *Voice of the Fugitive* some years earlier, when he denoted the differences between anti-black sentiment in the United States and that in Canada West. "Canadian Negro hate is incomparably MEANER than the Yankee article," wrote Bibb, "(for) Canadian Negro hate is not ORIGINAL. Copied, aped, deviltry is always meaner than the original diabolism.... A meaner set of negro haters, God in his inexplicable mercy, does not suffer to live, than these poor fools of Canadian second-generation imitations." Bibb's statement reflected the general opinion of the fugitive slaves, and was echoed by other contemporaries. Samuel Ringgold Ward claimed, "It is undeniable that Negrohate, to an almost fiendish degree, is to be found more in Canada and Nova Scotia." In Dresden, the white Reverend Mr. Hughes acknowledged that the Canadians carried their prejudice "to a more disagreeable extent than native-born Americans." Mary Ann Shadd also admitted that the fugitive slaves could effect no change on white Canadian opinion. She likened the "anti-slavery Negro hater" in the province to a rhinoceros, whose hide is so thick as to prevent any impression upon him.[14] Many of the refugees, then, simply decided to leave Canada West because they believed that white Canadian prejudice and discrimination would never be eradicated.

Other fugitives moved because they believed they could contribute to the process of Reconstruction. The Emancipation Proclamation and Lincoln's Reconstruction plans created optimism among the blacks to feel that American society could be rebuilt. Black ministers returned to the United States as missionaries to "supply their spiritual and temporal wants." The Reverend L.C. Chambers of the British Methodist Episcopal Church also induced members of his congregation to join him in meeting this "call" of divine Providence. Less idealistic refugees saw the economic opportunity of repatriation. According to John Hurst, formerly associated with the Colonial Church and School Society Mission, "Wages are higher there than in Canada, and work more continuous, and, of course, men with families must be expected to be influenced by these things." The black Bishop Willis Nazrey put it more bluntly. He accused the black opportunists of going "in search of fortunes and high and exalted positions."[15]

The return of the fugitive slaves fulfilled the prophecy of hostile white Canadians who had only viewed them as temporary guests in their province. As the *Advocate of Freedom* reported, the blacks considered themselves "but sojourners in the northern regions, and...many of them look with longing eyes to the native 'Sunny South.' " Essentially, these refugees perceived of themselves as American expatriots, and retained national identification with the United States. Robert Dale Owen, who accompanied Samuel Gridley Howe on his investigation tour, had predicted that once emancipation occurred, the "shivering" fugitives would "go home" because of the "primal law...of thermal lines." Though the unfavorable climate argument may have been of some influence, the blacks, themselves, consistently denied its validity.[16]

The overriding motive for the return of the blacks was, understandably, to rejoin "lost" family and relatives. As early as 1840, abolitionist Hiram Wilson foretold this event. He envisioned that after a general emancipation, "The majority would soon speed their way back to the embrace of their brethren and kindred at the south." At least one-third of Benjamin Drew's interviews with the fugitive slaves in 1856 contain some reference to absent relatives. Refugees Christopher Nichols and Henry Atkinson, both of St. Catharines, wanted but never expected to see their loved ones again and their neighbor David West sorely missed his wife and four children, who were "perpetually on my mind." Thoughts and memories of people from whom most of the refugees had been separated for less than a decade called them back. The blacks had not "taken firm root in Canada," wrote Samuel Gridley Howe, "and they earnestly desire(d) to go to the southern region of the United States, partly from love of warmth, but more from love of *home*."[17]

With this in mind, the fugitive slaves departed from Canada West almost en masse. From the peak figure of approximately 40,000 in 1859, the number of blacks dwindled to fewer than 15,000 by 1871. The precipitous decline in population had immediate reverberations on those refugees who remained. Bishop Nazrey explained the effect on the black churches: "Owing to the great rush of our people back to the United States just after the close of the war, our church ...seemed in quite a feeble state." Black cultural and benevolent societies disbanded, black separate schools closed, and black communities virtually disappeared. By 1869, for instance, it was determined that the blacks in Windsor "must be looked upon as simply forming a portion of a pastoral charge, and the Mission (there) considered a white one, with a sprinkling of coloured people." It became easy for white Canadians to once again neglect or ignore black problems in the province. The unfavorable circumstances surrounding the blacks in Canada would continue to decline until well after the turn of the century.[18]

Even the blacks who stayed at Elgin, the most successful black community in Canada West, developed a plan to buy 20,000 acres in the South and establish a colony there. Their proposal required the sale of their Canadian land, but it seemed a worthwhile endeavor to relocate if the new community could provide guidance and inspiration to southern blacks. In September 1865, the Reverend William King went to Washington to inquire for the fugitives about the feasibility of their project. Realizing the major difficulties that would face the blacks at a "New Buxton," General Oliver Otis Howard, Commissioner of the Freedmen's Bureau, advised against its establishment. King reported this to the blacks in Canada West, and suggested as an alternative that the educated individuals "go and give instruction to their brethren in ignorance."[19]

This they did. Most of the fugitive slaves from Elgin who were qualified to teach "went south," according to King, "and got good situations as teachers in the Schools of the Freedmen where they are now doing good service." Several with a higher degree of classical education attended the only university funded by the Freedmen's Bureau, Howard University in Washington, D.C., in preparation for the practice of law or medicine. Jerome Riley became a doctor in this manner and worked as a physician in the Freedmen's Hospital in Washington. His brother, John Riley, went to Louisville, Kentucky, where by 1870 he became minister to a large Baptist congregation. King reported that one of Elgin's black women also settled in Louisville, where she taught school for many years. Another teacher of a large school of emancipated slaves residing in Missouri also conducted a Sabbath school. Perhaps the most famous Elginite, James Rapier, returned to his native Alabama ostensibly to teach. There he became involved in state politics almost immediately, assisting in the drafting of the new state constitution. He then helped to compose the platform for the Alabama Republican Party, writing "We are the friends and advocates of free speech, free press, free schools,...and henceforth there is to be no discrimination made between the inhabitants of this state in civil and political rights, on account of color or previous condition." Eventually, Rapier became a union organizer, a journalist, and a United States Congressman.[20]

Other blacks from the province who had gained either secular or religious education also labored for the improvement of the emancipated slaves in the United States. W.H. Day was appointed first the Superintendent of Schools for the Freedmen's Bureau District of Maryland, and later the only black member of the Board of School Control in Harrisburg, Pennsylvania. The Reverend Charles Pearce of the British Methodist Episcopal Church organized the African Methodist Episcopal Church in Florida, and went on to serve as a state senator. A black Baptist preacher of Canada West, Henry P. Jacobs, established Baptist Associations in the western portion of Mississippi. T.W. Stringer also returned to Mississippi, acting as the General Superintendent of Missions and Presiding Elder for the A.M.E. Church. He too entered politics, participating in 1868 in the state's constitutional convention as "the most powerful political leader of his race"; ultimately he won an appointment as a Circuit Court judge in Mississippi.[21]

The members of the prominent Shadd family saw much success in the United States after the Civil War. Mary Ann Shadd Cary studied law at Howard University and received her degree in 1870 at the age of forty-seven. She set up a law office in Washington, D.C., and continued her political activism by crusading for women's rights. One brother, Abram D. Shadd, became a judge in Arkansas, but chose in the 1870s to resettle in Chatham while another, Isaac, gained membership to the Mississippi Legislature, and rose to the position of Speaker of the state's House of Representatives. Emaline, the youngest sibling, taught at Howard University before permanently relocating to Kent County, Ontario.[22]

The exile of the fugitive slaves in Canada West had indeed served certain individuals well. Even the minimal education provided by separate schools in the province gave those blacks an advantage over most American blacks. For the vast thousands of refugees, however, their visit to British North America was merely a waystation in their lives. Still poor, they traveled the routes of the Underground Railroad in reverse, fulfilling the claim "that if they could have the same privileges in the States that they have here, they would not remain a moment."[23]

In the final analysis, the only significant difference between the existence of blacks prior to 1860 in Canada West and their condition in the United States was the extension of legal rights to refugees by the Canadian Government. This one fact entitled Canada West to be described correctly as the fugitives' asylum. This one reality superseded in importance all of the Canadian abolitionists' rhetoric and the American slaveholders' expostulation. The privilege to vote, to take legal action in court, and to testify before the judiciary gave the refugees hope for a better life. Faced with widespread social discrimination both north and south of the forty-ninth parallel, thousands of blacks preferred to be governed by the Queen's law that did not exclude them. They fervently proclaimed, "That we have reason to thank God for the impartial character and administration of the laws of this our adopted country." Perhaps, though, it was even more basic than that. Legal freedom portended complete freedom. And, while the latter was never realized, the former had prompted Samuel Gridley Howe to see the fugitive slaves' situation in terms of a Biblical adaptation. "Each of them may say," he wrote, "as millions (in the United States) will soon say,—'When I was a *slave*, I spake as a *slave*, I understood as a *slave*, I thought as a *slave*; but when I became a *free man*, I put away slavish things.' "[24]

NOTES

1. Rolph, *Emigration and Colonization*, pp. 203-11.
2. *Annual Report of the Normal, Model and Common Schools in Upper Canada* (1871), p. 101;
    Toronto *Leader*, 12 December 1862; and
    Prentice and Houston, *Family, School and Society*, p. 235.
3. Toronto *Globe*, 3 January 1863.
4. *Provincial Freeman*, 6 May 1854, 7 April 1855, and 12 April 1856;
    Taylor Family Scrapbook, Fort Malden National Historic Park, Amherstburg, Ontario;
    Toronto City Directory, 1859-1860 (Toronto, 1860), p. 222;
    Hodgins, ed., *Documentary History*, XIV, p. 148.
5. *Provincial Freeman*, 3 June and 29 July 1854;
    Hamilton *Spectator*, 21 June 1824.
6. *Provincial Freeman*, 19 August and 28 October 1854, 5 and 12 April 1856;
    Minutes and Proceedings of the First Annual B.M.E. Conference (Chatham, 1856), p.

p. 17;

Martin R. Delany, *The Origin and Objects of Ancient Freemasonry, Its Introduction into the United States and Legitimacy Among Colored Men* (Pittsburgh, 1853), pp. 22-35; and

W. Sandfield Johnston, *Odd Fellowship in Ontario up to 1923* (Toronto, 1923), pp. 9-31.

7. *Provincial Freeman,* 17 April, 30 June, and 29 December 1855;
Drew, *North-Side View of Slavery,* pp. 236-37.

8. New York *Herald,* 9 February 1861;
Toronto *Leader,* 5 March 1861; and
Robin W. Winks, *Canada and the United States: The Civil War Years* (Baltimore, 1960), pp. 23-51.

9. *Provincial Freeman,* 12 August 1854 and 15 September 1855.
In Canada West, Southerners were found in St. Catharines, Toronto, London, and Niagara Falls. In these areas, black women found ready employment as cooks because of their knowledge of Southern dishes. In Montreal (Canada East), there was "a knot of Southern families, in a sort of American Siberia at a very comfortable hotel, who nurse their wrath against the Yankees.... They form a nucleus for sympathizing society to cluster around." A proposed meeting in Niagara of Southerners residing in the provinces never took place. However, Jacob Thompson of Toronto and other exiled Southerners became active Confederate agents in Canada. For more on this topic see
Fred Landon, *Western Ontario and the American Frontier* (Toronto, 1941), pp. 210-11.

10. Toronto *Globe,* as quoted in Simpson, "Blacks in Ontario," p. 895.

11. *Minutes of the Seventh Annual Conference of the B.M.E. Church* (Hamilton, 1863), p. 7;
"Recruitment Permit for the State of Indiana, August 15, 1864," in the Mary Ann Shadd Cary Papers, Moorland-Spingarn Research Center, Howard University, Washington, D.C.;
William King Autobiography, pp. 413-14, 416-19, in the King Papers, Public Archives of Canada, Ottawa.

12. Toronto *Globe,* 20 August 1864;
Toronto *Leader,* 5 May 1865;
A Thrilling Narrative from the Lips of the Sufferers of the Late Detroit Riot, March 6, 1863 (Detroit, 1863), pp. 12-13, 20;
David M. Katzman, *Before the Ghetto: Black Detroit in the Nineteenth Century* (Urbana, 1973), pp. 44-48.

13. Howe, *Refugees from Slavery in Canada West,* pp. 101-4.

14. *Voice of the Fugitive,* 4 November 1852;

Frederick Douglass' Paper, 20 April 1855;

Provincial Freeman, 7 June 1856;

Mission to the Colored Population in Canada 4 (1865), p. 67.

15. Amherstburg Baptist Association, *Minutes* (1867), p. 8, McMaster Divinity College, Hamilton, Ontario;

Mission to the Colored Population in Canada, *Annual Report* (1869), p. 10;

Minutes of the Ninth Annual Conference of the B.M.E. Church (June 1865), p. 3.

16. *Advocate of Freedom*, 14 May 1840; and

Robert Dale Owen, *The Wrong of Slavery, The Right of Emancipation and the Future of the African Race in the United States* (Philadelphia, 1864), pp. 210-11. For his opinion about the effect of the climate on blacks, Howe relied chiefly on two white Canadian physicians. Dr. Fisher of the Provincial Lunatic Asylum stated that "the colored people stand the climate very badly." Dr. T. Mack of St. Catharines declared of the fugitive slaves that "this climate will completely efface them." Both doctors went on to elaborate the specific physical problems produced by the change of climate. For more on this see

Howe, *Refugees from Slavery in Canada West*, pp. 21-22, 35-37, 101.

17. *Advocate of Freedom*, 29 October 1840;

Drew, *North-Side View of Slavery*, pp. 71, 82-89; and

Howe, *Refugees from Slavery in Canada West*, p. 102.

18. *Census of Canada*, p. 486;

Minutes of the Third General Conference of the B.M.E. Church (Hamilton, 1868), p. 5; and

Mission to the Colored Population of Canada, *Annual Report* (1869), p. 10.

19. William King Autobiography, p. 432, in the King Papers, Public Archives of Canada, Ottawa.

For more on General O.O. Howard see

William S. McFeely, *Yankee Stepfather: General O.O. Howard and the Freedmen* (New York, 1968).

20. William King Autobiography, pp. 124-25, 130, in the King Papers, Public Archives of Canada, Ottawa.

For more on Rapier, see

Eugene Feldman, *Black Power in Old Alabama: The Life and Stirring Times of James T. Rapier, Afro-American Congressman from Alabama, 1839-1883* (Chicago, 1968);

Loren Schweninger, *James T. Rapier and Reconstruction* (Chicago, 1978); and

idem, "A Fugitive Negro in the Promised Land: James Rapier in Canada, 1856-1864," *Ontario History* 67 (January 1975), pp. 29-44.

21. Simpson, "Blacks in Ontario," pp. 904-6; and

Vernon Lane Wharton, *The Negro in Mississippi 1865-1890* (Chapel Hill, N.C.,

1947), p. 149.

22.   *New National Era,* 26 February 1874;

       "Life Sketch of Mary Ann Shadd Cary" and "Notes on Other Members of the Family of Mary Ann Shadd," in the Mary Ann Shadd Cary Papers, Public Archives of Canada, Ottawa;

       unpublished manuscript, "Mary Ann Shadd Cary, 1823-1893" and "Family, Personal and Business Letters," in the Mary Ann Shadd Cary Papers, Moorland-Spingarn Research Center, Howard University, Washington, D.C.;

       Shadd Family Papers, 1837-1972, in the Mary Ann Shadd Cary Collection, American Missionary Association Archives, New Orleans; and

       Bearden and Butler, *Shadd,* pp. 209-23.

23.   Howe, *Refugees from Slavery in Canada West,* p. 44.

24.   Toronto *Globe,* 26 October 1852; and

       Howe, *Refugees from Slavery in Canada West,* p. iv.

BIBLIOGRAPHY

PRIMARY SOURCES

Manuscripts

American Missionary Association Archives, Dillard University, New Orleans
    Mary Ann Shadd Cary Papers
    Hiram Wilson Letters
Amherstburg, Ontario
    Alvin McCurdy Private Collection of Minutes of Public School Trustees, 1851-
    1882
Detroit Public Library, Burton Collection, Detroit
    Amherstburg History Files
    Blacks in Canada Files
Fort Malden National Historic Park Museum, Amherstburg, Ontario
    David Botsford Papers
    Fugitive Slave Files and Black Assessment Rolls
Hamilton Public Library, Hamilton, Ontario
    Black History Files
    Hiram Walker Historical Museum, Windsor, Ontario
    Black History Files
Historical Society of Pennsylvania, Philadelphia
    Journal of Pennsylvania Anti-Slavery Society Underground Railroad
    William Still Collection

Kent County Historical Museum, Kent, Ontario
    Buxton Presbyterian Church Records
    Chatham School Trustees, Memorandum, 1854-1861
    Session Book, Buxton North, 1858-1880
Library of Congress, Washington, D.C.
    American Anti-Slavery Society Minutes
    Carter G. Woodson Collection of Negro Papers
McMaster Divinity College, Hamilton, Ontario
    Amherstburg Baptist Association Minutes, 1841-1861
    James W. Johanson Papers on Amherstburg Baptist Association
    Sandwich Baptist Church Minutes
Moorland-Spingam Research Center, Howard University, Washington, D.C.
    Mary Ann Shadd Cary Papers
National Archives, Washington, D.C.
    American Freedmen's Inquiry Commission Interviews
    Department of the Interior's Records Pertaining to Slave Trade and Negro
    Colonization
North Buxton Museum, North Buxton, Ontario
    British Methodist Episcopal Church Records
    William King Diary of 1856 Trip to Louisiana
    Shadd Family Records
Ohio State Historical Society, Columbus
    Wilbur H. Siebert Papers on Fugitive Slaves in Canada
Ontario Provincial Archives, Toronto
    Mary Ann Shadd Cary Papers
    John Charlton Papers
    Crown Land Papers, Upper Canada, 1830-1841
    John George Hodgins Papers
    Mary O'Brien Journal
    Provincial Statutes, 1841-1866
    John Beverly Robinson Papers
    Peter Russell Papers
    Egerton Ryerson Papers
    John Graves Simcoe Papers
    Rev. William Wye Smith Papers
    John Strachan Papers, Letter Book, 1839-1868
    Toronto City Council Papers, 1834-1896, and accompanying petitions from
    black citizens
    Wesleyan Methodist Church (black) of Toronto, Minutes
    Western District Court Minutes, 1821-1870

Public Archives of Canada, Ottawa
 George Brown Papers, 1851-1867
 Canada Original Correspondence
 Canadian Acts
 Canadian Sessional Papers
 Mary Ann Shadd Cary Papers
 M.M. Dillon Papers, vol. 59 of Civil Secretary's Correspondence, 1840-1863
 Dispatches from the Colonial Office, 1794-1865
 Dispatches from the Lieutenant Governors to the Governor General, 1839-1841
 William King Papers
 Letter Book of Dispatches from the Colonial Office, 1842-1855
 Letter Book of Dispatches to the Colonial Office
 Minute Books of the Executive Council, 1841-1867
 Minutes of the Colonial and Continental Church Society
 Microfilm Hansard, clipping files of Parliamentary Debates
 James Murray Papers
 William Dummer Power Papers
 Upper Canada Land Petitions
 Upper Canada State Papers, 1791-1841
 Upper Canada Sundries, Calendars, 1837-1840
Public Library of Toronto, Toronto
 Anderson R. Abbott Papers
 William Jarvis Papers
 Elizabeth Russell Diary
 Wilberforce Lyceum Educating Society for Moral and Mental Improvement, Constitution and By-Laws
Public Library of Windsor, Windsor
 Black History Files
 Windsor Board of School Trustees, Minute Books
Schomburg Center for Black Culture, New York Public Library, New York City
 Robin W. Winks Collection on Blacks in Canada
University of Pennsylvania Library, Philadelphia
 Original run of the *Provincial Freeman*
University of Western Ontario Library, London
 Black History Files
 Fred Landon Papers
 Regional History—County Records Collections with accompanying petitions from black citizens
Victoria University (United Church of Canada Archives), Toronto

Minutes of Synod of Presbyterian Church of Canada, vol. 1: 1844-1852; vol. 2: 1852-1861

Printed Minutes, Letters, Directories, and Documents

Abel, Eloise, and Klingberg, Frank J.
> *A Sidelight on Anglo-American Relations, 1839-1858. Furnished by the Correspondence of Lewis Tappan and others with the British and Foreign Anti-Slavery Society.* Lancaster, Pa., 1927.

African Methodist Episcopal Church.
> *Minutes and Proceedings of the Annual Conferences of the African Methodist Episcopal Church, Canada District, 1853, 1855, 1856.*

"Banishment of the People of Color from Cincinnati."
> *Journal of Negro History* 8 (July 1923), pp. 331-32.

Blassingame, John W., ed.
> *Slave Testimony: Two Centuries of Letters, Speeches, Interviews, and Autobiographies.* Baton Rouge, 1977.

Calendar of Gerrit Smith Papers in the Syracuse University Library.
> Vol. 1 of Historical Record Survey. Albany, 1941.

Canada.
> Bureau of Statistics. *Census of Canada,* 1851, 1861, 1871.

Canada.
> *Journals of the Legislative Assembly,* 1849-1851.

Canada.
> *Journals of the Legislative Council,* 1850.

Canada.
> *Sessional Papers,* 1 Parliament, 2 session, II, 1842;
> 5 Parliament, 1 session, XIII, 1854;
> 6 Parliament, 4 session, IV, 1861.

Canada West.
> Education Office. *Annual Reports of Normal, Model and Common Schools in Upper Canada,* 1850-1870.

Canadian Anti-Slavery, Baptist Association.
> *Constitution, By-Laws, Minutes* for 1854.

Convention of the Colored Population.
> Report of the Convention Held at Drummondsville, August 1847. Toronto, 1847.

Cruikshank, Emest A., ed.
> *The Correspondence of Lieut. Governor John Graves Simcoe, with Allied Documents relating to His Administration of the Government of Upper*

Canada. Toronto, 1923.

————, ed.

"Petitions for Grants of Land in Upper Canada. Second Series, 1796-1799."
Ontario Historical Society Papers and Records 26 (1930), pp. 100-14.

"Documents Illustrating the Condition of Refugees From Slavery in Upper Canada Before 1860."
Journal of Negro History 13 (April 1928), pp. 199-207.

Duncombe, Charles.

Report Upon the Subject of Education Made to the Parliament of Upper Canada. Toronto, 1836.

Hodgins, John George.

Documentary History of Education in Upper Canada: From the Passing of the Constitutional Act of 1791 to the Close of Rev. Dr. Ryerson's Administration of the Education Department in 1876. 28 vols. Toronto, 1894-1910.

————.

Historical and Other Papers and Documents Illustrative of the Education System of Ontario, 1792-1871. 6 vols. Toronto, 1911-1921.

————.

The Legislation and History of Separate Schools in Upper Canada: From 1841 until 1876. Toronto, 1897.

"Letters of Henry Bibb and his wife to Gerrit Smith."
Journal of Negro History 27 (October 1942), p. 441.

"Letters of Hiram Wilson to Miss Hannah Gray concerning Missionary Work Among Refugees in Upper Canada."
Journal of Negro History 14 (July 1929), pp. 344-50.

"Letters of Negroes—Largely Personal and Private."
Journal of Negro History 11 (July 1926), pp. 62-214.

"Letters to Anti-Slavery Workers and Agencies."
Journal of Negro History 10 (July 1925), pp. 345-568.

Manning, William R., ed.

Diplomatic Correspondence of the United States: Canadian Relations, 1784-1860. 3 vols. Washington, D.C., 1940-1943.

Nichols, Charles H.

Black Men in Chains: Narratives of Escaped Slaves. New York, 1972.

————.

Many Thousand Gone: The Ex-Slaves' Account of Their Bondage and Freedom. Bloomington, Indiana, 1969.

"Petition of Coloured People Prepared at Ancaster, Upper Canada, July 25, 1828."
Journal of Negro History 15 (January 1930), pp. 115-16.

Railton's *Directory for the City of London, C.W.,* 1857.

Report of the Past History and Present Condition of The Common or Public Schools of the City of Toronto. Toronto, 1859.

Ryerson, Egerton.

    Special Report on the Separate School Provisions of the School Law of Upper Canada. Toronto, 1858.

Soutar, James ed.

    The Chatham Directory and County Gazetteer. Chatham, 1886.

Still, William.

    Underground Railroad Records. Philadelphia, 1886.

Western District.

    Municipal Council Minutes, 1843, 1844, 1845, 1848.

Woodson, Carter G.

    Free Negro Heads of Families in the United States in 1830: Together with a Brief Treatment of the Free Negro. Washington, D.C., 1925.

———.

    The Mind of the Negro as Reflected in Letters Written during the Crisis, 1800-1860. Washington, D.C., 1926.

Reports of Societies

American Anti-Slavery Society.

    Annual Reports. 1834-1840, 1855-1860.

American Colonization Society.

    Annual Reports. 1818-1860.

American and Foreign Anti-Slavery Society.

    Annual Reports. 1847-1853.

American Missionary Association.

    Annual Reports. 1846-1865.

Amherstburg Missionary Association.

    Quarterly Mission Journal. 1852.

Anti-Slavery Society of Canada.

    Annual Reports. 1852, 1853, 1857.

Anti-Slavery Society of Canada.

    Constitution and By-Laws. 1851.

British and Foreign Anti-Slavery Society.

    Annual Reports. London, 1840-1851, 1855-1863.

Canada Mission *Annual Reports.* 1842-1844.

Canadian Baptist Magazine. vols. 1-4. 1838-1841.

Colonial Church and School Society.

Annual Reports. 1853-1865.
Colonial Church and School Society.
    Occasional Papers. 1-4.
Elgin Association. *Annual Reports.*
Minutes and Proceedings of the General Convention for the Improvement of the Colored Inhabitants of Canada Held by Adjournments in Amherstburg, C.W., June 16th and 17th, 1853. Windsor, 1853.
Niagara Baptist Association.
    Minutes of the Thirty-Seventh Anniversary Meeting, 1856.
Report of the Refugees' Home Society, Held in Detroit, Michigan, August 25, 1852. Windsor, 1852.

Pamphlets

American Baptist Free Mission Society.
    Anti-Slavery Missions, A Brief View of the Origin, Principles and Operation of the American Baptist Free Mission Society. Bristol, 1851.
American Society of the Free Persons of Colour.
    Constitution of the American Society of the Free Persons of Colour, for Improving Their Condition in the United States, for Purchasing Lands; and for the Establishment of a Settlement in Upper Canada. Philadelphia, 1831.
Binga, Anthony.
    Binga's Addresses on Several Occasions. Virginia Union University, n.d.
———.
    Sermon and Address Delivered by A. Binga Jr., Pastor First Baptist Church Manchester, Va. Richmond, 1881.
British and Foreign Anti-Slavery Society.
    Proceedings of the General Anti-Slavery Convention Held in London, 1840. London, 1841.
Brown, George.
    The American War and Slavery: Speech of the Honourable George Brown at the Anniversary Meeting of the Anti-Slavery Society of Canada. Toronto, February 3, 1863. Manchester, 1863.
Brown, Paola.
    Speech on Slavery. Delivered at Hamilton City Hall, February 7, 1851.
Henning, Thomas.
    Slavery in the Churches, Religious Societies, etc. A Review:...with Prefatory Remarks by J.E. Linton. n.p., n.d.
Hutchinson, Edward.

The Fugitive Slave Circulars: or, England the Protector of the Negro Slave.
n.p., 1876.

King, William, and Robert Burns.
Fugitive Slaves in Canada, Elgin Settlement. 1860.

Linton, John J.E.
Slavery Question, Report of the New York General Association, 26 August 1855. Stratford, C.W., October 15, 1855.

Public Prayer for Civil Rulers and the Slavery Question Being a Contrast Between the Apologists for Slavery in the United States and the Ministers of Religion in Great Britain and Her Colonies.
By an anonymous correspondent of the *Ecclesiastical and Missionary Record.* (n.p., 1851).

Rochester Ladies Anti-Slavery Society.
Autographs for Freedom. Boston, 1853.

Scoble, John.
"Fugitive Settlement in Canada." *Uncle Tom's Cabin Almanac or Abolitionist Memento.* London, 1853.

Shreve, Dorthy Shadd.
Pathfinders of Liberty and Truth: A Century with the Amherstburg Regular Missionary Baptist Association. n.p., 1940.

Descriptive Works

Bigsby, John J.
The Shoe and Canoe, or Pictures of Travel in the Canadas, Illustrative of Their Scenery and Colonial Life. London, 1850.

Brown, James B.
Views of Canada and the Colonists. Edinburgh, 1851.

Carruthers, J.
Retrospect of Thirty-Six Years' Residence in Canada West; Being a Christian Journal and Narrative. Hamilton, 1861.

Darling, William S.
Sketches of Canadian Life, Lay and Ecclesiastical. London, 1849.

Delany, Martin Robison.
The Condition, Elevation, Emigration and Destiny of the Coloured People of the United States—Politically Considered. Philadelphia, 1852.

Drew, Benjamin.
The Refugee: A North-Side View of Slavery. Boston, 1856.

Emigration to Upper Canada from the Establishment of the Canada Company until the Present Period. London, 1842.

Gourlay, Robert.
  Statistical Account of Upper Canada and General Introduction. London, 1822.
Guillet, Edwin C.
  Early Life in Upper Canada. Toronto, 1963.
  The History of the County of Brant, Ontario. Toronto, 1883.
Hodgins, John George.
  The Establishment of Schools and Colleges in Ontario, 1792-1910. Toronto, 1910.
Hood, Bishop J.W.
  One Hundred Years of the African Methodist Episcopal Zion Church or the Centennial of African Methodism. New York, 1895.
Howe, Samuel Gridley.
  The Refugees from Slavery in Canada West: Report to the Freedman's Inquiry Commission. Boston, 1864.
Howison, John.
  Sketches of Upper Canada. Edinburgh, 1821.
Jameson, Anna.
  Sketches in Canada and Rambles among the Red Men. London, 1852.
Johnson, Homer.
  From Dixie to Canada: Romances and Realities of the Underground Railroad. Orwell, Ohio, 1896.
Kohl, J.G.
  Travels in Canada. 2 vols. London, 1861.
Logan, James.
  Notes of a Journey Through Canada, the United States of America and the West Indies. Edinburgh, 1838.
Mitchell, William M.
  The Underground Railroad from Slavery to Freedom. London, 1856.
Murray, Amelia M.
  Letters from the United States, Cuba and Canada. London, 1856.
Murray, Henry Anthony.
  Lands of the Slave and the Free: Or, Cuba, the United States and Canada. London, 1855.
Payne, Daniel A.
  The Semi-Centenary and the Retrospection of the African Methodist Episcopal Church in the United States of America. Baltimore, 1866.
———.
  History of the African Methodist Episcopal Church. Nashville, 1891.
Petitt, E.M.

Underground Railroad Sketches. Fredonia, New York, 1879.
Rolph, Thomas.
A Brief Account, Together with Observations Made During a Visit to the West Indies and a Tour through the United States of America, 1832-1833; Together with a Statistical Account of Upper Canada. Dundas, 1836.

————.

A Descriptive and Statistical Account of Canada: Showing Its Great Adaptation For British Emigration. London, 1841.

————.

Emigration and Colonization: Embodying the Results of a Mission to Great Britain and Ireland, During the Years 1839, 1840, 1841 and 1842. London, 1844.
Shadd, Mary Ann.
A Plea for Emigration or Notes on Canada West in Its Moral, Social and Political Aspects (with Suggestions Respecting Mexico, West Indies, and Vancouver Island) for the Information of Coloured Immigrants. Detroit, 1852.
Shaw, John.
A Ramble through the United States, Canada, and the West Indies. London, 1856.
Shirreff, Patrick.
A Tour through North America. Edinburgh, 1835.
Simms, James M.
The First Coloured Baptist Church in North America. Lippincott, c. 1880.
Smith, William H.
Canada: Past, Present and Future, being a Historical, Geographical and Statistical Account of Canada West. 2 vols. Toronto, 1851.
Still, William.
The Underground Railroad. Philadelphia, 1872.
Stowe, Harriet Beecher.
The Key to Uncle Tom's Cabin. London, 1853.

————.

Uncle Tom's Cabin or Life among the Lowly. Boston, 1852.
Stuart, Charles.
The Emigrant's Guide to Upper Canada; or Sketches of the Present State of That Province Collected from a Residence There During the Years 1817, 1819, 1820. London, 1820.

————.

Remarks on the Colony of Liberia and the American Colonization Society with Some Account of the Settlement of Coloured People at Wilberforce,

Upper Canada. London, 1832.
Talbot, Edward Allen.
Five Years' Residence in the Canadas. London, 1824.
Talbot, Rev. H.
A History of the Amherstburg Regular Baptist Association: Its Auxiliaries and Churches. London, 1844.
Troy, William.
Hair-Breadth Escapes From Slavery to Freedom. Manchester, 1861.
Wayman, Rev. A.W.
My Recollections of African Methodist Episcopal Ministers or Forty Years' Experience in the A.M.E. Church. Philadelphia, 1881.

Autobiographies and Memoirs

Bâby, William Lewis.
Souvenirs of the Past. Windsor, 1896.
Bethune, A.N.
Memoir of the Right Reverend John Strachan. Toronto, 1870.
Bibb, Henry.
Narrative of the Life and Adventures of Henry Bibb, an American Slave. New York, 1850.
Brown, William Wells.
Narrative of William W. Brown, A Fugitive Slave. Boston, 1847.
Burns, Reverend Robert.
The Life and Times of the Reverend Robert Burns. Toronto, 1872.
Coffin, Levi.
Reminiscences of Levi Coffin. Cincinnati, 1876.
Douglass, Frederick.
My Bondage and My Freedom. Boston, 1855.
———.
Narrative of the Life of Frederick Douglass, an American Slave, Written by Himself. Boston, 1845.
Fox, William S., ed.
Letters of William Davies, Toronto, 1854-1861. Toronto, 1945.
Galt, John.
The Autobiography of John Galt. London, 1833.
Haviland, Laura.
A Woman's Life Work. Cincinnati, 1882.
Head,, Sir Francis B.
A Narrative. London, 1839.

Henson, Josiah.

An Autobiography of the Rev. Josiah Henson (Mrs. Harriet Beecher Stowe's "Uncle Tom"): From 1789 to 1877, ed. John Lobb. London, 1878.

———.

The Life of Josiah Henson, Formerly a Slave, Now an Inhabitant of Canada, Narrated by Himself. Boston, 1849.

Jackman, Sydney, ed.

A Diary in America, with Remarks on Its Institutions by Frederick Marryat. New York, 1962.

Keilty, Greg, ed.

1837: Revolution In the Canadas, as told by William Lyon Mackenzie. Toronto, 1974.

King, Rev. William.

History of the King Family Who Settled in the Woods Near Where the Lage of Delta, Ohio, Now Stands in the Year, 1834. Delta, Ohio, 1893.

Loguen, Reverend Jeremiah W.

The Reverend J.W. Loguen as a Slave and Freeman. Syracuse, 1859.

Lundy, Benjamin.

The Life, Travels and Opinions of Benjamin Lundy. Philadelphia, 1847.

Mallory, William.

Old Plantation Days. Hamilton, 1902.

Miller, Audrey S., ed.

The Journals of Mary O'Brien, 1828-1838. Toronto, 1968.

Osofsky, Gilbert, ed.

Puttin' On Ole Massa: The Slave Narratives of Henry Bibb, William Wells Brown, and Solomon Northup. New York, 1969.

Perkin, Allan, ed.

North Into Freedom: The Autobiography of John Malvin, Free Negro, 1795-1880. Cleveland, 1966.

Pickering, Joseph.

Inquiries of an Immigrant; being the Narrative of an English Farmer from the Year 1824 to 1830. London, 1832.

Ross, Alexander M.

Recollections and Experiences of an Abolitionist. Toronto, 1876.

Silverman, Jason H. and Robin W. Winks, eds.

The Autobiography of William King. Athens, Georgia, forthcoming.

Steward, Austin.

Twenty Years a Slave and Forty Years a Freeman. Rochester, 1857.

Tiffany, Nina M.

"Narratives of Fugitive Slaves." New England Magazine 1 (June 1890), p.

524; 2 (July 1890), p. 569.

Ward, Samuel R.

Autobiography of a Fugitive Negro: His Anti-Slavery Labours in the United States, Canada and England. London, 1855.

Warren, Reverend Richard.

Narrative of the Life and Sufferings of Rev. Richard Warren (a fugitive slave) Written by Himself. Hamilton, 1850.

Williams, James.

Life and Adventures of James Williams, a Fugitive Slave, with a Full Description of the Underground Railroad. Philadelphia, 1893.

Winks, Robin (ed.)

Four Fugitive Slave Narratives. Reading, 1969.

Newspapers and Periodicals

American

African Repository and Colonial Journal. Washington, D.C., 1825-1864.
American Anti-Slavery Reporter. New York, 1833-1834.
American and Foreign Anti-Slavery Reporter. New York, 1844-1846.
American Missionary Association. *American Missionary,* 1846-1864.
Anglo-African Magazine. New York, 1859.
Anti-Slavery Examiner. New York, 1836-1845.
The Colored American. New York, 1837-1841.
Douglass' Monthly. Rochester, 1859-1863.
Evangelist. Oberlin, 1848-1853.
The Friend. Utica, 1820-1830.
The Friend of Man. New York, 1836-1838.
The Liberator. Boston, 1839-1861.
National Anti-Slavery Standard. New York, 1849-1851.
The North Star (from 1851, known as *Frederick Douglass' Paper*), Rochester, 1847-1855.

British

British and Foreign Anti-Slavery Reporter. London, 1840-1860.

Canadian

Chronicle. Chatham, 1849-1850.

Colonial Advocate. Toronto, 1824-1834.
Courier. Amherstburg, 1849-1850.
Constitution. St. Catharines, 1859-1869.
Ecclesiastical and Missionary Record. Toronto, 1844-1854.
Examiner. Toronto, 1854.
Expositor. Brantford, 1854-1865.
Gleaner. Chatham, 1844-1849.
Globe. Toronto, 1847-1861.
Herald. Windsor, 1855-1856.
Journal. Chatham, 1841-1844.
Journal of Education for Upper Canada. Toronto, 1848-1877.
Kent Advertiser. Chatham, 1849-1850.
Morning Chronicle. London, 1860.
Niagara Chronicle, 1837.
Niagara Reporter, 1833-1842.
Patriot. Toronto, 1851-1852.
Planet. Chatham, 1857-1868.
Provincial Freeman. Toronto, Chatham, 1853-1857.
True Royalist. Hamilton, 1860.
Voice of the Bondsman. Stratford, 1856-1857.
Voice of the Fugitive. Sandwich, Windsor, 1851-1852.
Western Planet. Chatham, 1853-1857.

Master's Theses and Doctoral Dissertations

Brooks, Catherine L.
"Negro Colonization Projects and Settlements in Canada Until 1865." M.A. thesis, Howard University, 1945.
Brooks, Maxwell R.
"A Sociological Interpretation of the Negro Newspaper." M.A. thesis, Ohio State University, 1937.
Burnet, Jean R.
"Ethnic Groups in Upper Canada." M.A. thesis, University of Toronto, 1943.
Carlesimo, Peter.
"The Refugee Home Society: Its Origin, Operation, and Results, 1851-1876." M.A. thesis, University of Windsor, 1973.
Carlton, Sylvia.
"Egerton Ryerson and Education in Ontario, 1844-1877." Ph.D. dissertation, University of Pennsylvania, 1950.
Chatters, Harriet.

"Negro Education in Kent County." M.A. thesis, Howard University, 1956.

Farrell, John K.A.
"The History of the Negro Community in Chatham, Ontario, 1787-1867." Ph.D. dissertation, University of Ottawa, 1955.

Fisher, James W.
"Proposals for Negro Colonization of the Western Hemisphere, 1850-1867." M.A. thesis, Howard University, 1937.

Hill, Daniel G.
"Negroes in Toronto: A Sociological Study of a Minority Group." Ph.D. dissertation, University of Toronto, 1960.

Houston, Susan E.
"Politics, Schools, and Social Change in Upper Canada between 1836 and 1847." M.A. thesis, University of Toronto, 1967.

Jackson, Margaret Y.
"An Investigation of Biographies and Autobiographies of American Slaves Published Between 1840 and 1860." Ph.D. dissertation, Cornell University, 1954.

Jensen, Carole.
"History of the Negro Community in Essex County, 1850-1860." M.A. thesis, University of Windsor, 1966.

Johnson, Lulu M.
"The Negro in Canada, Slave and Free." M.A. thesis, University of Iowa, 1930.

Krauter, Joseph F.
"Civil Liberties and the Canadian Minorities." Ph.D. dissertation, University of Illinois, 1968.

Landon, Fred.
"The Relation of Canada to the Anti-Slavery and Abolition Movements in the United States." M.A. thesis, University of Western Ontario, 1919.

Lewis, James K.
"The Religious Life of the Fugitive Slaves and the Rise of the Coloured Baptist Churches, 1820-1865 in what is now Known as Ontario." B.D. thesis, McMaster University, 1965.

Murray, Alexander L.
"Canada and the Anglo-American Anti-Slavery Movement: A Study in International Philanthropy." Ph.D. dissertation, University of Pennsylvania, 1960.

Pemberton, I.C.
"The Anti-Slavery Society of Canada." M.A. thesis, University of Toronto, 1967.

Purdy, J.D.
  "John Strachan and Education in Canada, 1800-1851." Ph.D. dissertation,
  University of Toronto, 1962.
Sheffield, Wilfred.
  "Background and Development of Negro Baptists in Ontario." B.D. thesis,
  McMaster University, 1952.
Simpson, Donald G.
  "Negroes in Ontario From Early Times To 1870." Ph.D. dissertation,
  University of Western Ontario, 1971.
Temperly, Howard R.
  "The British and Foreign Anti-Slavery Society, 1839-1868." Ph.D. disserta-
  tion, Yale University, 1960.
Walton, Jonathan.
  "Blacks in Buxton and Chatham, 1830-1890: Did the 49th Parallel Make a
  Difference?" Ph.D. dissertation, Princeton University, 1979.
Wilson, Ruth.
  "Canadian Colonies of Descendants of American Slaves." M.A. thesis, New
  York University, 1948.
Yanuck, Julius.
  "The Fugitive Slave Law and the Constitution." Ph.D. dissertation, Colum-
  bia University, 1953.

SECONDARY SOURCES

Books

American Missionary Association.
  History of the American Missionary Association. New York, 1874.
Aptheker, Herbert.
  American Negro Slave Revolts. New York, 1963.
———.
  History of the Negro People. New York, 1964.
———, ed.
  A Documentary History of the Negro People in the United States. 2 vols.
  New York, 1965.
Beard, Augustus Field.
  *A Crusade of Brotherhood: A History of the American Missionary
  Association.* Boston, 1909.
Bearden, Jim and Linda Jean Butler.

Shadd: The Life and Times of Mary Ann Shadd Cary. Toronto, 1977.
Beattie, Jessie L.
Black Moses. Toronto, 1957.
Bennett, Lerone, Jr.
Before the Mayflower: A History of the Negro in America, 1619-1964, rev. ed. Chicago, 1964.
Boyd, Frank S., Jr.
McKerrow: A Brief History of the Coloured Baptists of Nova Scotia, 1783-1895. Halifax, 1976.
Braithwaite, Rella, ed.
The Black Woman in Canada. n.d., n.p.
Bradford, Sarah.
Scenes in the Life of Harriet Tubman. New York, 1869.
Brebner, J. Bartlet.
Canada: A Modern History. Ann Arbor, 1960.
Brown, Hallie Q.
Homespun Heroines and Other Women of Distinction. Xenia, Ohio, 1926.
Brownlee, Frederick L.
Heritage of Freedom. Philadelphia, 1963.
Bryce, George.
Short History of the Canadian People. Toronto, 1914.
Buckmaster, Henrietta.
Let My People Go: The Story of the Underground Railroad and the Growth of the Abolition Movement. Boston, 1948.
Burkholder, Mabel.
The Story of Hamilton. Hamilton, 1938.
Burwash, Nathaniel.
Egerton Ryerson. Toronto, 1910.
Campbell, C.T.
Pioneer Days in London. London, 1921.
Campbell, Marjorie.
A Mountain and a City: A Story of Hamilton. Toronto, 1966.
Campbell, Stanley W.
The Slave Catchers: Enforcement of the Fugitive Slave Law, 1850-1860. New York, 1968.
Caniff, William.
History of the Province of Ontario. Toronto, 1872.
———.
History of the Province of Upper Canada. Toronto, 1869.
Careless, J.M.S.

Brown of the Globe. Toronto, 1959.

———.

The Union of the Canadas. Toronto, 1967.

Carter, Francis.
Judicial Decisions on Denominational Schools. Toronto, 1962.

Catterall, Helen T.
Judicial Cases Concerning American Slavery and the Negro. 5 vols. Washington, D.C., 1937.

Clairmont, Donald and Dennis Magill.
Nova Scotian Blacks: An Historical and Structural Overview. Halifax, 1970.

———.

Africville: The Life and Death of a Canadian Black Community. Toronto, 1974.

Cochrane, Honora M.
Centennial Story: The Board of Education for the City of Toronto, 1850-1950. Toronto, 1950.

Coles, Howard W.
The Cradle of Freedom: A History of the Negro in Rochester, Western New York and Canada. Rochester, 1941.

Craig, Gerald M.
Upper Canada—The Formative Years, 1784-1841. Toronto, 1963.

Creighton, Donald G.
Dominion of the North. Toronto, 1962.

———.

Towards the Discovery of Canada. Toronto, 1972.

Dabney, Wendell P.
Cincinnati's Colored Citizens. Cincinnati, 1926.

Dorland, Arthur G.
A History of the Society of Friends in Canada. Toronto, 1927.

Edwards, S.J., Celestine.
From Slavery to a Bishopric or The Life of Bishop Walter Hawkins. London, 1891.

Elgee, William H.
The Social Teachings of the Canadian Churches: Protestant, the Early Years, Before 1850. Toronto, 1964.

Farrell, John K.A.
The Ontario Negro: An Outline of Negro History and Development. Windsor, 1965.

Farrison, William E.

William Wells Brown, Author and Reformer. Chicago, 1969.

Firth, Edith G., ed.
Early Toronto Newspapers, 1793-1867. Toronto, 1961.

Fitch, E.R.
The Baptists of Canada. Toronto, 1911.

Franklin, John Hope.
From Slavery to Freedom: A History of Negro Americans. New York, 1980.

French, Gary E.
Men of Colour: An Historical Account of the Black Settlement in Oro Township, Simcoe County, Ontario, 1819-1849. Stroud, Ontario, 1978.

French, G.S.
Parsons and Politics: The Role of the Wesleyan Methodists in Upper Canada and the Maritimes from 1780-1855. Toronto, 1962.

Gara, Larry.
The Liberty Line: The Legend of the Underground Railroad. Lexington, Ky., 1961.

Gates, Lillian F.
Land Policies of Upper Canada. Toronto, 1968.

Glazebrook, G.P. de T.
Life in Ontario: A Social History. Toronto, 1968.

Greaves, I.C.
The Negro in Canada. McGill University Economic Studies No. 16. Montreal, 1930.

Gregg, William.
A Short History of the Presbyterian Church in the Dominion of Canada. Toronto, 1893.

Gregg, William R.
The African in North America: Their Welfare After Freedom as Effected and Influenced by the Life of William King. Ashtabula, Ohio, 1933.

Gross, Bella.
Clarion Call: The History and Development of the Negro People's Convention Movement in the United States from 1817-1840. New York, 1947.

Guillet, Edwin C.
In the Cause of Education: Centennial History of the Ontario Educational Association, 1861-1960. Toronto, 1960.

Hallam, W.T.
Slave Days in Canada. Toronto, 1919.

Hamil, Frederick Coyne.
The Valley of the Lower Thames, 1640-1850. Toronto, 1951.

Hansen, M.L., and J.B. Brebner.
  The Mingling of the Canadian and American Peoples. New Haven, 1940.
Hardy, E.A., and Honora M. Cochrane.
  Centennial Story: The Board of Education for the City of Toronto, 1850-1950. Toronto, 1950.
Harris, A.M.
  A Sketch of the Buxton Mission and Elgin Settlement, Raleigh, Canada West. Birmingham, 1866.
Harris, Robin S.
  "Egerton Ryerson," in *Our Living Tradition.* Toronto, 1959.
Harrow and Colchester South Township School Board.
  A Story of Public Schools in Colchester South Township. Harrow, 1966.
Hassard, A.R.
  Famous Canadian Trials. Toronto, 1924.
Head, Wilson.
The Black Presence in the Canadian Mosaic: A Study of Perception and the Practice of Discrimination Against Blacks in Metropolitan Toronto. Toronto, 1975.
Henry, Francis.
  Forgotten Canadians: The Blacks of Nova Scotia. Don Mills, Ontario, 1973.
Henderson, J.L.H.
  John Strachan. Toronto, 1969.
Hill, Daniel G.
  The Freedom Seekers: Blacks in Early Canada. Agincourt, Ontario, 1981.
History of Middlesex. London, Ontario, 1889.
Hunter, Andrew.
  A History of Simcoe County, Ontario, Canada. 2 vols. Barrie, Ontario, 1909.
Illustrated Atlas of the Dominion of Canada Together with a General Descriptive History. . . and Local Maps.
  Prepared under the direction of D. MacDonald, Toronto Co., 1881.
Jain, Sushil K.
  The Negro in Canada. Regina, Ontario, 1967.
Jamieson, Annie Straith.
  William King: Friend and Champion of Slaves. Toronto, 1925.
Johnston, G.M.
  Brant County. Toronto, 1967.
Jordan, Winthrop.
  White Over Black: American Attitudes Toward the Negro, 1550-1812. Chapel Hill, 1969.

Katz, Michael B.

> *The People of Hamilton, Canada West: Family and Class in a Mid-Nineteenth Century City.* Cambridge, Mass., 1975.

Kentiana, The Story of the Settlement and Development of the County of Kent. n.p. 1939.

Killian, Crawford.

> *Go Do Some Great Things: The Black Pioneers of British Columbia.* North Vancouver, B.C., 1978.

Lajevnesse, Ernest J.

> *The Windsor Border Region.* Toronto, 1960.

Landon, Fred.

> *Western Ontario and the American Frontier.* Toronto, 1941.

Laskin, Richard, ed.

> *Social Problems: A Canadian Profile.* Toronto, 1964.

Lauriston, Victor.

> *Romantic Kent: More Than Three Centuries of History, 1626-1952.* Chatham, 1952.

Lewis, John.

> *George Brown.* Toronto, 1907.

Litwack, Leon.

> *North of Slavery: The Negro in the Free States, 1790-1860.* Chicago, 1961.

Macdonald, Helen Grace.

> *Canadian Public Opinion on the American Civil War.* New York, 1926.

MacDonald, Norman.

> *Canada 1763-1841: Immigration and Settlement.* Toronto, 1939.

Masters, D.C.

> *Protestant Church Colleges in Canada.* Toronto, 1966.

———.

> *The Rise of Toronto, 1850-1890.* Toronto, 1947.

McDougall, Marion G.

> *Fugitive Slaves, 1619-1865.* Boston, 1891.

MacLachlin, K. Gordon.

> *A History of Dawn Township and Its Origin.* n.d., n.p.

Mealing, Stanley R.

> "John Graves Simcoe," in *Our Living Tradition.* Toronto, 1959.

Middleton, Jesse E., and Fred Landon.

> *The Province of Ontario, A History.* Toronto, 1927.

Moir, John S.

> *Church and State in Canada, 1627-1867.* Toronto, 1967.

———.

Church and State in Canada West. Toronto, 1959.
Moore, John B.
A Treatise on Extradition and Interstate Rendition. Boston, 1891.
Ontario Educational Communication Authority.
Identity: The Black Experience in Canada. Toronto, 1979.
Pease, William H., and Jane H. Pease.
Black Utopia: Negro Communal Experiments in America. Madison, 1963.
Penn, Irvine Garland.
The Afro-American Press and Its Editors. Springfield, Mass., 1891.
Perry, Charlotte B.
The Long Road: The History of the Coloured Canadian in Windsor, Ontario, 1867-1967. Windsor, 1967.
Phillips, C.E.
The Development of Education in Canada. Toronto, 1957.
Prentice, Alison L. and Susan E. Houston, eds.
Family, School, and Society in Nineteenth-Century Canada. Toronto, 1975.
Presbyterian Church in Canada.
Historic Sketches of the Pioneer: Work and the Missionary, Educational and Benevolent Agencies of the Presbyterian Church in Canada. Toronto, 1975.
Putnam, John Harold.
Egerton Ryerson and Education in Upper Canada. Toronto, 1912.
Quilton, Frank V.
Colour Line in Ohio. Ann Arbor, 1913.
Reville, F. Douglass.
History of the County of Brant. Brantford, 1926.
Richardson, Harry.
Dark Glory. New York, 1947.
Rice, C. Duncan.
The Rise and Fall of Black Slavery. Baton Rouge, 1975.
Riddell, William Renwick.
The Legal Profession in Upper Canada in Its Early Periods. Toronto, 1916.
———.

The Life of John Graves Simcoe, First Lieutenant Governor of the Province of Upper Canada, 1792-93. Toronto, 1926.
———.

The Slave in Canada. Washington, D.C., 1920.
———.

Upper Canada Sketches: Incidents in the Early Times of the Province.

Toronto, 1922.

Robinson, C.W.
  Life of Sir John Beverly Robinson, Chief Justice of Upper Canada.
  Edinburgh, 1904.

Ross, George W.
  The School System of Ontario (Canada). New York, 1896.

Schmeiser, D.
  Civil Liberties in Canada. New York, 1964.

Schwartz, Harold.
  Samuel Gridley Howe, Social Reformer, 1801-1876. Cambridge, Mass.,
  1956.

Siebert, Wilbur H.
  The Underground Railroad From Slavery to Freedom. New York, 1898.

Sissons, Charles B.
  Church and State in Canadian Education. Toronto, 1959.

———.
  Egerton Ryerson, His Life and Letters. Toronto, 1937.

Spalding, L.T.
  History and Romance of Education (Hamilton), 1816-1950. Hamilton,
  1951.

Spicer, Elizabeth, ed.
  Descriptions of London and Its Environs. London, Ontario, n.d.

Spray, William.
  Blacks in New Brunswick. Fredericton, 1972.

Tanser, Henry.
  The Settlement of Negroes in Kent County, Ontario. Chatham, 1939.

Thomas, Clara E.
  Ryerson of Upper Canada. Toronto, 1969.

Thompson, Colin.
  Blacks in Deep Snow: Black Pioneers in Canada. Don Mills, Ontario, 1979.

Thompson, H.P.
  Thomas Bray. London, 1954.

Toronto Centennial Committee.
  Toronto Normal School, 1847-1947. Toronto, 1947.

Tulloch, Headley.
  Black Canadians: A Long Line of Fighters. Toronto, 1975.

Ullman, Victor.
  Look to the North Star: A Life of William King. Boston, 1969.

Urquhart, M.C., and K.A.H. Buckley, eds.
  Historical Statistics of Canada. Cambridge, England, 1965.

Walker, James W. St. G.
>   *The Black Loyalists: The Search For a Promised Land in Nova Scotia and Sierra Leone, 1783-1870.* New York, 1976.

―――.
>   *A History of Blacks in Canada: A Study Guide for Teachers and Students.* Hull, Quebec, 1980.

Wilson, J.D., R.M. Stamp, and Louis-Philippe Audet.
>   *Canadian Education: A History.* Scarborough, Ontario, 1970.

Winks, Robin W.
>   *The Blacks in Canada: A History.* New Haven, 1971.

―――.
>   *Canada and the United States: The Civil War Years.* Baltimore, 1960.

Wittke, Carl.
>   *A History of Canada.* New York, 1928.

Wise, S.F. and Robert C. Brown.
>   *Canada Views the United States: Nineteenth Century Political Attitudes.* Seattle, 1967.

Woodson, Carter G.
>   *A Century of Negro Migration.* Washington, 1918.

―――.
>   *The Education of the Negro Prior to 1861.* New York, 1915.

―――.
>   *The History of the Negro Church.* Washington, 1921.

―――.
>   *The Mis-Education of the Negro.* Washington, 1933.

Work, Monroe N.
>   *A Bibliography of the Negro in Africa and America.* New York, 1928.

Articles

Amstrong, Fred H.
>   "The Toronto Directories and the Negro Community in the Late 1840's." *Ontario History* 61 (June 1969), pp. 101-19.

Arthurs, H.W.
>   "Civil Liberties—Public Schools—Segregation of Negro Students." *Canadian Bar Review* 41 (September 1963), pp. 453-57.

Baughman, A.J.
>   "The Underground Railway." *Ohio Archaeological and Historical Society Publication* 15 (April 1906), pp. 189-91.

Bell, Howard H.

"The Negro Emigration Movement, 1849-1854: A Phase of Negro Nationalism." *The Phylon Quarterly* 20 (Summer 1959), pp. 132-42.

———.

"Expressions of Negro Militancy in the North, 1840-1860." *Journal of Negro History* 45 (January 1960), pp. 11-20.

———.

"Negro Nationalism: A Factor in Emigration Projects, 1858-1861." *Journal of Negro History* 47 (January 1962), pp. 42-53.

Careless, J.M.S.

"Mid-Victorian Liberalism in Central Canadian Newspapers, 1850-1867." *The Canadian Historical Review* 31 (September 1950), pp. 221-36.

Carnochan, Janet.

"Slave Rescue in Niagara, Sixty Years Ago." *Niagara Historical Society Publication,* No. 2 (1897), pp. 8-18.

Chamberlaine, A.D.

"Coloured Citizens of Toronto." *Women's Canadian Historical Society* (Toronto), No. 8 (1914), pp. 10-15.

Champion, Thomas E.

"The Underground Railroad and One of its Operators." *Canadian Magazine* 4 (May 1895).

Cooper, John I.

"The Mission to the Fugitive Slaves at London." *Ontario History* 46 (April 1954), pp. 133-39.

Eames, Frank.

"Pioneer Schools of Upper Canada." *Ontario Historical Society Papers and Records* 18 (1920).

Edward, C.B.

"London Public Schools, 1848-1871." *London and Middlesex Historical Society Transactions* 5 (1914).

Farrell, John K.A.

"Schemes for the Transplanting of Refugee American Negroes from Upper Canada in the 1840's." *Ontario History* 52 (December 1960), pp. 245-49.

———.

"Some Opinions of Christian Europeans Regarding Negro Slavery in the Seventeenth and Early Eighteenth Centuries." *The Canadian Historical Association Report* (1958), pp. 13-22.

Gara, Larry.

"Propaganda Uses of the Underground Railway." *Mid-America* 34 (July 1952), pp. 155-71.

———.

"The Underground Railway: Legend or Reality?" *Proceedings of the American Philosophical Society* 105 (1961), pp. 334-39.

Green, Ernest.
"Upper Canada's Black Defenders." *Ontario Historical Society Papers and Records* 27 (1931), pp. 365-91.

Gregg, William R.
"Mrs. Stowe's Originals in Canada." *Toronto Sunday World,* 6 July 1924.

Hamilton, J.C.
"The African in Canada." *Proceedings of the American Association for the Advancement of Science* 33 (1890).

———.
"The African in Canada: The Reverend William King and the Elgin Association." *Knox College Monthly and Presbyterian Magazine* 11 (November 1889), pp. 30-37.

———.
"John Brown in Canada." *Canadian Magazine* 4 (May 1895), pp. 119-40.

———.
"Slavery in Canada." *Magazine of American History* 25 (March 1891), pp. 233-38.

Hancock, Harold B.
"Mary Ann Shadd: Negro Editor, Educator, and Lawyer." *Delaware History* 15 (April 1973), pp. 187-94.

Hartgrove, W.B.
"Josiah Henson." *Journal of Negro History* 3 (January 1918), pp. 1-21.

Hill, Daniel.
"Negroes in Toronto, 1793-1865." *Ontario History* 55 (June 1963), pp. 73-91.

——— and Arnold Bruner.
"Heritage of Overcoming: The 350th Anniversary of Blacks in Canada." *(Toronto) Globe and Mail,* 19 August 1978.

Hill, Hilda.
"Henry Bibb, the Colonizer." *Negro History Bulletin* 4 (April 1941), p. 148.

"History of the Negro Population at Collingwood."
Huron Institute Papers and Records (January 1909), pp. 40-42.

Hite, Roger W.
"Voice of the Fugitive: Henry Bibb and Antebellum Black Separatism." *Journal of Black Studies* 4 (March 1974), pp. 269-84.

Jack, I.A.
"Loyalists and Slavery in New Brunswick." *Transactions of the Royal Society of Canada* 2d series, 4 (1898), pp. 137-85.

James, C.C.
"The First Legislator of Upper Canada." *Transactions of the Royal Society of Canada* 2d series, 8 (1902), pp. 131-40.

Johnson, Clifton.
"Mary Ann Shadd: Crusader for the Freedom of Man." *Crisis* 78 (April/May 1971), pp. 89-90.

Knaplund, Paul.
"Sir James Stephen: The Friend of the Negro." *Journal of Negro History* 35 (October 1950), pp. 368-407.

Landon, Fred.
"Abolitionist Interest in Upper Canada." *Ontario History* 44 (October 1952), pp. 165-77.

————.
"Agriculture Among the Negro Refugees in Upper Canada." *Journal of Negro History* 21 (July 1936), pp. 304-12.

————.
"Amherstburg, Terminus of the Underground Railroad." *Journal of Negro History* 10 (January 1925), pp. 1-11.

————.
"The Anderson Fugitive Case." *Journal of Negro History* 7 (July 1922), pp. 233-42.

————.
"Anthony Burns in Canada." *Ontario Historical Society Papers and Records* 22 (1925), pp. 160-66.

————.
"The Anti-Slavery Society of Canada." *Journal of Negro History* 4 (January 1919), pp. 33-40.

————.
"The Anti-Slavery Society of Canada." *Ontario History* 48 (July 1956), pp. 125-31.

————.
"Benjamin Lundy, Abolitionist." *Dalhousie Review* 7 (July 1927), pp. 189-97.

————.
"The Buxton Settlement in Canada." *Journal of Negro History* 4 (October 1918), pp. 360-67.

————.
"Canada and the Underground Railroad." *Kingston Historical Society, Reports and Proceedings* (1923), pp. 17-31.

————.

"Canada's Part in Freeing the Slaves." *Ontario Historical Society Papers and Records* 17 (1919), pp. 74-84.

————.

"The Canadian Anti-Slavery Group Before the Civil War." *University Magazine* 18 (December 1918), pp. 540-47.

————.

"Canadian Negroes and the John Brown Raid." *Journal of Negro History* 6 (April 1921), pp. 174-82.

————.

"Canadian Negroes and the Rebellion of 1837." *Journal of Negro History* 7 (October 1922), pp. 377-79.

————.

"Captain Charles Stuart, Abolitionist." *Western Ontario History Nuggets* 24 (1956), p. 19.

————.

"From Chatham to Harper's Ferry." *Canadian Magazine* 53 (October 1919), pp. 441-48.

————.

"A Daring Canadian Abolitionist: Alexander Milton Ross." *Michigan Historical Magazine* 5 (July-October 1921), pp. 364-73.

————, ed.

"The Diary of Benjamin Lundy, Written During his Journey Through Upper Canada, January 1832." *Ontario Historical Society Papers and Records* 19 (1921), pp. 110-33.

————.

"Fugitive Slaves in Ontario." *Northwest Ohio Quarterly* 8 (April 1936), pp. 1-12.

————.

"The Fugitive Slave Law and the Detroit River Frontier." *Bulletin of the Detroit Historical Society* 7 (1950), pp. 5-9.

————.

"Fugitive Slave in Canada." *University Magazine* 18 (April 1919), pp. 270-79.

————.

"Fugitive Slaves in London Before 1860." *Transactions of the London and Middlesex Historical Society* 10 (1919), pp. 25-38.

————.

"Henry Bibb." *Journal of Negro History* 5 (October 1920), pp. 437-47.

————.

"History of the Wilberforce Refugee Colony in Middlesex County." *Transac-*

tions of the London and Middlesex Historical Society 9 (1918), pp. 30-44.

———.

"Negro Colonization Schemes in Upper Canada Before 1860." *Transactions of the Royal Society of Canada* 3d series, section II, 23 (1929), pp. 73-80.

———.

"The Negro Migration to Canada after the Passing of the Fugitive Slave Act." *Journal of Negro History* 5 (January 1920), pp. 22-36.

———.

"In an Old Ontario Cemetery." *Dalhousie Review* 5 (1926), pp. 523-31.

———.

"Over Lake Erie to Freedom." *Northwest Ohio Quarterly* 17 (October 1945), pp. 132-38.

———.

"A Pioneer Abolitionist in Upper Canada." *Ontario History* 52 (June 1960), pp. 77-83.

———.

"The Reverend Josiah Henson." *Kent Historical Society, Papers and Addresses* 7 (1951), pp. 44-52.

———.

"Social Conditions Amongst Negroes in Upper Canada, Before 1865." *Ontario Historical Society Papers and Records* 12 (1925), pp. 144-61.

———.

"When Uncle Tom's Cabin Came to Canada." *Ontario History* 44 (January 1952), pp. 1-5.

———.

"Wilberforce, An Experiment in the Colonization of Freed Negroes in Upper Canada." *Transactions of the Royal Society of Canada* 3d series, section II, 31 (1937), pp. 69-78.

———.

"The Work of the American Missionary Association Among the Negro Refugees in Canada West, 1848-1864." *Ontario Historical Society Papers and Records* 21 (1924), pp. 198-205.

Leask, J. MacKenzie.

"Jesse Happy, a Fugitive Slave from Kentucky." *Ontario History* 54 (June 1962), pp. 87-98.

Lefroy, Catharine F.

"Recollections of Mary Warren Breckenridge of Clarke Township." *Ontario Historical Society Papers and Records* 3 (1901), pp. 110-13.

Lewis, James K.

"Religious Nature of Early Negro Migration to Canada and the Amherstburg

Baptist Association." *Ontario History* 58 (June 1966), pp. 117-32.

Lindsay, Arnett G.

"Diplomatic Relations Between the United States and Great Britain Bearing on the Return of Negro Slaves, 1788-1828." *Journal of Negro History* 5 (October 1920), pp. 391-419.

McCurdy, Alvin.

"Henry Walton Bibb." *Negro History Bulletin* 22 (October 1958), pp. 19-21.

Murray, Alexander L.

"The Extradition of Fugitive Slaves from Canada: A Re-evaluation." *The Canadian Historical Review* 43 (December 1962), pp. 298-314.

———.

"The Provincial Freeman: A New Source for the History of the Negro in Canada and the United States." *Journal of Negro History* 44 (April 1959), pp. 123-35.

Neilson, Hubert.

"Slavery in Old Canada: Before and After the Conquest." *Quebec Historical Society Transactions* 26 (1906), pp. 19-45.

O'Brien, W.E.

"Early Days in Oro." *Simcoe County Pioneer and Historical Society, Pioneer Papers* 1 (1908), pp. 22-27.

Pease, William H., and Jane H. Pease.

"Opposition to the Founding of the Elgin Settlement." *The Canadian Historical Review* 38 (September 1957), pp. 202-18.

———.

"Uncle Tom and Clayton: Fact, Fiction, and Mystery." *Ontario History* 50 (April 1958), pp. 61-73.

———.

"William King: From Master to Servant." *Rensselaer Review of Graduate Studies* 16 (May 1959), pp. 3-10.

Proudfoot, Wiliam.

"The Proudfoot Diaries." *Ontario Historical Society Papers and Records* 27-32 (1931-1936).

Riddell, William Renwick.

"Additional Notes on Slavery." *Journal of Negro History* 17 (July 1932), pp. 368-73.

———.

"Baptism of Slaves in Prince Edward Island." *Journal of Negro History* 6 (July 1921), pp. 307-9.

———.

"Further Notes on the Slave in Canada." *Journal of Negro History* 9

(January 1924), pp. 26-33.

———.

"Interesting Notes on Great Britain and Canada with Respect to the Negro." *Journal of Negro History* 13 (April 1928), pp. 185-98.

———.

"An International Complication Between Illinois and Canada Arising Out of Slavery." *Journal of the Illinois State Historical Society* 25 (October 1932), pp. 25-32.

———.

"Le Code Noir: Application of in Canada." *Journal of Negro History* 10 (July 1925), pp. 321-29.

———.

"Notes on Slavery in Canada." *Journal of Negro History* 4 (October 1919), pp. 396-411.

———.

"Notes on the Slave in Nouvelle France." *Journal of Negro History* 7 (July 1923), pp. 316-30.

———.

"Reciprocity of Slaves Between Michigan and Upper Canada." *Journal of Negro History* 17 (July 1932), pp. 368-77.

———.

"The Slave in Canada." *Journal of Negro History* 5 (July 1920), pp. 261-377.

———.

"The Slave in Upper Canada." *Journal of Negro History* 4 (October 1919), pp. 372-95.

———.

"Slavery in Upper Canada." *Journal of Criminal Law* 14 (August 1923), pp. 249-78.

———.

"Slaves in Upper Canada." *Canadian Magazine* 54 (March 1920), pp. 377-81.

———.

"Some References to Negroes in Upper Canada." *Ontario Historical Society Papers and Records* 19 (1929), pp. 144-46.

———.

"When Human Beings Were Real Estate." *Canadian Magazine* 57 (June 1921), pp. 147-49.

Sexsmith, William N.

"Some Notes on the Buxton Settlement, Raleigh, Kent County." *Kent*

Historical Society, Papers and Addresses, (1919), pp. 40-44.

Silverman, Jason H.

"The American Fugitive Slave in Canada: Myths and Realities." *Southern Studies* 19 (Fall 1980), pp. 215-27.

———.

"Kentucky, Canada, and Extradition: The Jesse Happy Case." *The Filson Club History Quarterly* 54 (January 1980), pp. 50-60.

———.

"Mary Ann Shadd and the Search for Equality" in *Black Leaders of the Nineteenth Century,* eds., August Meier and Leon Litwack. Urbana, Ill., forthcoming.

———.

" 'We Shall Be Heard!': The Development of the Fugitive Slave Press in Canada." *The Canadian Historical Review* 65 (March 1984), pp. 54-69.

——— and Donna J. Gillie.

" 'The Pursuit of Knowledge Under Difficulties': Education and the Fugitive Slave in Canada." *Ontario History* 74 (June 1982), pp. 95-112.

Smith, T. Watson.

"The Slave in Canada." *Collections of the Nova Scotia Historical Society for the Years 1896-1898* 10 (1899), pp. 1-161.

Spragge, G.W.

"Elementary Education in Upper Canada, 1820-1840." *Ontario History* 43 (1951).

———.

"John Strachan's Contributions to Education, 1800-1823." *The Canadian Historical Review* 22 (1941).

Styles, William A.

"Slave Days in Canada." *Canadian Magazine* 83 (January 1935).

Talman, James J.

"The Newspaper Press of Canada West, 1850-1860." *Transactions of the Royal Society of Canada* 2d series, 33 (1939), pp. 117-31.

———.

"The Newspapers of Upper Canada." *The Canadian Historical Review* 19 (March 1938), pp. 65-73.

Wade, Richard C.

"The Negro in Cincinnati, 1800-1830." *Journal of Negro History* 29 (January 1954), pp. 43-59.

Walker, James W. St. G.

"The Establishment of a Free Black Community in Nova Scotia, 1783-1840" in *The African Diaspora: Interpretive Essays,* eds. Martin L. Kilson and

Robert I. Rothberg. Cambridge, Mass., 1976, pp. 205-36.

Winks, Robin W.

"The Canadian Negro: A Historical Assessment." *Journal of Negro History* 53 (October 1968), pp. 283-300; 54 (January 1969), pp. 1-18.

———.

"Negroes in the Maritimes: An Introductory Survey." *Dalhousie Review* 48 (Winter 1968), pp. 453-71.

———.

"Negro School Segregation in Ontario and Nova Scotia." *The Canadian Historical Review* 50 (June 1969), pp. 164-91.

———.

" 'A Sacred Animosity': Abolitionism in Canada," in *The Antislavery Vanguard: New Essays on the Abolitionists*, ed., Martin Duberman. Princeton, 1965, pp. 301-42.

Withrow, W.H.

"The Underground Railroad." *Transactions of the Royal Society of Canada* 2d series 8 (1902), pp. 49-78.

Yeigh, Frank.

"Famous Canadian Trials, VIII—Anderson, the Fugitive Slave." *Canadian Magazine* 45 (December 1915), pp. 397-401.

Zorn, Roman J.

"An Arkansas Fugitive Slave Incident and Its International Repercussions." *Arkansas Historical Quarterly* 16 (Summer 1957), pp. 133-40.

———.

"Criminal Extradition Menaces the Canadian Haven for Fugitive Slaves." *The Canadian Historical Review* 38 (December 1957), pp. 284-94.

INDEX